European Monographs in Social Psychology

Levels of explanation in social psychology

European Monographs in Social Psychology

Executive Editors:
J. RICHARD EISER and KLAUS R. SCHERER
Sponsored by the European Association of Experimental Social Psychology

This series, first published by Academic Press (who will continue to distribute the numbered volumes), appeared under the joint imprint of Cambridge University Press and the Maison des Sciences de l'Homme in 1985 as an amalgamation of the Academic Press series and The European Studies in Social Psychology, published by Cambridge and the Maison in collaboration with the Laboratoire Européen de Psychologie Sociale of the Maison.

The original aims of the two series still very much apply today: to provide a forum for the best European research in different fields of social psychology and to foster the interchange of ideas between different developments and different traditions. The Executive Editors also expect that it will have an important role to play as a European forum for international work.

Other titles in this series:

Unemployment by Peter Kelvin and Joanna E. Jarrett
National characteristics by Dean Peabody
Experiencing emotion by Klaus R. Scherer, Harald G. Wallbott and
   Angela B. Summerfield

Levels of explanation in social psychology

Willem Doise
Department of Psychology,
University of Geneva

Translated from the French by
Elizabeth Mapstone
Department of Psychology,
University of Oxford

The right of the
University of Cambridge
to print and sell
all manner of books
was granted by
Henry VIII in 1534.
The University has printed
and published continuously
since 1584.

Cambridge University Press
Cambridge
London   New York   New Rochelle
Melbourne   Sydney

Editions de la Maison des Sciences de l'Homme
Paris

Published by the Press Syndicate of the University of Cambridge
The Pitt Building, Trumpington Street, Cambridge CB2 1RP
32 East 57th Street, New York, NY 10022, USA
10 Stamford Road, Oakleigh, Melbourne 3166, Australia
and Editions de la Maison des Sciences de l'Homme
54 Boulevard Raspail, 75270 Paris Cedex 06

Originally published in French as *L'explication en psychologie sociale*
by Presses Universitaires de France, 1982
and © Presses Universitaires de France
First published in English by Editions de la Maison des Sciences de l'Homme and
Cambridge University Press 1986 as *Levels of Explanation in Social Psychology*
English translation © Willem Doise 1986

Printed in Great Britain by the University Press, Cambridge

British Library cataloguing in publication data

Doise, Willem
Levels of explanation in social psychology. –
(European monographs in social psychology)
1. Social psychology
I. Title II. Series III. L'explication en
psychologie sociale. *English*
302'.01   HM251

Library of Congress cataloguing in publication data

Doise, Willem, 1935–
Levels of explanation in social psychology.
(European monographs in social psychology)
Translation of L'explication en psychologie sociale.
Bibliography.
Includes index.
1. Social psychology. I. Title. II. Series.
HM251.D62813   1986   302   85-30943

ISBN 0 521 30748 1 hard covers
ISBN 0 521 31485 2 paperback

ISBN 2 7351 0142 8 hard covers (France only)
ISBN 2 7351 0141 X paperback (France only)

UP

Contents

Preface

Social psychology, and especially experimental social psychology, has produced a multitude of explanations which appear to have very little connection with one another. Theoretical approaches are so diverse that most are left with very restricted areas of application, while in the case of the few theories with wider scope, it appears to be impossible to arbitrate between rivals. The aim of this book is not to obscure this diversity, but rather to try to bring some order into it. We shall find we can distinguish four kinds of explanation in social psychological studies: the first is limited to 'psychological' or 'intra-personal' processes which take account of the way the individual organises her/his experience of the social world. A second looks at the dynamics of 'inter-personal' or 'intra-situational' processes which occur between individuals considered as interchangeable actors. A third type of explanation introduces the notion of social position or status to deal with differences in situational interactions, where individuals are not treated as interchangeable. Finally, a fourth type of research starts with an analysis of the general concepts concerning social relations brought to the situation by the individuals under study, and shows how such 'universalist ideological beliefs' lead to differentiated or discriminatory mental representations and behaviour.

But if we distinguish four levels of analysis, this is better to defend our thesis that they closely overlap in many studies, and that the articulation of levels of analysis should be treated as a topic of social psychological research in its own right.

The notion of articulation of levels of analysis was developed in an earlier book (Doise, 1978a) where it was applied to a particular area, that of inter-group relations. We will show that this kind of articulation of levels occurs in other research areas and will make the notion of articulation clear by showing how it knits together the four levels of analysis that we now distinguish, and not just the more widely distinguished levels of psychological and social explanations.

Our constant endeavour in this work has been to incorporate as far as possible ideas developed in the work of social psychologists, and especially that of experimentalists. There are several reasons for our preference for experimental research: it provides a means of investigation which is

relatively easy to circumscribe, and which furthermore requires the investigator to make her/his theoretic assumptions specific. On the other hand,
experiments seem to favour analysis on a intra- or inter-personal level. If
we can show that experiments can go beyond these two levels of analysis,
this would provide stronger support for our theory of different levels of
analysis and their articulation.

A preference for experiment in no way implies that field studies or clinical
investigations are not amenable to the same levels of analysis: but it seems
better to begin our study of levels of explanation in social psychology with
those which are formulated in a direct and unambiguous manner because
of the need to make experimental predictions.

Development of our theme will not be linear, for all that we are following
a single line of thought. It will be more like a piece of music where a number
of main themes are introduced at the beginning, and reintroduced, developed,
interwoven many times over as the piece proceeds. So Chapter 1 will give
a description of the four levels of analysis and introduce the theme of their
articulation. The three following chapters will look at three different areas
of research, each of which seems to require a particular type of explanation
but is nevertheless enriched by the other types of analysis. These areas (in
which the writer and his colleagues at the University of Geneva have carried
out considerable work) are: social factors in cognitive development, social
influence and intergroup relations. Chapter 5 will give more details about
our concept of the social psychological experiment, illustrating key points
with typical examples.

This edition has not been very greatly changed from the French language
edition. In some places, more recent publications have been mentioned or
briefly commented on when they illustrate some aspect of our thesis. Among
these we must make special note of a chapter by McGuire (1983) on
contextualism. It is true that in his chapter McGuire begins by explicitly
defending a philosophical position, and this is an area we have avoided in
this book. We are, of course, perfectly aware that our thesis implies a
philosophical stance. But rather than working on a philosophical synthesis,
we thought it more important to carry out a classification and structuring
of relations between the different sorts of explanations proposed by social
psychologists. It will nevertheless be seen that our book, written before we
learned of McGuire's theories, is the product of preoccupations very similar
to his. Here we will simply list the major similarities between his approach
and our own. They bear upon the importance of abandoning 'the logical
empiricist position that the empirical confrontation is a test of whether a
given theory is correct (or better, in the method of strong inference, which
of several opposed theories is correct and which wrong)' in favour of the
position which holds 'rather that empirical confrontation is a discovery

process to make clear the meaning of the hypothesis, disclosing its hidden assumptions and thus clarifying circumstances under which the hypothesis is true and those under which it is false' (McGuire, 1983:7). However, we would not accept as it stands his statement that contradictory hypotheses can be valid. But it is precisely because we believe that a hypothesis only has meaning through its implicit – and preferably explicit – articulation with other hypotheses that we also share the view 'that an adequate understanding of either a phenomenon or a theory requires that it be investigated through a program of research planned to reveal the wide range of circumstances that affect the phenomenon and the rich set of implicit assumptions that limit the theory, thus making explicit the contexts in which one or another relationship obtains' (1983:22). In effect, the implicit assumptions necessarily become hypotheses or theoretical conjectures when they are invoked to explain modifications or to describe the conditions under which processes under investigation will hold. We believe that McGuire has illustrated not only the contextualist approach but also our concept of the articulation of analyses at the same or at different levels, when he writes:

Adding multiple independent variables, each uniquely predicted by a different theory to produce an interaction effect, helps the researcher to appreciate that explanation is not a zero-sum game: however firmly one believes in Boyle's Law, one need not reject Charles's Law. A diverse set of theorized processes may be operative with wide variation from situation to situation in the proportion of common variance contributed by each of the mediators...A research design that includes interaction variables each suggested by a different theory is an example of the heuristic value of the contextualist approach. (1983:27)

Elsewhere we have used the term 'grand theory' (Doise, 1983) for those general concepts which inspire and guide the description of more specific psychological dynamics. McGuire uses the term 'guiding idea theories' in a similar sense. However, we believe we have gone one step further by proposing a structure whereby explanations inspired by different theoretic approaches may be articulated.

The long list of references at the back of this book will bear witness to how much we owe also to two leading social psychologists in Europe, Serge Moscovici and Henri Tajfel, as well as to Gabriel Mugny, who was to a large extent joint creator of the Genevan school of social psychology, and in particular, joint author of an earlier version of chapter 3 (Mugny & Doise, 1979a). Much of the work mentioned was carried out thanks to four grants from the Fonds national de la Recherche scientifique suisse, which we shared with Jean-Claude Deschamps, Gabriel Mugny or Anne-Nelly Perret-Clermont. Graham Vaughan of Auckland, New Zealand, and John Rijsman of Tilburg, Holland, both kindly invited us to spend an extended period in their universities where we were able to find the perspectives of time and distance so necessary to complete this work. But we trust that all our colleagues cited in the long bibliography appreciate that this book is based upon respect for their work. Progress in experimental work is achieved by questioning and criticism, but a time for integration and synthesis is essential as well. Of course, neither of these aspects of scientific investigation can ever be considered definitive. We hope nonetheless that this work will present a perspective of at least momentary utility in the development of experimental social psychology, and that at the same time it may make the task easier for those who wish to get to know something about this area of human science.

Translator's note

Articulation is a key concept in this book. Because the French term carries richer associations than the English, it seems important at the outset to attempt to convey some of the associated notions which go somewhat beyond the English sense of 'The action of jointing; the state of being jointed; mode of jointing or junction.'[1]

Le Petit Robert[2] lists a number of figurative meanings for this term. For the purposes of this text, the most important are:

'Organisation of the separate elements which contribute to the functioning of a whole.'
'Interlinking of two processes.'

Articulation might be translated variously as 'integration', 'interlinking', 'enlacement', 'interpenetration' and so on, depending on the context. Professor Doise preferred to use a single term throughout the text, to avoid dissipating his message. 'Articulation' in its richest sense is already employed by many literary theorists: now psychologists will find it a valuable addition to their vocabulary.

---

[1] *Shorter Oxford English Dictionary*, 1972. C. T. Onions, ed., p. 103, meaning 1.
[2] *Dictionnaire Le Robert*, 1979. A. Rey & J. Ray-Debove, eds. Paris: Société du Nouveau Littré, 109.

1 Levels of analysis

The current debate about social psychology leaves a number of questions still unanswered. Is experimentation desirable in social psychology, or even viable? What are the links between social psychology, psychology and sociology? What use is social psychology? Is social psychology fundamentally reductionist, does it aim to explain social phenomena in terms of non-social factors? In the final analysis, is it not all mystification, a widespread attempt to give scientific respectability to ideological notions whose principle aim is legitimisation of the established social order?

These questions have been raised repeatedly over the past years. Just recall a few names: Ring (1967), McGuire (1967, 1973), Pêcheux (1969–70), Smith (1972), Tajfel (1972), Moscovici (1972), Gergen (1973), Armistead (1974), Steiner (1974), Plon (1974), Pepitone (1976), Taylor & Brown (1979). This list is far from exhaustive, but does show how regularly social psychologists, especially experimentalists, have questioned the very foundations of their discipline. Is this perhaps a crisis in Kuhn's (1962) sense, signalling the beginning of a new era of creativity? Possibly. But the crisis has been around for a long time, a fact which scarcely arouses optimism as to the imminence of its passing.

I. A long-standing crisis

Wundt's two contributions

A hundred years ago, Wundt founded the first experimental psychology laboratory. In addition, he produced some ten volumes on *Völkerpsychologie* (folk psychology), translated into English with his approval as 'social psychology':

All mental products of a general character presuppose as their condition the existence of a mental *community* composed of many individuals, though of course their deepest sources are the psychical attributes of the individual. Because of this dependence on the community, in particular on the social community, the whole department of psychological investigation here involved is designated as *social psychology*, and is distinguished from individual psychology, or as it may be called because of its predominating method, experimental psychology. (Wundt, 1902:27)

I

Right from the beginning, a marriage between experimental and social psychology appeared to face serious difficulties:

In the present stage of the science these two branches of psychology are generally taken up in different treatises, although they are not so much different departments as different *methods*. So-called social psychology corresponds to the method of pure observation, the objects of observation in this case being the mental products. The necessary connection of these products with social communities, which has given to social psychology its name, is due to the fact that the mental products of the individual are of too variable a character to be the subjects of objective observation. The phenomena gain the necessary degree of constancy only when they become collective. (Wundt, 1902:27)

So the first answer to the question, 'Are experiments possible in social psychology?' appears to have been 'No.' It should be noted however that the problem itself has since somewhat altered in character: experiments are no longer restricted to the study of elementary psychic phenomena such as sensory perception or word associations, but may now be used to investigate complex thinking processes; while at the same time the fundamental involvement of such processes in our collective existence is ignored. We will return to this problem in Chapter 2.

Writers in conflict

The relationship between psychology and sociology was at the heart of a long debate between Tarde and Durkheim at the beginning of this century. The former maintained that facts of social life could be studied as psychological phenomena, and in particular, as processes of imitation: the latter believed that collective phenomena, and in particular social representations, had their own dynamic and should be studied separately, that collective phenomena were only to be explained in terms of other collective phenomena. This argument has never been resolved. Neither side won a decisive victory, and the controversy flares up again at regular intervals, as for example in the debate over the existence of a 'group mind'. McDougall (1920:6) wrote:

Only when the general principles of group life have been applied to the understanding of particular societies, of nations and the manifold system of groups within the nation, will it be possible for Social Psychology to return upon the individual life and give of it an adequate account in all its concrete fullness... [For] the aggregate which is a society has, in virtue of its past history, positive qualities which it does not derive from the units which compose it at any one time; and in virtue of these qualities it acts upon its units in a manner very different from that in which the units as such interact with one another. Further, each unit, when it becomes a member of a group, displays properties or modes of reaction which it does not display, which remain latent or potential only, so long as it remains outside that group. It is possible, therefore, to discover these potentialities of the units only by studying them as elements in the life of the whole. That is to say, the aggregate which is a society has a certain individuality, is a true whole which in great measure determines the nature and the modes of activity of its parts; it is an organic whole. The society has a mental life which is not the mere sum of the mental lives of its units existing as independent units; and a complete knowledge of the units, if and in so far as they could be known as isolated units, would not enable us to deduce the nature of the life of the whole.

A reply from F. Allport (1924:5) soon appeared:

given the *situation of the crowd* – that is, of a number of persons within stimulating distance of one another – we shall find that the actions of all *are* nothing more than the sum of the actions of each taken separately. (italics in original)

Half a century later, the same argument was still going on. Indeed, positions had become so entrenched that Tajfel (1972:97) had only to paraphrase a passage by Berkowitz (1962:167) to contrast the approaches of 'collectivist' and 'individualist.' We are thus able to illustrate both positions in a single quotation: the original text is by Berkowitz, with Tajfel's suggested modifications of the italicised portions shown in brackets.

Granting all this, the present writer is still inclined to emphasize the importance of *individualistic considerations in the field of group relations* [H.T. considering the field of group relations in terms of social structure]. Dealings between groups *ultimately become problems of the psychology of the individual* [H.T. cannot be accounted for by the psychology of the individual]. *Individuals* [H.T. Governments] decide to go to war; battles are fought by *individuals* [H.T. armies]; and peace is established by *individuals* [H.T. governments]. *It is the individual who adopts the beliefs prevailing in his society, even though the extent to which these opinions are shared by many people is a factor governing his readiness to adopt them, and he then transmits these views to other individuals* [H.T. The social conditions in which groups of people live largely determine their beliefs and the extent to which they are shared]. Ultimately, *it is the single person who attacks the feared and disliked ethnic minority group, even though many other people around* [H.T. a single person's attack on an ethnic minority groups that he dislikes or fears would remain a trivial occurrence had it not been for the fact that he acts in unison with others who] share his feelings and are very important in determining his willingness to aggress against this minority. Theoretical principles can be formulated *referring to the group* [H.T. based on the individual] as a unit and these can be very helpful in understanding hostility between groups. But such abstractions *refer to collections of people* [H.T. could only refer to unstructured collections of people] and are [H.T. only] made possible by inter-individual uniformities in behaviour [H.T. which are due to the fact that people live in a social context which has its own laws and structure].

Origins of the controversy

The other questions posed at the beginning of this chapter have been around for some time too. For example, Le Bon's book on crowds (1895) raised the question of the ideological determination of would-be scientific research. But we think it more important for the time being to examine the nature of the opposition between Tarde and Durkheim, or Allport and McDougall, or Berkowitz and Tajfel, and of course many others.

A short-term explanation would be that this persistent controversy merely reflects an institutionally constructed division within the universities, between the work of psychologists and sociologists, with social psychologists finding themselves stranded in the no-man's-land between the two. Certainly this division within the universities may contribute to the current polarisation of debate, but to take this as the only explanation is to forget that originally these academic divisions were not nearly so clear-cut (Durkheim had to teach a subject that looked remarkably like today's educational science); furthermore today it is psychologists like Tajfel who advocate a more social approach and sociologists like Boudon (1977, 1979) who try to explain collective phenomena by the cumulative 'perverse effects' of purely individual strategies. In fact, the conflict is much more fundamental because, while each side is scientific, and each elaborates different explanatory theories, each stance is fundamentally ideological.

Our society needs, on the one hand, to promote the idea of the autonomous individual, master of his own acts, capable of resisting social determinism so that he may play a responsible part in numerous social contracts: this was Rousseau's vision. What could be more obvious to the observer than the existence of autonomous individuals, responsible for their own social acts? Equally, what could be more clearly evident than the real existence of groups like nations, cultures, churches, races, groups separated by barriers which are designed to instil respect for social differences and to safeguard various interests, held to be of more importance than purely personal ones? Both sides in this controversy are constantly and forcefully reaffirmed, whether it be by common sense assertion or academic discussion (see Billig, 1982). This does not mean that explanations of a psychological or a sociological nature are illegitimate. Indeed, there are scientific theories which describe organisational structures at the level of the individual or at the level of society and which are investigated as such. But some way of articulating these two levels needs to be invented because social processes can only occur via processes in the individual, and these are in no way like uncoordinated 'Brownian' movements, nor are the contributions of the individual unaffected by the social structure which generates and guides individual activities.

Does this mean that up to now no social psychologist has worked on this articulation and that there is none whose work has demonstrated how it is possible to go beyond the opposition between the individual and the group? Such an assertion would ignore the work of pioneers like Sherif and Lewin;

it would also entail dismissing recent claims by certain leading European experimental social psychologists as being nothing but declarations of intent.

II. Attempts to articulate psychology and sociology

The work of Sherif

The work of Muzafer Sherif is very varied and now stretches over nearly half a century. We cannot hope to present a complete review of his work here, and so will limit ourselves to describing those areas which demonstrate an attempt to forge a link between psychological and sociological explanations. Sherif's first experiments (1935) looked at the creation of social norms and will be examined in more detail in a later chapter. What should be borne in mind here is that Sherif had no hesitation in studying a social phenomenon via experimentation. It is true that in his first experiments he approached the problem of how a norm is created at the personal and the inter-personal levels. Later, in his famous experiments on group relations, Sherif (1966) studied the same problem in an inter-group context. One of his pupils (Sampson, 1968) carried on this line of research elsewhere. The entire body of work is a demonstration of how an important collective phenomenon, which results from a combination of intra-personal, inter-personal and inter-group processes, can be studied experimentally.

Attitude measurement took pride of place in the American social psychology of the thirties, but the approach was mainly descriptive and documentary. Then Sherif & Cantril (1945, 1946) elaborated a theory based on the twin concepts of frame of reference and anchoring which allowed them to study attitudes experimentally. Work with Hovland (Sherif & Hovland, 1961) refined the model, and led to investigation of its function within the framework of the theory of reference groups, applied especially to adolescent groups (Sherif & Sherif, 1964). Attitudes were no longer seen just as personal dispositions, but also as anchored to one's social group affiliations and to relations between these groups. Research on cooperation and competition between groups again provided the best illustration of this social concept of attitude. Sherif frequently emphasised the inadequacy of individualistic theories in explaining the consistencies found in inter-group relations. He was aware of going against the current:

Especially in societies such as the United States, in which cultural and intellectual heritage stresses the importance of individuals and interpersonal relations, we often fail to see that many contacts among individuals are cases of intergroup relations. Failing to appreciate the distinctive properties of the in-group and relations between groups, we are then puzzled about failures in communication, misunderstandings, the obstinacy of certain individuals, and other events that would seem outlandish in the usual give-and-take among members within the same group. (Sherif & Sherif, 1969:222)

He makes this idea clearer by going on to reject successively explanations of inter-group relations based on instinct, on possible links between frustration and aggression, on displacement of aggression onto a scapegoat, or on deviant or pathological behaviour. He concludes: 'The crux of the problem is the existence of prejudices and hostilities and the participation of the bulk of the membership in them...The major problem, therefore, is such participation – not the ravings of a few deviate individuals.' (1969:227). The above could be an extension of Tajfel's adaptation of the quotation from Berkowitz cited above.

The question that inevitably arises after this brief resumé of Sherif's work is: Does this look like the social psychology referred to by the diagnosticians of crisis? We think not, and Sherif's work is rarely mentioned in articles about the crisis in the discipline. Must we then conclude that Sherif's work has no influence in modern social psychology, especially in America? Important though rudimentary signs suggest the contrary. The author index for the authoritative five-volume work on social psychology edited by Lindzey & Aronson (1969) took no less than 16 lines for references to Sherif, as many as for Freud. Only six other writers are mentioned more often: Festinger (22 lines), Kelley (19 lines), Newcomb (18 lines), Berkowitz, Campbell and Hovland (17 lines each). However, it may be that this impressive seventh place in itself provides the answer to our question about Sherif's status in the eyes of critics of social psychology: it could be that this position means he is not a dominant figure in social psychology. Though he has a very important place, he is not identified with mainstream thought, which is the object of criticism. We believe that this mainstream finds its best expression in the handbook by Jones & Gerard (1967), in which 40 writers are cited on more pages than Sherif. Probably because he is so little identified with dominant ideas, Sherif has escaped the criticisms directed at them.

The work of Lewin

In the preface to a collection of articles by her husband, G. Lewin (Lewin, 1948:xvi) recalls how Lewin, in one of his first publications on the will (K. Lewin, 1926), compared the task of linking theory and the full reality of the individual case to building a bridge across a gorge. And she continues, recalling the excitement Lewin expressed every time he crossed one of America's great bridges:

No doubt he conceived of his particular field of research as equally capable of joining what seemed such widely separated stretches of territory. The connection of theory and the profoundly disturbing social issues of our reality especially led him to experience this intense, persistent 'tension'.

The history of Lewin's work shows how he strove to bring about a closer connection between theory and praxis, and between the individualist and the social approach. Dissatisfied with the association theories which ruled German laboratories in the period following Wundt, Lewin began his psychological investigations by studying the will, or motivation to use a more current term. Since associationism required the intervention of some dynamic, Lewin hoped that his approach might lead to integration of both the whole and the elements making up the whole, as required by the Gestalt theories being developed at the same time. His book (Lewin, 1935) proposing a dynamic theory of personality demonstrates how this interest led his colleagues to what is now known as the Zeigarnik Effect (in which interruption has a facilitating effect in a memory task) and to study of levels of aspiration, today still an important area of social psychology. But it was more especially when he studied the role of environment in child development that Lewin (1933) began to be interested in the social factors which needed to be described 'as they affect the particular individual concerned. For the "objective" social factors here have no more an ambiguous relation to the psychological individual than objective physical factors have.' (1933:595). The notion of field, with its diagrams and vectors and topological representations, was first elaborated as description of psychological dynamics and subsequently developed into the notion of social field. Events in Nazi Germany, which forced Lewin to emigrate to the U.S., also directly influenced his scientific concerns. In 1935, he published an article which might be considered his first paper on social psychology, entitled 'Psychosociological problems of a minority group'. The divisions between Jews and non-Jews, in a ghetto situation and in liberal Germany at the beginning of the twentieth century, are presented in terms of two different diagrams. On the one hand, Jews in the ghetto are subject to pressure as a group from the surrounding society; on the other, in the more mixed society, it is the individual Jew who finds himself isolated and subject to pressures. Problems of identity are explicitly expressed within the general framework of group membership and in the more specific framework of the salience within a given situation of membership of a particular group.

During most of his life the adult acts not purely as an individual but as a member of a social group. However, the different groups a person belongs to are not all equally important at a given moment. Sometimes his belonging to one group is dominant, sometimes his belonging to another. He may, for instance, in one situation feel and act as a member of his political group; at other times as a member of his family, religious, or business group. Generally, in every situation the person seems to know what group he belongs to and to what group he does not belong. He knows more or less clearly where he stands, and this position largely determines his behaviour. (Lewin, 1948:146)

Hence the problems which can arise for people who occupy positions where several social groups intersect. To see how greatly these problems influenced Lewin we have only to look at the general titles given by G. Lewin to the collection of papers by her husband: Part I, Problems of changing culture; Part II, Conflicts in face-to-face groups; Part III, Inter-group conflicts and group belongingness.

It was in this context that Lewin, Lippit & White (1939) carried out their famous experiment on democratic, *laissez-faire* and authoritarian climates in groups. Lewin (1948:73), writing about this experiment, briefly discusses the problem of 'group mind'. His position is clear:

Groups are sociological wholes; the unity of these sociological wholes can be defined operationally in the same way as a unity of any other dynamic whole, namely, by the interdependence of its parts. Such a definition takes mysticism out of the group conception and brings the problem down to a thoroughly empirical and testable basis. At the same time it means a full recognition of the fact that properties of a social group, such as its organization, its stability, its goals, are something different from the organization, the stability, and the goals of the individuals in it.

Lewin's great merit here is that he has shown how one can overcome the dichotomy between the personal and the collective experimentally, by creating collective situations with defined properties which influence the interactions between the individuals taking part in a specific way.

Another famous piece of research (Lewin, 1943) was about changes in eating habits. Norms which govern behaviour are social and must be changed collectively by 'gatekeepers' who control movement of foodstuffs from production to the family table. It is true that from a strictly method-ological point of view one can find much to criticise in this experiment, which compares two conditions which vary on several dimensions. Nevertheless, it inspired a whole body of research (Radke & Klisurich, 1947; Bennett, 1955; Pennington, Harary & Bass, 1958) which did elucidate the roles of the different variables involved in the original work. The important thing was to start research into the social dynamics of change, and for this 'there is nothing so practical as a good theory': this was, yet again, that the collective and the personal, social practice and individual behaviour are intimately intertwined.

When he became Director of the Research Center for Group Dynamics at M.I.T., Lewin had already built up a large group of collaborators and his new position allowed him to attract many others. Their names are among the best-known in American social psychology: Bavelas, Cartwright, Deutsch, Festinger, French, Kelley, Lippitt, Schachter, Thibaut. According to Lewin, 'there is nothing so practical as a good theory', and it is certainly true that his ideas proved their worth by inspiring the work of others. So the question arises once more: where does the present crisis, or malaise, in the world of social psychology come from? Let us try yet again to find an answer.

Pitfalls of the experimental method

It is striking to note that Lewin does not figure in the top ten cited in Lindzey & Aronson (1968). Certainly, his relatively short life and career can partly explain his somewhat modest position within the social psychologists' hierarchy. But we believe there was a more fundamental cause: Lewin's message, his attempt (like Sherif's) to articulate psychology and sociology, was not understood. The direction taken by his best-known colleagues demonstrates this. Their paradigms emphasise intra-personal processes, or else inter-personal processes which are completed in the here and now, within the experimental situation itself. This is true, for example, of the processes described by cognitive dissonance theory, or by game theory: the experimenter manipulates his independent variables in such a way as to have complete control over the processes under investigation, and tends to forget their insertion into a social context which goes well beyond the experimental situation.

The development of Festinger's work, as described by Faucheux (1976:271), is a particularly good illustration of the progressive elimination of all that is social.

it is possible to contend that, since Lewin, theoretical social psychology has drifted progressively toward a sort of cognitive general psychology, leaving aside the characteristically social phenomena which Lewin had suggested, and becoming increasingly interested in more strictly psychological phenomena. The evolution of Leon Festinger in this respect is particularly worth noticing for, although being the person who since Lewin has contributed the most to theoretical progress in social psychology, he nevertheless has deserted the discipline after having moved successively from the study of intragroup mechanisms (*Informal social communication*, 1950), to the study of interpersonal processes (*A theory of social comparison*, 1954), of intrapersonal processes (*Theory of cognitive dissonance*, 1957), and he now devotes himself to the study of vision.

If we are to study the articulation of psychological and sociological processes, explanatory theories must take account of variables which exist prior to the experimental situation, such as power relations, relative dominance of social categories or subjects' ideological preconceptions. Sherif and Lewin themselves perhaps did not sufficiently emphasise these different levels of analysis and how they inevitably interact in a properly social psychological experiment. In some of their experiments, they did not show explicitly how these different levels of analysis are articulated. In fact, if one rereads the reports of experiments by Sherif or Lewin, one is struck by a shared characteristic. Sherif, in his studies of inter-group relations, emphasises that they all have in common something quite independent of the specific nature of these relations, which can be revealed by experiment: 'Yet, if there is a *social psychology* of intergroup relations, it should not be altogether different when we consider small groups, ethnic groups, labor and management groups, or nationalities.' (Sherif & Sherif, 1969:223). Similarly, Lewin studied, for example, the democratic or the authoritarian climate as such. Both authors give the impression that their experiments are investigating entities in themselves, this in spite of all the care they take to explain the necessity of studying social phenomena in a particular framework or context. The experimental paradigm tends to isolate and reify elements of a more complex process. In some ways one might say that Sherif's experiments on intergroup relations and Lewin's on climates and social change were primarily simulations or scale models rather than experimental analyses of the dynamics of interdependence between artificially created situations and a social context. While on this subject, it is striking to note that in Lewin (1948) topological figures illustrating social inclusions and overlappings abound when he is investigating social phenomena like antisemitism, but are replaced by graphs when he writes of experiments on group climate or levels of aspiration. It is as though the experiment produced at the graphic level as well as at the theoretic a schematic and impoverished representation of social reality.

Finally, the reason for Sherif and Lewin's very relative lack of success may be an important characteristic of the experimental approach itself, which tends to eliminate all it cannot directly control. This has led to concentration on paradigms and neglect of the social context. Once again it looks as though the opposition between the psychological, as studied experimentally, and the social, apparently uncapturable by experiment, has carried the day. Does this mean then that Wundt was right? This would be so if experiments really were necessarily limited to the study of intra-personal or inter-personal processes and unable to focus on the articulation of these processes with more social dynamics. However, the rest of this book will demonstrate that experiments can investigate the articulation of processes at different levels.

III. Levels of analysis in experimental social psychology

When Hovland & Sherif (1952) examined the ratings by different social groups of statements expressing more or less favourable attitudes to Blacks, they were dealing with a serious social problem, but their explanation only used an intra-personal theory concerning contrast and assimilation effects in judgement. To a certain extent, these authors even forgot that the scale used for rating (from favourable to unfavourable to Blacks) is in itself a reflection of an important social reality, having its own connotations and producing therefore very different reactions from extremists on both sides. In a subsequent chapter, we will see that Zavalloni (1964) and Eiser (1971a) incorporate this social meaning into their analyses, and they are thus able to explain how an intra-personal process can operate differently in members of different social groups. Hovland & Sherif left out an important level of analysis, just as Lewin did in his investigation into food habit changes, when he appeared to attach no importance to the fact that the leader of the discussion group argued a case related to the war effort which itself was not unconnected with the cause (the Red Cross) which brought the discussion group members together.

Let us now try to look at the problem of different levels of analysis in a more systematic way. We will distinguish four levels, and will show how they are important in many paradigm experiments in social psychology. Let us be quite clear from the start: we are not talking about four different levels of reality, but of four different levels of analysis. Theories are designed to capture different aspects of reality, and we are in no way trying to suggest that reality itself is structured on four levels.

The intra-personal level

A first level of analysis looked at in experimental social psychology is concerned with intra-personal processes. The theories describe how individuals organise their perception, their evaluation of their social milieu and their behaviour within this environment. In such theories, the interaction between individual and social environment is not dealt with directly, and only the mechanisms by which the individual organises her/his experience are analysed. The current research into cognitive development by the Piagetian school is at this level, as is research into perception of complex stimuli in social psychology. As examples, we may cite the work of Anderson (1965, 1971) or Fishbein & Hunter (1964). In general, their studies begin by measuring the value subjects attach to particular personality traits presented in isolation (e.g. friendly, cheerful, hardworking) and attempt to determine how these isolated evaluations are integrated into an overall evaluation where different traits are all attributed to one person. Mathematical models have been proposed to describe how these elements are combined: some models use an averaging procedure for combining elements, others use an additive process, still others weight different elements with different values. What all models have in common is that they treat the individual as an information processor which follows certain rules which may be discovered. Formulae will of course always be found to take account, with varying degrees of approximation, of empirical results. Different variables may be introduced, such as the time factor (how recent is the information) or its relevance or plausibility.

Better known are those investigations – on the same level of analysis – which are based on balance theory (Heider, 1946; Cartwright & Harary, 1956), cognitive congruence (Osgood & Tannenbaum, 1955) or cognitive dissonance (Festinger, 1957). All these theories, with varying degrees of formalised strictness, postulate a need within the individual to establish an equilibrium between the different cognitive elements in a given situation. This tendency towards balance affects a person's concept of the social situation and may lead to behaviour designed to modify the environment so as to maintain or achieve balance.

Like theories dealing with integration of information or cognitive balance, the theory about the categorisation process deals primarily with the ways in which the individual organises her/his experience of the social environment. This theory, presented in its definitive form by Tajfel & Wilkes (1963), describes how category membership leads to an accentuation of resemblances between stimuli in the same category and of differences between those belonging to different categories, when subjects are required to make judgements on these stimuli in certain conditions. This process is held to account for certain formal characteristics of social stereotypes (Tajfel, Sheikh & Gardner, 1964; Doise, Deschamps & Meyer, 1979).

The inter-personal and situational level

A second level of analysis is concerned with inter-personal processes as they occur within a given situation. The different social positions occupied by individuals outside this particular situation are not taken into account. Most experimental research into game theory is at this level. The object of study is the dynamics of the relations established at a given moment by given individuals in a given situation. It is possible to show the spiralling of processes which can lead to conflict and tension between individuals.

An older paradigm, using level II analyses, is the communication network studied by Bavelas (1950), who was one of Lewin's co-workers. These networks have often been used to show how the different communications systems which may exist between a number of people allow them to coordinate the information available in a more or less efficient way in problem solving. Once again relations between individuals are the focus of analysis: depending on their position in such a network, participants are found to be more or less satisfied with their contribution to group output (Leavitt, 1949).

Another pupil of Lewin's, Kelley (1967) also employs a theoretical model – attribution theory – which belongs essentially to the level of the study of inter-personal relations. To account for how people attribute intentions to one another, he proposed a model based on analysis of variance, which takes account of the consistency of the other's behaviour in different situations. Jones & Davis (1965) showed that other factors intervene, such as the importance for the observer of the other's action. Jones & Nisbett (1972) drew attention to the fact that it is important to study the point of view of the observer as such and as different from that of the actor: the latter tends to attribute more importance to situational factors, the former to the intentions of the actor he is observing.

The positional level

However, a third level comes into many investigations into attribution: it is made explicit in explanations which bring in differences in social position which exist prior to the interaction between different categories of subject. The effect of *differences in social position* on interaction was the subject of one of the first experiments on attribution (Thibaut & Riecken, 1955) which was therefore not just restricted to the study of elements in the experimental situation alone. This experiment is exemplary in the sense that it articulates one aspect of inter-personal relations, that of persuasion, and pre-existing status differences. Subjects were required to persuade two other subjects in the same experiment to give blood to the Red Cross. In fact, the two other subjects were confederates: one was introduced as being of higher status, the other of lower status compared to the target subject. Each time, the false subjects allowed themselves to be persuaded by the subjects, who completed a questionnaire about their companions at both the beginning and the end of the session. Results showed that manipulation of social status created a difference in the situation: subjects believed the low-status subject had really been convinced by their argument, whereas the high-status person was seen as more autonomous and as acting as he did for his own reasons. A given act with identical results nevertheless produced quite different attributions depending on the status relationships introduced into the situation.

In the same vein, Taylor & Jaggi (1974) studied the nature of causality attributions made by Hindus about members of their own group or about Muslims; they found that the proportions of attribution in terms of internal or external causality were reversed, depending on whether the question concerned a socially desirable or undesirable behaviour, by a member of one's own group or of the other. These are examples of the sort of effect membership of social groups outside the experiment can have on a given situation. It is interesting to note here that Kelley, who used a model based on analysis of variance in which the between-groups effect is usually important, does not introduce into his model any factor to account for inter-group effects. More recently Deschamps (1983) and Hewstone & Jaspars (1982) have demonstrated in a number of experiments the specificity of attributions in an inter-group context.

Let us look at a further example of how level III explanations are often grafted onto explanations at level II. Festinger's theory of social comparison, which starts with the fundamental need of the individual for self-esteem, though itself not explained in social terms, is based nevertheless upon inter-personal comparisons and therefore operates at level II: to evaluate his abilities, the individual often needs to compare himself with others, and prefers to make such comparisons with those who are similar to himself but marginally superior. What happens to this comparison process when it occurs in a relationship between groups of very different social status, as with Chicanos or Blacks on the one hand and Whites on the other in the United States? Aboud (1976) investigated this and she found that direction of comparison by individuals differed depending on which social category they belonged to and who they were confronted with. Blacks and Chicanos systematically behaved in a specific way when it was a matter of comparing oneself with someone who had succeeded more, or less, than oneself and when they could make comparison with one of their own group or a White. When they compared themselves with someone less successful, they tried significantly more often to compare themselves with a White. It appeared to be more gratifying to their self-esteem to compare themselves with people who were inferior but belonged nevertheless to a more prestigious group. Simply setting in motion the mechanism postulated by Festinger in an inter-group context showed that at least one of Festinger's propositions needs revision: the one which asserts that we always prefer to compare ourselves with those most similar to us.

The social experiences and social positions of subjects taking part in an experiment, which are a function of pre-existing social relations, may correlate to differing degrees with the dynamics of their specific insertion into a given situation. All variations, however temporary or limited, introduced into an experimental situation will be affected by pre-existing dynamics and thus tell us something about their nature. Frequently the effects of a given situation in an experiment can only be studied in terms of changes in a pre-existing dynamic. A process created experimentally may reinforce or counteract a social dynamic. At a theoretic level, therefore, we must articulate sociological explanations and explanations dealing with the dynamics of the specific experimental situation, i.e. explanations at levels II and III.

The ideological level

Lerner's (1971) experiments dealing with 'the innocent victim' brought in a fourth level of analysis. Every society develops its own ideologies, its own systems of beliefs and representations, values and norms, which validate and maintain the established social order. An example of such a belief is that which holds that reward and punishment, positive and negative sanctions, are not distributed by chance. Lerner's research is based on this general belief in a just world. Certainly his investigations manipulated situational variables: subjects took part in a learning experiment during which electric shocks were inflicted on a student who made mistakes: the latter might or might not do this for the benefit of the subjects, he might or might not receive a fee, might or might not expect further suffering. These variables had an important effect on subjects' attitudes towards the victim: he was more depreciated by those who were directly implicated, if he had to carry on suffering or if he received no fee. The basic explanation proposed for these results invokes the existence within subjects of a profound conviction that the world they live in is just and that people who suffer must deserve their fate. Therefore someone who suffers without apparent reason and who must continue to suffer is endowed by subjects with bad traits, suggesting that he deserves the suffering undergone. Recent literature on victimisation (Janoff-Bulman & Hanson Frieze, 1983) is based on a similar assumption.

Milgram (1974) invoked the prestige of science in his attempt to interpret his findings that people recruited at random through newspaper advertisements were prepared to torture others when the experimenter insisted they do so: 'the idea of science and its acceptance as a legitimate social enterprise provide the overarching ideological justification for the experiment' (Milgram, 1974:142).

The work of Lerner and Milgram shows that if we are to understand what is going on in the experimental situation, we need to invoke factors which go beyond the levels of analysis so far described and which permit a more global view:

Such institutions as business, the church, the government, and the educational establishment provide other legitimate realms of activity, each justified by the values and needs of society, and also from the standpoint of the typical person, accepted because they exist as part of the world in which he is born and grows up. (Milgram, 1974:142)

Let us note that these widespread beliefs lead to justification for whatever happens to those taking part. It is this conviction of universal applicability which paradoxically lays the foundation for social differentiation and discrimination.

Cross-cultural research also operates with analyses at our level IV when it deals with hypotheses about values or norms more or less shared by members of the same culture. Such research often articulates situational and cultural analyses in an ingenious way, as for example in Berry's (1967) investigations into conformity in two different cultures.

Articulation of analyses

Finally there is the problem of articulating the different levels of analysis. This will be illustrated in the rest of this book. We should note that analysis at each level is legitimate in its own right; one could look on each level as a filter which captures one aspect of reality while others escape. All science inevitably involves abstraction and can never capture the whole of reality. On the other hand, to restrict oneself to a single theory is always an impoverishment and it is often necessary to use complementary analyses at different levels in order to account for changes in a process described by a particular theory.

Articulation thus may be of two kinds: there is articulation of analyses at different levels or of analyses at the same level. An example will make this distinction clear. As we have already pointed out, the theory of cognitive dissonance deals typically with level I explanations because reduction of contradictions between incompatible cognitions is investigated primarily as a process of cognitive organisation in the individual. However, the need to maintain one's self-image in relation to another (see, for example, Frey & Irle, 1972) and the importance of 'definitional attitudes' linked to group membership (Cooper & Mackie, 1983) both influence the process and seem to call for articulation of analyses at levels II and III. Articulations with level IV have been proposed by Beauvois & Joule (1981) and by Poitou (1974) in the sense that the former looked at the process of reduction in dissonance as forming part of the function of ideology, and the latter looked at it as the product of an ideology which sees the individual as autonomous and consistent.

While cognitive dissonance theory and learning theory have frequently been said to contradict each other, articulation of different levels of explanation would allow investigators to make explicit the conditions in which the process described by one or other theory may be found. Because researchers rarely make such articulations between levels explicit, the rest of this book will deal with this kind of articulation.

However, within-level articulation is equally important and is more frequently attempted by investigators. This is most often done by linking different processes via a reinterpretation based on a more general or more fundamental process. This was the procedure adopted by Nuttin (1975) when he explained the attitude changes obtained in a situation of forced compliance as due to contagion of responses in a situation of arousal. He was then able to explain both phenomena which were in accord with cognitive dissonance theory (change of attitude when rewards are very low) and which were in accord with learning theory (change of attitude due to reinforcement by very large reward). Gerard *et al.* (1974) also suggested a sort of intra-level articulation though they did not invoke an alternative theory. They claimed essentially that the strength of justification for having carried out some action is a result of several factors and that the resulting justification must pass a number of thresholds: below the first threshold, justification is insufficient, at the first threshold it becomes just sufficient but contains many dissonant elements; at a second threshold, justification becomes comfortable due to a balance between positive and negative consequences of the proposed action; justification increases up to a third threshold where it becomes more than adequate. Dissonance would occur between the first and second threshold, while beyond the third, all additional rewards would have the effect of making subjects more well-disposed towards the situation and the position they are called on to defend. Cognitive dissonance theory and learning theory are therefore seen as not mutually exclusive but as operating at different levels of strength of justification provided by a social situation. Two theories generally considered incompatible can thus be integrated.

IV. Is there an inherently European approach to social psychology?

The preceding pages have demonstrated that there is no single school of American social psychology. The work reported is varied and operates at several levels, as indeed does the work of the European psychologists we will now describe. However, while we believe that there are several American social psychologies and several European ones, we nevertheless do think there is a dominant trend in American social psychology. The levels of explanation distinction allows us to describe it: it is a tendency to limit analysis to levels I and II. Festinger and Kelley, the two most cited in Lindzey & Aronson (1968–69), illustrate this point. It is true that this statement needs modifying since we know that Festinger began by investigating race relations and apocalyptic movements; nevertheless, the most important theories he developed are level I (cognitive dissonance) and level II (social comparison).

This same tendency is also strongest in Europe, numerically speaking, at least if one takes as an index the articles published in the *European Journal of Social Psychology* (Doise, 1980). Nevertheless, numbers which express an actual state of affairs are not necessarily a good indication of future trends, especially since social psychologists like Moscovici (1970, 1972, 1984) and

Tajfel (1972, 1974, 1978, 1979, 1981) have repeatedly and strongly argued for a social psychology different from that predominant in U.S.A. Are their words merely expressions of pious hope, declarations of intent without substance? Or can we really see a specifically European approach being developed? We believe one can realistically speak of a European trend in social psychology: its distinguishing characteristic would be the introduction of level III and IV analyses into its theories and experimental research.

Let us nevertheless be clear right from the start: the same trend can also be discerned in the U.S. The only difference is that in Europe, in recent years, some relatively highpowered and prestigious people have argued for 'a more social social psychology'. We have seen that Sherif and Lewin had already done so in the past, but perhaps present circumstances in Europe are more propitious for such a message to be heard.

We will not rehearse here the manifestos of the new school of European social psychology nor will we produce a new one of our own. The cases of Sherif and Lewin teach that more than that is needed for a new approach to carry the day: we must produce paradigms which deal with articulation of levels, otherwise experiments will again be restricted to analyses at levels I and II only. We will show that such paradigms already exist, that a dozen different directions of research in Europe involve articulation of levels III and IV with levels I and II in experimental investigations. In the three following chapters, we will describe in more detail some important research areas where these articulations are being elaborated.

We should immediately warn the reader that the accounts that follow are not intended to be exhaustive and that they are certainly biased by the fact that we have prefered to deal with those investigations with which we are best acquainted. Thus the comparatively high frequency of French examples in the research about to be described does not necessarily mean that French social psychologists are more typical of this 'new European school' than their colleagues in other countries on this side of the Atlantic. The dearth of references to contemporary social psychologists from Eastern European countries is explicable for the same reasons. In addition, in many cases it would be belabouring the obvious to show that their theoretic framework is to be found at our levels III or IV; this does not of itself anyway offer any better guarantee of success in attempts to articulate the sociological and the psychological than theories restricted to levels I or II.

Social mobility and social change

One of the best illustrations of the new trend in European social psychological research is the collection of work recently published by Tajfel (1978) on differentiation between groups. We shall return to this research in a subsequent chapter. But here it is important to note the theoretic concepts proposed by Tajfel (1974) in support of his experimental paradigm for the study of inter-group relations. He distinguished between a condition of inter-group relations where there is possibility of social mobility and where there is social change:

In each individual's life there will be situations in which he acts, exclusively or mainly, as an individual rather than as a member of a group; there will be others in which he acts, exclusively or mainly, in terms of his group membership. One of the important determinants of an individual's choice to act in terms of self rather than in terms of his group is what we shall refer to in this discussion as 'social mobility' as contrasted with 'social change'. The former refers to situations in which it is relatively easy to move individually from one social group to another; so that if a group does not contribute adequately to an individual's social identity, one of the more obvious solutions for him is to move, or attempt to move, to another group. In the latter class are those situations in which, for whatever reasons, passing from one group to another is very difficult or impossible. It may be expected that, in these situations, there will be many occasions (and constraints) leading an individual to act as a member of his group, or at least in the knowledge that he is categorized as such. Social change (as distinct from social mobility) refers therefore in this discussion to changes in the relationships between the groups as a whole, to expectations, fears or desires of such changes, to actions aiming at inducing or preventing them, or to intentions and plans to engage in these actions. (Tajfel, 1974:78)

Of even greater importance for a putative European social psychology is the fact that this distinction is explicitly associated with two very different ideological systems. It was Tajfel's discovery of the work of the American sociologist Hirschman (1970) which led to this link:

if Hirschman, Hofstadter (1945) and others are correct about 'the hold which exit has had on the national imagination' and about success having 'been long conceived in terms of evolutionary individualism', than it follows that 'most of our social psychology of intergroup behaviour' *should* apply 'to the behaviour of individuals who are assumed to have the belief structure of social mobility'...The American tradition of exit developed against a background of belief in individual mobility which, although it is by no means exclusively American, has probably been more salient in the social history of the United States than almost anywhere else...This being the case, the question arises whether findings derived from a social context overwhelmingly dominated by the exit (or social mobility) option can be said to have a wider general validity. (Tajfel, 1975:107)

Tajfel than went on to create an experimental instrument which also allowed him to study the psychological phenomena characteristic of a situation of social change: the Minimal Group paradigm (Tajfel, 1978), which we will describe in detail later.

While Tajfel, as initiator of a large body of research, links his approach directly to an ideological concept, it was clearly his intention, not to 'test' this ideology nor to show its superiority in relation to social mobility, which would have made no sense within his proposed framework, but to illuminate some of the possible psychological processes involved. The interest of this research lies not so much in the fact that it reminds us, as Sherif and Lewin did, that people often act in terms of their category or group membership, but rather that it provides a paradigm for studying different ways in which this important aspect of social identity might function.

We should add to this first body of research Giles's (1977) experiments on inter-group relations at the level of their linguistic expression. It is true that Lambert (1967) in Canada and Labov (1972) in the U.S. originated this kind of research, but it was in Europe that its articulation with social identity theory was outstandingly successful and the process of linguistic divergence was demonstrated experimentally (Bourhis *et al.*, 1978; Ball, Giles & Hewstone, 1984).

Social representations

Every ideology functions through a set of social representations which constitute so many collective definitions of social reality as elaborated within the society. Moscovici (1961), in his book on social representations of psychoanalysis, analysed newspaper articles, interviews and public opinion surveys so as to demonstrate that the dynamics of social elaboration of a representation differ depending on the interests of the group creating the propaganda (Communist party, Catholic Church, major newspaper interests). Other social psychologists followed him, Kaes (1968) and Herzlich (1973) among the first, and the study of representations now extends in many directions (see Farr & Moscovici, 1984). But what is of most immediate interest to us is the experimental use of this concept. Clearly this is another example of the articulation of different levels of analysis, and, in particular, of the effect of certain more general representations on personal interactions. For example, this applies in mixed motivation games (Abric, Faucheux, Moscovici & Plon, 1967; Faucheux & Moscovici, 1968) where simple manipulation of representations of one's opponent (subject plays against chance or nature, a machine or a person) demonstrates that subjects' strategies vary considerably even when their opponent's strategies remain the same in every case. Similarly, in a task which required a collective solution, Codol (1984) showed correlations between representations of this task, social relations established during interaction and behaviour during exchange of information. Abric (1984) also reports a series of studies showing the causal role of social representations in personal interactions.

Sources of cognitive balance

One characteristic of social representations studied at a personal level is their tendency to seek a balance. But what is the origin of this tendency to equilibrium, described for example by Heider (1958) and Cartwright & Harary (1956), which leads to systematic preferences for statements of the type: the friends of my friends are my friends, the enemies of my enemies are my friends? A fundamental property distinguishes the two sentences: one is based on the transitivity of positive relations – if A likes B and B likes C, then A likes C; the other is based on the intransitivity of negative relations – if A dislikes B and B dislikes C, it is not true that A dislikes C. Flament (1984) and several of his colleagues have shown that these two principles of balanced structures operate in different ways in different social situations. The former expresses an idealisation of reality – the group united in brotherhood – the other a Manichean view of the world as divided into two camps. This leads back to the study of general ideas which are activated in different situations. In a calm situation where subjects are reassured by their task success, the first view predominates; in a situation of tension or comparative failure, the second view prevails (Rossignol & Flament, 1975). Where social cleavage is invoked, the second is stronger than where such cleavage is absent (Pichevin & Poitou, 1974). A further set of studies shows that situating affective relations within a framework of hierarchical relations weakens the trend towards balance and strengthens a trend towards congruence, or the establishment of similar affective relations between individuals at the same distance within the hierarchy (Flament & Monnier, 1971). Once again an ideological view of hierarchical relations appears to determine the circumstances in which the trend towards balance will occur. We should also note the work of Leonard (1975) which begins with an ideological analysis of the bias of balance and which shows consistency of response in subjects does not occur spontaneously, but only in situations which evoke a need for rationality.

Power

One specific social representation is that of social power. The work of Mulder (1972) studied the dynamics of this representation experimentally, using a model based on the tendency in people with intermediate power status to reduce differences in power in relation to their superiors. The model is somewhat analogous to Festinger's social comparison theory, but lays greater emphasis on asymmetric processes. Mulder (1977) is now using it to study the social psychology of organisations, and again stresses articulation with explanations at level III by distinguishing different kinds of power which activate more or less strongly the tendency to reduce differences in power. Ng (1977), in research begun in Bristol, has been trying to articulate Mulder's theory with Tajfel's social identity theory.

Polarisation of groups

Another body of research appears to show that people who need to agree on decisions which imply a certain risk take more risky decisions as a group than as individuals. Brown (1965) proposed an explanation of 'risky shift' in terms of value: in our society, risk is valued more highly than prudence. Such a collective value would lead to a dual consequence at the level of interaction: (1) more arguments would be put forward in favour of a risky choice than in favour of a more prudent one; (2) the most risky responses would inform the most prudent individuals that their responses, contrary to what they supposed, are not valuing risk highly enough. The combined effect would therefore lead to a change in response for prudent individuals but not for bold ones. This explanation does articulate different levels of analysis, for all that it originated in America. However, it is significant that a similar articulation of explanations worked out in Europe by Moscovici & Zavalloni (1969) led to a reformulation of the problem of the risky shift: it is now considered to be a special case of group polarisation, which arises when people involved in a discussion are led to express their opinions in a more extreme form than they otherwise would if not in a confrontation situation. Thus it has been possible to show that situational factors which favour confrontation (being seated round a table rather than side by side, absence of time or procedural constraints) lead to a greater polarisation of available responses (Moscovici & Lecuyer, 1972; Moscovici, Doise & Dulong, 1972). We were even able to show that an American experiment (Kogan & Wallach, 1966) which did not use material about risk-taking, and which had appeared to lead to moderation in group response, had nevertheless led to polarisation (Doise, 1971). Since then, group polarisation has been found by many researchers, particularly in the U.S. (Myers & Bishop, 1970; McCauley, 1972). Meanwhile, investigations are under way into the bipolarisation which arises when the situational dynamic counteracts the pressures of a social norm (Paicheler, 1977).

Minority influence

Moscovici's research into minority influence (1979), which will be presented at greater length in a subsequent chapter, is also based on reinterpretation of a classic paradigm: Asch's (1956) pressure to conformity paradigm. If one looks at the Asch situation outside its social context, one could suppose that this experiment deals with majority pressure, but the responses of the numerical majority in the experiment are very strongly those of a minority, not to say a deviant minority, when looked at in a non-experimental context. A series of experiments by Moscovici (1976b) studied the specific effects of an influence which ran counter to the dominant norms in a given society. Mugny (1981) looked at the influence exercised by a minority when faced with 'populations' which subscribe to certain themes in the dominant ideology.

Contrasts in social judgement

One problem which preoccupied social psychologists for a long time was the difference in judgements made by extremists on opposite sides when they were asked to rate favourable or unfavourable opinions about an attitude object. A solution was only found when they invoked the notion of social value, related to social representation, i.e. shared evaluations by members of a society which govern social attitudes, such as tolerance, for example. The theory of assimilation and contrast proposed by Sherif & Hovland (1961) predicted that people with extreme attitudes for or against an attitude object should judge clearly favourable or unfavourable opinions as extremist in a symmetric way and more strongly than less involved or neutral subjects. But this is not what Hovland & Sherif (1952) or Zavalloni & Cook (1965) found when they asked militant anti-segregationists, militant segregationists and neutrals to rate statements about Blacks or about segregation problems as more or less pro- or anti-Black, on an 11-point scale. Only the anti-segregationists emphasised more than neutrals differences between pro-Black and anti-Black opinions. Similar results were found with students in favour of non-medical use of drugs who gave more extreme ratings than those not in favour of such use (Eiser, 1971).

How were these systematic differences between those in favour and those opposed to a cause explained? Zavalloni (1964) made a distinction between two types of judgement which might intervene in the same situation: direct judgement which expresses the actual attitude of the subject doing the judging, and indirect judgement whereby the subject places the opinion to be judged on the scale provided by the experimenter. The former, which the subject is not asked to express but which nevertheless intervenes in her/his response, determines how far the subject accepts or rejects the opinions s/he must judge, to the extent that s/he is favourably or unfavourably disposed towards the particular social issue. Even if the experimenter appears uninterested in a subject's own opinion, it nevertheless plays a part. Eiser (1971) makes a similar analysis and shows, as does Zavalloni, that there may be congruence or non-congruence between the two kinds of judgement.

For pro-Blacks or pro-drug subjects there would have been congruence: they could judge in a positive manner (favourable to, tolerant) statements with which they agreed. The situation was different for anti-Black or anti-drug subjects: they had to judge as negative (unfavourable, intolerant) opinions they shared and to judge as positive opinions they rejected: whence the hesitation to produce extreme judgements by the latter, a hesitation which would not have been shared by the former. A particular social value, the general meaning attributed by a society to being favourably disposed to the groups which make it up as well as to being tolerant, would be shared by all subjects and would explain their variable extremism in the requested ratings. In addition, Eiser (1973) worked out an experimental technique which permitted confirmation of this explanation: all that was needed was to reverse the value of the experimental rating scales. Thus, instead of only rating opinions about drugs on scales such as tolerant–intolerant/liberal–authoritarian/openminded–narrowminded, all of which allow only subjects in favour of drugs to evaluate opinions which they share positively, subjects must also rate the same statements on scales like immoral–moral/decadent–decent which permit anti-drug subjects to judge statements they share as positive. As expected, in the first case pro-drug subjects push their judgements to an extreme, while in the second case it is anti-drugs subjects who do so. This group of investigations seems to provide a particularly good illustration of the need for a level of analysis which deals with social values, so as to account for the results of research which was intended to deal only with intra-personal processes.

Religious orthodoxy

Ideologies are the result of historical conditions characteristic of a society which are unmodifiable by social psychological experimentation. The best way to study ideologies is to look at social upheavals at the historical level. Experiments nevertheless need not be reduced to simply demonstrating the basic principles of these ideologies, as for example in Lerner's work (1971) cited above. Some experiments seem to deal with the processes of regulation characteristic of certain ideological demands. Deconchy's (1973, 1980, 1984) experiments on religious orthodoxy are a case in point.

The theoretic presuppositions of this work are based on three definitions, summarised as follows:

We shall refer to an individual as 'orthodox' if he accepts, or even requests, that his thoughts, his language and his behaviour be regulated by the ideological group to which he belongs, and particularly so by the power apparatus of that group. We shall refer to a group as 'orthodox' if it ensures this type of regulation and when the axiological and technological basis of this regulation is itself part and parcel of the 'doctrine' accepted by the group. An 'orthodox' system consists of all the social and psychosocial arrangements which regulate the activity of the orthodox individual in an orthodox group. (Deconchy, 1984:429)

The basic hypothesis of the research which is of interest to us deals with a characteristic of the operation of the orthodox system: 'In an orthodox system, logical flaws in information are compensated by strength of regulation' (Deconchy, 1980:32) and this regulation is essentially social in nature.

One experiment described by Deconchy (1980) tried to increase perception of the logical flaws in certain religious propositions in students of theology or priests, individuals with clearly defined positions in the Catholic orthodox system: for all subjects, agreement or disagreement with the propositions became as a result a stronger criterion for membership of or exclusion from the group. In a second experiment, social regulation itself was manipulated: subjects were made to believe that acceptance or rejection was not a true criterion for determining membership of the group. This weakening of the social norm resulted in subjects' seeing more clearly the logical flaws in different religious propositions. In a similar manner, a third and fourth experiment confirmed that questioning the rationality of certain propositions led to a more coherent and unified representation of the doctrinal corpus to which they belonged and that, on the other hand, weakening of coherence, when subjects were made to believe that the corpus was less unified and coherent than they had thought, diminished the power of the social norm and showed up the logical weaknesses in their beliefs. The logical weakness of orthodox statements is thus said to be compensated for by strength of social pressure; when this gives way, the logical weakness becomes more apparent.

Deconchy's experiments thus demonstrate some of the mechanisms whereby adherence by individuals to their beliefs can interfere with social regulation. This is precisely how ideologies can reinforce social relationships, and particularly so when their links with these relationships are not understood.

Applied social psychology

To end this list of research paradigms which have been enriched by incorporation of analyses at different levels, let us leave the field of experiment proper for a moment to make a brief excursion into the field of applied social psychology. No doubt it is not by chance that the most explicit attempts to integrate analyses at different levels have been made when considering how to apply psychology or social psychology in practice. As we have shown elsewhere (Doise & Frésard, 1981), practical application requires enrichment of a given theoretic model by other models so as to construct a more complete approach to reality by reduction of the unexplained in each model. Breakwell & Rowett (1982) tried to work out a system for such an approach by distinguishing four levels of analysis or description of a problem and four processes as central to all social behaviour. Their four levels of analysis, in fact, are restricted to our first three levels, their levels 3 and 4 being, as it were, two variations of our level III. Let us quote:

With reference to the experience and behaviour of individuals in social context, the processes of analysis and explanation can operate at four levels: (1) the intrapsychic – with phenomena whose realm of operation is within the single person; (2) the interpersonal – with phenomena whose realm of operation lies in the interaction and relationships between people; (3) the intragroup – with phenomena whose realm of operation lies within the group; (4) the intergroup – with phenomena whose realm of operations rests in relationships and interactions between groups. (Breakwell & Rowett, 1982:101)

The social worker must try to define and explain the problem s/he is confronted with at these four levels, at the same time bearing in mind the four key processes which they term construal, consistency, comparison and conformity. We give below the main points in their definition:

> *Construal:* The construal process is the way in which people make sense of the world. Construal involves assimilating information, categorising it according to a classification system evolved through experience, and endowing it with personal meaning...
> *Consistency:* People seek stability. They wish to maintain their thought, feelings and actions in a state of equilibrium. Inconsistencies between any of these three elements result in distress because inconsistency threatens the person's ability to predict experience and thus understand it...
> *Comparison:* People seek to validate their understanding of the world. When possible, they use objective evidence in order to confirm their understandings. If this is not available, they compare their understandings with those of other people: a process of social comparison. As long as the process yields consensus the understanding is validated...
> *Conformity:* The process of conformity is founded in two sources. The first concerns the desire that people have to receive social approval which is necessary in some form if self-esteem is to be maintained. People conform in order to receive social acceptance. The second concerns the desire people have to enforce conformity upon others. (Breakwell & Rowett, 1982:103–4)

These processes are interrelated: 'People pressure others to conform (to think, feel, or act as expected) so that their expectations can be met and their construals verified, the need for consistency sated, and favourable comparisons maintained.' However, they do not necessarily work in harmony: 'Where the processes come into conflict it has to be resolved or else the individual will not function effectively. The processes themselves initiate change but conflict between them is a more powerful motivator of change. Such change will involve an adjustment in the relative salience of each process in that particular context.' (1982:104–5)

Several examples of social intervention are given to illustrate a typical outcome in three stages:

1. Analysis of the problem at four levels: intrapsychic; interpersonal; intragroup; and intergroup; and in terms of four key targets: identity; relationship; groups; and environment.
2. Explanation of the problem in terms of processes of construal, consistency, comparison and conformity.
3. Intervention in order to generate change using techniques based on the motive power of construal, consistency, comparison and conformity. (1982:106)

So Breakwell & Rowett (1982) recommend to social workers an approach which articulates analyses explicitly taking into account our first three levels, and also implicitly including our fourth by adding the bias of the pressures to conformity.

Theirs is not the only move in this direction even though other writers do not explicitly use the notion of levels of analysis. Gale & Chapman (1984) collected 15 contributions on psychological intervention into problems of childhood, criminal behaviour, failures of academic achievement, unemployment, satisfaction at work, industrial relations, accidents, depression, sexual difficulties, drug and alcohol dependence, smoking, inter-group conflict, blindness and deafness, mental subnormality and ageing. In all these areas, the twenty-odd contributors produced titles for subsections in their papers like: 'The extent of the problem, Concepts of the person and models of human behaviour, Individual assessment, The immediate social and emotional environment, The wider social and organizational environment, Problems of ethics, The role of other disciplines and professions...' The fact that over twenty writers could adopt, for very different problems, the same procedure of including a number of different conceptual approaches is a strong indication in favour of our thesis that theory about applied psychology necessarily requires articulation of many different kinds of analysis.

V. Preliminary assessment of levels of analysis

At the end of this first chapter we can already conclude that the traditional opposition between psychological and sociological explanations does not correspond to the real nature of explanations put forward in the various bodies of work in experimental social psychology. But while we distinguish four kinds of explanation, we do not wish to replace a dichotomy by a larger set of opposing analyses. On the contrary, we have shown on many occasions how introduction of a new type of analysis has led to a better account of the operation of processes which a single type of analysis was intended to explain. The analyses at different levels are complementary: when Flament introduced ideology to account for the process of cognitive balance, he at the same time also described a psychological process more exactly by distinguishing the intervention of two axioms; when Moscovici redescribed the Asch situation by analysing it in relation to the non-experimental context, he introduced at the same time a very important notion, that of consistency, into the study of intra-situations dynamics. When Tajfel made a distinction between ideologies advocating individual mobility and social change, he also made explicit the operation of a paradigm which allowed evaluation of the respective weight of inter-personal and inter-group decision strategies.

By introducing analyses at a different level to phenomena usually studied at a given level, the investigators mentioned enriched our understanding. If there is a case for distinguishing four levels of analysis, it is in order to unite them better in future research. It is precisely this articulation which in our opinion constitutes the task of experimental social psychology: without this, the proposed explanations necessarily remain incomplete. In the rest of the book, we will illustrate this theory in three different areas, in which we and our colleagues have done considerable work. Each of these areas traditionally employs a specific level of analysis: the intra-personal level for the study of intelligence, the inter-personal level for social influence, the positional level for inter-group study. We will show that study of each area remains incomplete without introduction of analyses belonging to levels other than those usually applied.

Let us nevertheless be clear that we do not intend to present complete and exhaustive accounts of different bodies of research in experimental social psychology. Our argument will be better developed by selecting for study a number of typical examples. However, the concept of levels of analysis and their articulation does not just apply to a number of examples chosen *ad hoc*. It offers a grid of analyses which can also be applied to an exhaustive study of very widely varying bodies of research. We have shown this by systematically analysing all the experimental studies published in the first nine volumes of the *European Journal of Social Psychology* (Doise, 1980). On this occasion different uses of levels analysis were found to be possible: if such analysis served in the first place to study theoretical approaches, it may also be used to examine experimental paradigms and, in particular, to analyse relations between dependent and independent variables. Study of such relations provides useful indicators of theoretical articulations not made explicit by the experimenter.

2 Levels of explanation in the study of intelligence

It would be difficult to give a definition of intelligence without appealing to notions that relate to the individual's organisation of experience and knowledge. So the study of intelligence requires analysis at level I. In this chapter we will show that such an analysis is not fully adequate: in fact, it only deals with the momentary expression at the level of the individual of a process which is social in nature and which must therefore also be analysed as such. Widespread neglect of the social aspect of intelligence has given rise to dilemmas over important issues, e.g. the question of possible differences in intellectual capacity between members of different socio-economic, racial or cultural groups. Indeed, most studies treat intelligence as a purely individual trait which can be measured in an individual test, and this very fact alone abstracts out the social function of intelligence. Often, studies of differences between the intellectual abilities of members of different social groups turn to biological explanations which invoke differences in genetic inheritance and ignore the complex interactions between heredity and factors in the environment. While statistical models have now been proposed which take better account of such interactions (Jaspars & de Leeuw, 1980), we still have no models or theories which describe the nature of this interaction between the individual and the collective, and how it might operate. Our aim is to fill this gap, at least partially, by looking at the intervention of social factors in the construction of intelligence. We will try to reformulate a problem which has for too long been restricted to analyses at level I by demonstrating the relevance of analyses carried out at the other three levels. However, experimental illustration has to be limited almost entirely to analyses at level II, or more precisely, to the articulation of level I and level II analyses. Experiments using the two other levels are still too rare, though articulation of these levels does appear to be possible.

I. Consensus on the social nature of intelligence

Mead

In the early 1930s, a number of psychologists starting out with very different points of view all came to the conclusion that intelligence was essentially social in origin. G. H. Mead (1934) elaborated a theory which linked inter-personal interactions and intellectual development. He began with the notion of the conversation of gestures: even before consciousness of self or thought properly so-called appear, exchange of actions between two individuals provides a foundation for the construction of symbolic thought. The action of one individual in relation to another is adapted to the reaction of the other, and is thus in some sense like a signifier which refers to a signified. 'Just as in fencing the parry is an interpretation of the thrust, so, in the social act, the adjustive response of one organism to the gesture of another is the interpretation of that gesture by that organism – it is the meaning of that gesture' (Mead, 1934: 78). Thought is internalization of the conversation of gestures:

The internalization in our experience of the external conversations of gestures which we carry on with other individuals in the social process is the essence of thinking; and the gestures thus internalized are significant symbols because they have the same meanings for all individual members of the given society or social group, i.e. they respectively arouse the same attitudes in the individuals making them that they arouse in the individuals responding to them: otherwise the individual could not internalize them. (1934:47)

This internalisation would be facilitated when verbal exchanges are added to the conversation of gestures:

If the individual does himself make use of something answering to the same gesture he observes, saying it over again to himself, putting himself in the role of the person who is speaking to him, then he has the meaning of what he hears, he has the idea: the meaning has become his. (1934:109)

Piaget

For Piaget, 'intellectual operations are interiorised actions, reversible (as to inversion or reciprocity at the level of concrete operations, and in combination at the level of formal operations) and coordinated into structural systems (elementary "groupings" between 7 and 12 years, network and set of four transformations from 11 or 12 years)' (Piaget, 1976c:187). He also emphasises in numerous passages the need for inter-personal interaction so that the child may free himself from his own centrations and integrate his perceptions into a coordinated whole. Cooperation between individuals is 'the first of a series of forms of behaviour which are important for the constitution and development of logic' (Piaget, 1950:163) and 'human intelligence develops in the individual as a function of social interactions which are too often neglected' (Piaget, 1971:260). When he wishes to list the factors which intervene in cognitive development, social factors of inter-personal coordination are described at the same time as factors of biological maturation, of equilibration of actions affecting the physical environment and of cultural transmission by education (Piaget, 1966).

At about the same time that Mead proposed his concept of the social genesis of thought, Piaget put forward his ideas on the same question. In a paper on logic and sociology, published first in 1928, Piaget made a distinction between *autism*, which was taken to be an extreme form of egocentric thought, *social constraint* which leads to conformist, non-autonomous thinking, and *cooperation*, defined as:

all relations between two or more persons who are equal or believe themselves to be so, in other words all social relations in which no element of authority or prestige intervenes. It goes without saying that it is difficult to classify behaviour except in terms of degrees of cooperation and coercion: the product of cooperation may end up being imposed by constraint, and so on. But in law the distinction is intelligible, and in practice, one can make an adequate enough estimate for this discussion. That being said, we believe that only cooperation constitutes a process which generates reasoning, with autism and social constraint attaining only the pre-logical in all its forms. (Piaget, 1976a:67)

And the paper ends:

In conclusion, we believe that social life is a necessary condition for the development of logic. We believe therefore that social life transforms the individual fundamentally, changing him from an autistic state to the state of a personality. When speaking of cooperation we are therefore thinking of a creative process leading to new realities and not of a simple exchange between two fully developed individuals...Social constraint is only a stage on the way to socialisation. Cooperation alone can ensure that spiritual balance which allows one to distinguish between facts which belong to the domain of psychological processes and rights which belong to the domain of the rational ideal. (1976a:80)

At a conference in 1931, Piaget summed up his ideas on the role of inter-personal cooperation in the development of intellectual functions in this way:

In conclusion, cooperation is the source of three sorts of transformation in individual thought, all three being such that they allow the individual a greater consciousness of the reasoning immanent in all intellectual activity. First, cooperation is a source of reflection and of self-consciousness. Here it marks an inversion of sense, not only in relation to the sensorimotor intelligence of the individual himself, but also in relation to social authority, which engenders imposed belief and not true deliberation. Second, cooperation dissociates the subjective from the objective. It is thus a source of objectivity and changes immediate experience into scientific experience, whereas social constraint can only consolidate the former by elevating egocentrism to the rank of sociomorphism. Third, cooperation is a source of regulatory processes. Transcending the simple regularity perceived by an individual and the heteronomous rule imposed by constraint in both knowledge and morality, it establishes the autonomous rule or rule of pure reciprocity, which is a factor of logical thought and a principle of the system of notions and signs. (Piaget, 1976b:114)

Vygotsky

In 1934, the year L. S. Vygotsky died, there appeared a work later translated into English as *Thought and Language* (trans. 1962). In it, Vygotsky attacked some of Piaget's ideas about children's language: he claimed that the Swiss psychologist laid too much emphasis on the egocentricity of early language (monologue, lack of coordination between simultaneous discourse of different children). For Vygotsky,

Egocentric speech as a separate linguistic form is the highly important genetic link in the transition from vocal to inner speech, an intermediate stage between the differentiation of the functions of vocal speech and the final transformation of one part of vocal speech into inner speech. It is this transitional role of egocentric speech that lends it such great theoretical interest. The whole conception of speech development differs profoundly in accordance with the interpretation given to the role of egocentric speech. Thus our schema of development – first social, then egocentric, then inner speech – contrasts both with the traditional behaviorist schema – vocal speech, whisper, inner speech – and with Piaget's sequence – from nonverbal autistic thought through egocentric thought and speech to socialized speech and logical thinking. In our conception, the true direction of the development of thinking is not from the individual to the socialized, but from the social to the individual. (Vygotsky, 1962:19)

There are other important differences between the theories proposed by Piaget and Vygotsky. The latter lays more emphasis on acquisition of a cultural heritage within the school system, an aspect totally ignored by Piaget. According to the Russian writer:

In the child's development...imitation and instruction play a major role. They bring out the specifically human qualities of the mind and lead the child to new development levels. In learning to speak, as in learning school subjects, imitation is indispensable. What the child can do in cooperation today he can do alone tomorrow. Therefore the only good kind of instruction is that which marches ahead of development and leads it; it must be aimed not so much at the ripe as at the ripening functions. (1962:104)

And then?

So in the early 1930s, three writers, whose names are today among the most highly respected in psychology, proposed three theories which certainly differed but which had in common a strong emphasis on the importance of social factors in cognitive development. What has become of these theories half a century later? What research programmes did they inspire? They ought no doubt to have prompted work which articulated levels I and II at least in the explanation of cognitive development. But this can scarcely be said to be so.

As far as Mead is concerned, his notions about the conversation of gestures as the origin of symbolic thought have not inspired any systematic research. It is mostly the other aspect of his work, on the social origins of the idea of self and on the interiorisation of values, which has interested investigators and led to work which appeals to symbolic interactionism.

Vygotsky was still living when Luria (trans. 1976) completed his famous study of changes in ways of reasoning following major social changes, at the time of collectivisation and literacy campaigns in Uzbekhistan. Similar results to his were found by Cole *et al.* (1971) at times of cultural change in other countries. However, it would not be true to say that Luria's research succeeded in throwing light on the specific processes which linked changes at the level of reasoning to changes at so historic and global a level as collectivisation of the means of production. On the other hand, this research was not pursued for political reasons and publication was only possible after the death of Stalin. In broad terms, we can say that research along the lines suggested by Mead and the lines suggested by Vygotsky have failed to integrate psychological and sociological analyses of cognitive development: in the former case, because interest was focussed only on classical areas of social psychology, and in the latter, because the approach could not explain how socio-cultural changes mediated cognitive functioning. Neither Mead nor Vygotsky produced a paradigm which permitted study of this kind of articulation. But what about the Piagetian approach?

II. Epistemology and overcoming contradictions in Piaget

Piaget's social psychology

Let us first look at the development of Piagetian ideas and research which deals most explicitly with the articulation of the psychological and the social. When Piaget (1932) studied the development of moral judgement, he went about it like a social psychologist: he did not just study the interactions of children who played marbles, their use of rules and their reaction to stories which dealt essentially with social interactions, but what is more important, the way he set about explaining his findings derives exclusively from social psychology. The transition from submission to rules to mastery of them, which can lead to children's changing the rules of a game, is explained by the large number of cooperative interactions between equals participated in by children in our society:

And if, at a given moment, cooperation takes the place of constraint, or autonomy that of conformity, it is because the child, as he grows older, becomes progressively free from adult supervision. This came out very clearly in the game of marbles. Children of 11 to 13 have no others above them in this game, since it is one that is only played in the lower school. (Piaget, 1932:98)

The same explanation is given for the development of attitudes towards lying:

For the need to speak the truth and even to seek it for oneself is only conceivable in so far as the individual thinks and acts as one of a society, and not of any society (for it is just the constraining relations between superior and inferior that often drive the latter to prevarication) but of a society founded on reciprocity and mutual respect, and therefore on cooperation. (1932:160)

Attribution of responsibility by only taking into account the effects of an act also changes to taking account of the actor's intentions through the effects of cooperation: 'It is cooperation which leads to the primacy of intentionality, by forcing the individual to be constantly occupied with the point of view of other people so as to compare it with his own' (Piaget, 1932:187). When it comes to ideas of equality and justice, 'it may be the case that, far from being the direct result of parental or scholastic pressure, the idea of equality develops essentially through children's reactions to each other and sometimes even at the adult's expense' (1932:274).

The child, at first incapable of cooperation and autonomy, spontaneously attributes the origin of rules of a game to adults, or even to God himself, rather than agree that rules might have been invented by children. A parallel is drawn between this development in the child and ideological concepts:

To the residuum peculiar to the conforming attitude of the little one correspond the derivations 'divine or adult origin' and 'permanence in history'. To the residuum peculiar to the more democratic attitude of the older children correspond the derivations 'natural (childish) origin' and 'progress'. (1932:68)

In the final chapters of his book, Piaget as a psychologist had no hesitation in making explicit the links between his own theory and those of the sociologist Durkheim. The latter tended to attribute an externality to the social constraints on the individual. According to Piaget, such constraints, however attenuated, could not provide the explanatory principle for autonomy. But on the other hand, constraint does have a role to play:

Without this unilateral respect [which the younger child feels for the older, and for its parents] one simply does not see how the ethics and the logic peculiar to social constraint and conformity could ever have come into being. In the moral sphere, it may very well be that such facts as ritual obligations and prohibitions, moral realism and objective responsibility would not exist without the respect which the child feels for the adult. (1932:349)

These are certainly explanations which attempt to link the social and the psychological and therefore constitute articulations of different levels of explanation.

A plausible explanation

If Piaget in the passages we have cited invokes a social explanation for cognitive development proper, it is nevertheless striking that this is never done in passages which analyse directly the performance of children under observation, contrary to his procedure in the study of the development of moral development. When he does turn to a social explanation for empirical findings, it is to explain differences in findings by other people. For example, he does this when offering an explanation for the intellectual backwardness found in children in Martinique. Their backwardness was not due to cultural factors: 'since they followed the same primary school programme as in France and...gave evidence nevertheless of a delay of about four years in the principal operational tests; here the delay seems to be attributable to the general characteristics of social interaction' (Piaget, 1966; 10).

At first sight, the differences between his book on moral judgement and this brief passage are numerous: the former does not deal directly with cognitive development but with a detailed analysis of moral development, while the other deals with problems of cross-cultural comparison which Piaget only touches on in passing; the former is an early work, the latter relatively recent and published first in 1966. However, what both these fragments of the Piagetian opus have in common is what comes out most clearly in the later text: while he does appeal to inter-personal interaction there, it only serves to provide a plausible explanation. All things considered, and despite the large number of investigations reported in *The development of moral judgment*, the role of cooperation in its development can only have the status of a plausible interpretation there as well. So that Piaget (1932) did not succeed any better than his two contemporaries in creating an experimental paradigm which would allow us to study the articulation of the psychological and the social in moral or cognitive development. Can this be just chance?

Rejection of a causal explanation

Another aspect of the links between social interaction and cognitive development appears in Piaget's writings. It shows that a more fundamental position is reflected in this absence of paradigm allowing direct investigation of the effects of inter-personal coordination or cooperation in child development. This position is most clearly set out in *Etudes sociologiques* (1965). There Piaget poses once again 'the question so often discussed as to the social or personal nature of logic' (Piaget, 1965:143). Having published his celebrated studies of different forms of operational thought, Piaget once again looked at the problem of the links between social life and cognitive development' by adding a new fact to the case: the existence of operational "groupings", whose role in the formation of reason may be discerned in their psychological origins' (1965). The same logico-mathematical models can account for the cognitive activities the child of 7 to 10 years is capable of carrying out on his physical environment, and for the social activities, such as intellectual exchange in argument or exchange of value judgements, of which he is also capable. So there is nothing surprising in the fact that 'the operational period coincides with...marked progress in socialisation: the child becomes capable of cooperation, that is, he no longer only thinks of himself but also of real or possible coordination with other points of view' (1965:157). In other words, there is a correlation between cognitive development and social development, though one cannot speak of a causal connection:

If progress in logic goes hand in hand with progress in socialisation, must we say that the child becomes capable of rational operations because his social development makes him capable of cooperation, or must we accept on the contrary that it is his personal acquisition of logic which allows him to understand others and which thus brings him to cooperate? Since both aspects of progress proceed exactly on a par with one another, the question appears to be impossible to answer, except by saying that they are two aspects of the one reality, which is both social and personal, and thus indivisible. (1965:158)

Epistemology as the answer

How are we to reconcile this position with that strongly affirmed earlier, and taken up again later, on the role of social interaction in cognitive development? We should note immediately that these two positions do not appear contradictory to Piaget himself, since they occur in the same texts. Thus when in 1928 he laid emphasis on the role of cooperation, he was already asking the question which was to recur in *Etudes sociologiques*:

We see that at exactly the age when the social life of the child is developing, he acquires the ability to enter into the point of view of the other, he practises reciprocity and discovers how to manage the logic of relationships. Should we ask here if it is the logic of relationships which leads to reciprocity, or the opposite? This is the problem of the chicken and the egg. There are two sides to every process: cooperation is the empirical fact of which reciprocity is the logical ideal. (1976a:79)

Question and answer remained the same when recently he wrote, commenting on our research into the sociogenesis of cognitive operations:

Whether it is a question of causality or of development...it is clear that coordination of actions and of operations are identical whether the links be intra- or inter-personal, and all the more so since the individual is himself socialised, and reciprocally collective work could never be undertaken if each member of the group did not have a nervous system and the psychobiological regulators required. In other words, the operational 'structure' involved is of a general or 'communal' nature and therefore biopsychosociological, and for that reason is fundamentally logical. (1976d:226)

The fact is that two different ways of thinking can be found in some of Piaget's writings. One is psychological and deals with the frequently minute analyses of systematic observations; the other is more philosophical, and deals with the epistemological implications of different theories. In practically all his writings on the links between social life and knowledge, Piaget begins by sketching out an opposing view: he describes on the one hand a position attributed to Durkheim, which accentuates the socially contingent aspect of logic, and on the other, a Rousseauian or nativist position, which proposes that the cognitive capacities of individuals develop autonomously and independently. At this epistemological level, Piaget opts for a third approach, as he does elsewhere when opposing Idealism and Empiricism, Gestalt Psychology and Positivism, Lamarckianism and Darwinism. At the level of these epistemological syntheses, it is clearly not a question of studying precise mechanisms, nor the operation of one variable on another. When he deals with a synthesis of Darwinism and Lamarckianism, he proposes a very general notion, that of the phenocopy: this biological phenomenon, the precise mechanics of which he leaves for biologists to study, is defined 'as a replacement of a phenotype, due to pressures of the surroundings, by a genotype caused by the organism's genic activities which then reproduces endogenously the characteristics of the initial phenotype' (Piaget, 1978:198). Piaget's (1980) contribution therefore is to provide observations which can be interpreted by such a hypothetic construction.

Inter-personal coordination, or cooperation, has a similar structure: it is never operationalised and remains to some degree an idealised notion which is intended to link phenomena of different kinds between which one can only observe parallels. The effect of empirical 'cooperation' is never studied experimentally. One of our objectives will be precisely that of making 'cooperation' functional at an operational level so as to study its mechanisms and effects in different conditions. But before we demonstrate this, let us give some examples of articulations of social interaction and cognitive development limited to pointing out the parallels. Later, with this as background, the specificity of our approach will be seen more clearly.

III. Socio-cognitive parallels

The Genevan school

A great deal of research has looked at the link between cognitive and social development, though it has done little more than demonstrate parallels between the two processes. The furthest this research has gone is to treat the social behaviour of subjects as a reflection of their cognitive capacities. We shall begin by citing research done in Geneva. First, let us look at the work of Nielsen (1951) who used a simple but ingenious technique: two children had to do a drawing with two pencils joined by a string, which meant they had to coordinate their actions. These studies aimed to look at how the social life of the child is constructed 'as intellectual activity with several participants' (Nielsen, 1951:139). When she worked with children from 6 to 13 years, Nielsen came to the conclusion: 'If we set aside the very rare examples of success...the real solution to social problems belongs to levels beyond the ages we studied' (1951:140). In effect, in the task with the apparatus described, strong competition seemed to counter the assignment which was to finish the drawing at the same time. Even though from 11 years practically all the children were shown to understand the assignment, it was also from this age that certain blocks appeared more frequently, especially in interactions with discussion. This is indeed proof that factors other than simple comprehension intervene in the task. Nevertheless, in other forms of collaboration, 'if we compare our results with Piaget's, we are surprised to find almost perfect convergence between his experiments and ours, which all show a turning point in social development around 7 to 8 years' (Nielsen, 1951:159).

Dami carried on this tradition of Genevan research by studying the evolution of strategies as a function of age in different competitive games between two children. While their strategies change with age, children do not necessarily adopt the most rational when they have become capable of them. The presence of an opponent has its own effect on the actions of the player, in two ways:

On the one hand, it exercised a positive and constructive influence by allowing the subject to perceive the situation in an increasingly diversified way, and develop increasing mobility (need to change tactics frequently because of the opponent's choices); on the other, it exercised a negative and inhibiting effect because the action of the opponent was constantly in opposition to that of the subject, preventing him from reaching the goal he had set himself. (Dami, 1975:158)

One characteristic of game playing is that it leads the player to invent strategies which are unpredictable so as to maintain indeterminacy and risk for the other. This is perhaps a primary reason why Nielsen and Dami did not always find the expected strategies in older children. On the other hand, behaviour which appears antisocial may nevertheless presuppose a high level of social intelligence. We should point to the work of Moessinger (1974, 1975) in this connection, and his studies in Geneva of sharing behaviour as a function of age. While the youngest children are very little concerned with exploiting all the resources available to both parties, egalitarian and equitable forms of behaviour make their appearance before that highly elaborated and anti-social form of social conduct, extortion, which only appears in children who have reached the stage of formal thinking.

All this research in the tradition of the Genevan Master does no more than demonstrate a parallelism between cognitive and social development, without trying to invent experimental situations which might permit the discovery of a causal link. Where there are considerations of interdependance or reciprocal influence, they remain at a high level of generality like that in the quotation from Dami. The least one can say is that this research has scarcely made explicit the notion of inter-personal cooperation or coordination as a factor in cognitive development.

Flavell

Outside Geneva, approaches to the investigation of links between cognitive development and social interaction are not fundamentally different. As an example, we will look at the work of Flavell *et al.* (1968): the development of some of the cognitive mechanisms which intervene in social interaction is studied for the most part using situations where the child has to coordinate his actions with those of an experimenter. Flavell describes his approach as that of a 'developmental naturalist' (p.2) or as 'developmental descriptive' (p. 207): without attempting a causal analysis, he wants to describe development of roletaking and communication skills. His experimental tasks seem to be typical of this line of research, so we will describe them in some detail.

In one experiment, the child was given two containers, whose tops were labelled to show that one contained one coin, the other two. The child had to remove the money from one of the containers and predict the choice of a confederate who was told that now only one container had money in it. Three principal strategies were found, depending on whether the child took account of: (a) the material aspect only (5 to 8 or 9 years); (b) the purpose that the other might attribute to the child, which therefore leads the child to change his plan (from 10 to 11 years); (c) the possibility that the other might take account of strategy (b), which would lead the child to stick to his first plan (very rare). Normal development is therefore taken to be progress from centring on the object towards integration of the child's own purpose and the fact that the other could take it into account.

A second task was similar to the Three Mountains test invented by Piaget and Inhelder (1956): different objects were arranged in front of the child who had to reproduce their arrangements from the point of view of the experimenter on the other side of the table. Results showed that the ability to discover the point of view of the other develops with age. Still another task looked at the ability to decentre from one's own viewpoint: a series of seven drawings was shown to the child who was asked to tell a story about them. Three drawings were then removed and the child had to suggest what story a new person would produce based on the four remaining drawings. Decentration from the original story was frequent around 9 to 10 years.

A fourth and fifth test confirmed that the older child can take into account the characteristics of his audience by comparing the descriptions of a target object to a person who can see the object and to one who cannot, or by comparing the elements of information necessary to decipher a code given to members of groups who can or cannot say what elements they already know. A second series of studies using tasks very similar to those described confirmed these results.

A completely new experiment produced very clear results: in two different situations, the child had to try to convince another person who was not present. The number of different arguments increased very significantly with age: older children also produced more persuasive arguments and appealed to the interests of the other person. Results of a second new experiment were less clear: children were asked to tell the same story twice, once as a 'timid' child, and once as a 'brave' one. By 6 to 7 years, stories were very different, and this difference did not increase significantly with age. Perhaps it is easier to play a particular role oneself than to take account of particular traits in another person.

Flavell's book also reports a series of experiments with younger children from 3 to 6 years. These experiments were less well adapted, but nevertheless showed that before 6 years many children are not aware that other perspectives than their own exist, and that most children are aware of this from 6 years on. To know that the point of view of the other is different does not of itself mean knowing in what way it is different.

Flavell's purpose was descriptive. Several of his colleagues, whose experiments are reported in this book, went further and tried to improve children's communication. They were not very successful. More important in our view, however, is the list, produced by Flavell (1968:208), of factors which can help a child make progress in the course of an interaction, e.g. the fact that interaction introduces continuity of another person's viewpoint into the situation. But once again, these factors are only presented as hypothetical constructs which, like cooperation with Piaget, are not subjected to experimental test.

Feffer, Waller and Damon

In Flavell's work, the notion of role does not have the social content usually attributed to it. Other writers have devoted themselves more specifically to the study of developmental mastery of social roles. We will first look at the approach of Feffer (1959) who developed a task called the 'Role Taking Task' (RTT). Using dolls and props, the subject creates a scene in the street or in a house with at least three characters, and then describes the scene from the point of view of each participant. The different versions are analysed according to the changes in the features mentioned for each character as seen by a different actor, and according to the integration of points of view in the different accounts: progress is greatest between 8 and 11 years. In a theoretical paper, Feffer (1970) discusses Piaget's notions of centration and decentration and Asch's Gestaltist concepts, and arrives at a developmental model of social interaction which entails coordination of elementary bipolar schemata. These schemata are at first isolated from each other and give rise to conflicting and fluctuating viewpoints. As with conservation of physical quantities, progress occurs when different polar dimensions are coordinated, e.g. give–receive, question–answer, dominate–obey.

Waller (1978) also set out to study socialisation from a cognitive perspective, and attacked the problem of differentiation between behaviour linked to status or social role and behaviour linked to a particular system of inter-personal relations. Subjects were presented with situations which varied, on the one hand as to sex and age of the two protagonists, and on the other as to particular aspects of the situation, such as how threatening it was and whether it could be changed. Let us give an example of a problem given to the children: a girl and a boy are both doing an errand for their mother, both discover they no longer have the money their mother had given them. The girl thinks: I left it at home. The boy thinks: I lost it while playing. Which child cries? Which does not? If subjects reply in terms of social stereotypes, they say the girl cries; if they reply in terms of the irreversibility and threat in the situation, then the boy is said to cry. A developmental trend was found: children of 6 to 9 years took more account of the details of the situation than those of 4 to 5 years. While decentration in relation to well-established stereotypes became possible with increasing age, these stereotypes nevertheless tended to gain strength with age when not counteracted by particular aspects in the situation.

Many investigations into the link between cognitive and moral development are in the same vein. Let us mention here the work of Damon (1977) who has the merit of using better experimental instruments than Piaget's (1932) or Kohlberg's (1963) hypothetical stories. Unfortunately, this line of research is usually limited to showing the existence of a link between cognitive and social development. The explanation given for this correspondence is that increased mastery of cognitive skills permits a more successful participation in increasingly complex social interactions. A counter-reaction of social interaction on cognitive development is rarely envisaged. This remains true for most current research into the development of social cognition (see Doise, 1985a).

IV. Social interaction and cognitive development

There is no dearth of research which demonstrates a certain correspondence between cognitive and social development. But none attack the question of causality: their paradigms do not allow this anyway, for only an experimental approach which explicitly manipulates different aspects of social interaction could show the possible influence of social regulatory mechanisms on cognitive ones. In our research we therefore explicitly introduce kinds of social interaction as an independent variable into the experimental design, in order to study their effects on particular aspects of cognitive development.

To claim that social interaction plays a causal role in cognitive development does not entail acceptance of the idea that the individual is passively fashioned by regulatory mechanisms imposed from outside. Our concept is interactionist and constructivist: by acting on her/his environment, the individual develops systems for the organisation of such action on the real world. In most cases, s/he is not alone in confronting reality: it is precisely by coordinating her/his own actions with those of others that s/he elaborates systems of coordination of actions and is subsequently able to repeat such actions when alone. The causality that we attribute to social interaction is therefore not unidirectional but circular, proceeding in spiral: interaction allows the individual to master certain coordinations which then lead to ability to participate in more elaborate social interactions, which in turn become a source of cognitive development for the individual. Thus at given levels of cognitive development, certain social interactions operate in a way similar to inducers of embryogenesis by providing the conditions for development of new cognitive organisation. It is in this sense that we want to illustrate experimentally the thesis that, at certain levels of development, social interaction produces cognitive structures which the individual could not master before the interaction but can master after. Coordination of actions between individuals precedes individual cognitive coordination of certain actions.

The research carried out by our team in this field has been in several stages. In the first phase, we wanted to assess differences in cognitive performance between individuals who were working together on a given apparatus and those who were working alone on the same apparatus. More particularly, we needed to show that groups organise their activities more than do individuals, and especially when certain cognitive coordinations are being developed in individuals who are members of the group. In a second phase, we wanted to show that coordinations elaborated in social interaction are subsequently mastered by the individual alone. A third series tried to show more explicitly that it is the need to resolve conflicts between opposing perspectives which gives rise to new cognitive structures.

These three preliminary phases are sometimes intermingled in our research. We will deal with them separately, not only because broadly speaking they correspond to stages which followed one another in our research, but principally so as to make our findings clearer. One consequence is that at first the effect of social interaction was studied in general terms and later we tried to separate out which particular aspects of the interaction were a source of progress.

Our concept of the articulation of levels I and II in the study of intelligence is illustrated better by the complete body of research rather than by each experiment taken in isolation. A recent book (Doise & Mugny, 1984) gives full details.

Constructive interaction within groups

Our first set of results bears on the constructive aspect of social interaction. We mean by this that individuals who interact with one another to solve a given problem come to give better performances, at least at certain stages in development, than individuals acting alone. Different tasks have been used, notably ones involving motor coordination and spatial transformations.

Research on motor coordination (Doise & Mugny, 1975) was carried out to test the hypothesis that differences which are favourable to a group compared to the individual only arise at a certain level of development, group and individual performances being similar when the individual has mastered the coordination in question. To test this hypothesis, we used a task of interdependent motor coordination called *jeu cooperatif* (cooperative game). Subjects had to make a moving object follow a given track by pulling cords on pulleys. The task was 'cooperative' in that success required coordination of the actions executed jointly on both pulleys, which either unrolled, rolled up or blocked the cord. Performance of subjects was recorded by a felt-tip pen fixed to the moving object so that subjects were given direct feedback as to their coordination. At the end, a score was calculated according to whether the trace was in the middle of the track (one point) or off the track (minus point).

Subjects were placed in front of the apparatus either alone or in pairs. In the lone condition, the child was asked to complete a first track using two pulleys, then a second symmetric in form to the first. With the pairs, children were required to complete the same two tracks but each child manipulated a single pulley. They were told they could talk. Subjects were 7 to 8 or 9 to 10 years. Results showed a significant difference between individuals and pairs in younger children but not in the older. The pairs produced better coordinated actions than the individuals but only at a given development stage, this superiority being cancelled out by normal development. This squares well with the thesis that operations are first elaborated via social interaction and are only later acquired by the individual alone.

Using the same apparatus, group situations were particularised by imposing a leader or by preventing verbal communication. For the younger children such manipulations were very disrupting, but not for the older ones who had already mastered the coordinations used in the task.

A different task, using spatial transformations, was an adaptation of Piaget & Inhelder's (1956) Three Mountains test. The apparatus used consisted of two identical sets of three houses. One set was arranged by the experimenter on a stand and the child had to copy the village exactly on a separate stand with the other set of houses. Four lay-outs (villages) had to be copied: two were easy, with the stands for model and copy oriented in the same direction, and two difficult, with the stand for the copy turned round 180° in relation to the model. The children made copies either alone or in pairs. The experimental measure was the number of houses correctly placed. Results showed that pairs succeeded better than single subjects, especially with the difficult copies: appropriate analyses showed that this was not a simple artefact due to the greater probability that, in pairs, one of the two was likely to be at a level to complete the task alone.

A second experiment (Mugny & Doise, 1978a) with the same apparatus, but with a pre-test, showed even more clearly the productivity of the group performance. Thus, for example, half the pairs made up of one child who managed no transformation and of one child who produced an incomplete transformation in the pre-test did succeed in at least one complete copy of one of the two difficult transformations when working together.

So it is clear from this first set of experiments that, at certain moments in cognitive development, social coordination of actions on reality is in advance of individual coordination of the same actions.

Effects on individuals of social coordination of actions

If, by interacting with others, children produce cognitive coordinations they were not previously capable of, we still need to show that after social interaction children have improved in their mastery of cognitive coordinations. Anne-Nelly Perret-Clermont (1979) has concentrated mainly on this issue.

A first experiment (Doise, Mugny & Perret-Clermont, 1975) tried to show that non-conserving and intermediate children in a liquid transformation task (Piaget & Szeminska, 1952) would show improvement in this test if they participated in a task of sharing liquids with two children who were conservers. Results showed the effect of social interaction: in the experimental condition, 24 out of 37 children improved. Comparison with the control group, in which 2 out of 12 improved, shows that a simple factor of maturation or of uncontrolled social interaction is unlikely to be responsible for the high percentage (64.8%) who did show improvement.

Results of a second post-test showed that this improvement was fairly stable. To demonstrate that it was not just simple effect of memory but was mastery of new operations, responses of experimental subjects in post-tests were compared with the different arguments given by conserving subjects during the social interaction. More than half the subjects who showed conservation in post-tests introduced into their own explanations one or more arguments which had not appeared in the social interaction.

Similar results have been obtained since, not only in the second experiment on spatial transformations (Mugny & Doise, 1978a) but also in a new conservation experiment with liquids and with number (Perret-Clermont, 1979). Every time improvement between pre- and post-test was found in subjects who, in the intervening period, had taken part in certain forms of social interaction. In addition, the new experiment on conservation of liquids showed that experimentally induced improvement went hand in hand with improvement in other operational tests, just as in the 'natural' development studied by the Genevan school. On the other hand, several experiments also showed that a given interaction does not bring about development in just any individual: a minimal competence is required which allows the subject to take part in a socio-cognitive interaction. This competence will have been acquired in the course of previous interactions.

This second group of experiments shows that children who have participated in a social interaction which produced coordinations new to them do become capable of reproducing them subsequently when alone. Tests of generalisation and analysis of the children's justifications at post-test also showed that progress is 'authentic'.

Socio-cognitive conflict in cognitive development

In a third group of experiments, we tried to make more explicit the constructivist concepts on which our theory about the links between social interaction and cognitive development is based. Articulation of the collective and the personal in no way requires that we accept a simple projection of one onto the other, nor that we treat the genesis of cognitive operations in the individual as the passive acquisition of a social heritage. Without denying the importance of this heritage, our thesis is that, at certain stages in development, joint action by several individuals, entailing resolution of conflicts between their different perspectives, leads to construction of new coordinations. This has an important consequence; during an interaction between two individuals who are in process of elaborating certain modes of coordination of their actions, the more advanced as well as the less so can make progress. This thesis of course goes counter to all social learning theories which tend to explain learning by modelling or by acquisition of external rules.

We have been able to observe on many occasions the construction of new coordinations during the reproduction of the villages described earlier, and reported in Doise, Mugny and Perret-Clermont (1975). The level attained by pairs was more advanced than that expected if one took account of the most advanced member of the dyad. This result was confirmed using the same apparatus (Mugny & Doise, 1978a).

How can we explain these results? We look for an explanation in the direction suggested by Smedslund (1966) when he dealt with the social origins of decentration. With him, we think that the dynamics of development principally derive from a conflict in social communication: in an interaction between several individuals, centrations come into more direct conflict than where a single individual must act on the real world. For the interaction to come to a satisfactory conclusion, people need to coordinate their opposing perspectives. An experiment by Mugny, Doise & Perret-Clermont (1975–76) illustrates clearly how conflict in communication can lead to new structuration as the result of countersuggestion in a conservation test of length.

We know that, at a certain stage of development, a child accepts that two straight rulers placed parallel in front of him with ends clearly level are the same length, but not the same when one of the rulers is displaced. Using an ordinal evaluation schema already at his disposal, the child estimates that the displaced ruler is longer. In effect, he centres on one end of the displaced ruler which does in fact extend beyond the end of the other, but he does not take account of the inverse displacement at the other end.

In our experiment, we wanted to study the effect of a conflict of perspective introduced socially to non-length-conserving children. After a classic pre-test (Inhelder, Sinclair & Bovet, 1974), new test material was used: two wooden rails of the same length from a miniature railway. Once their equality had been confirmed by the child, one of the rails was displaced as in the classic test. After the child had said that one rail was longer than the other, the experimental manipulation was carried out: in one condition, an adult confederate contradicted the child by giving the correct response and showed that the amount of overlap at one end was cancelled out by loss at the other (positive conflict): in a second condition, the adult contradicted the child but gave an incorrect response by pointing to the increased length at the other end of the rail not chosen by the child (negative conflict): in a control group, there was no contradiction, but the same material was presented to subjects first with ends together, then one shifted, return to starting position and displacement of the other; so that children might pick up the contradiction in their own judgements.

If the conflict hypothesis is valid, improvement is expected in both experimental conditions; if modelling is correct, only the first (positive conflict) condition should lead to improvement. To test this, children immediately took part in a new conservation test using rulers of the same length, and also two chains of different lengths, to test conservation of inequality when the longer chain is folded so that both ends are within the span of the shorter chain (see Inhelder, Sinclair & Bovet, 1974). This post-test was repeated ten days later by an experimenter who did not know the children's original assignment to groups. Results showed that social conflict of centrations certainly is a source of progress. Both children confronted with of false response (negative conflict) and those given the correct response (positive conflict) showed improvement. Conflict of communication (Smedslund, 1966) therefore does generate new constructions even when the subject has not been exposed to more highly developed behaviour.

Similar results have been found since on a number of occasions. Using the same conservation test, Mugny, Giroud & Doise (1978–79) found similar results by opposing one child against another. Here two children, neither conservers in length conservation tests, sat opposite each other and judged displacements of rulers performed by the experimenter. It was found that their opposed centrations led to a socio-cognitive conflict and to improvement in post-test. The importance of socio-cognitive conflict was also shown using a spatial transformation task (Doise & Mugny, 1979).

Corroboration from other investigators

Let us note before ending this section that several other writers have obtained results which corroborate our principal hypothesis as to the importance of social interaction for cognitive development. For example,

F. B. Murray published a paper in 1972 which reported that children who responded to different conservation problems in a consensus situation subsequently showed individual progress. Silverman & Stone (1972) also confirmed significant improvement after interaction on a test of conservation of space: Silverman & Geiringer (1973) confirmed that social interaction in one test situation can lead to improved performance in other tests. Maitland & Goldman (1974) also found improvement with interaction on problems of moral judgement, while Miller & Brownell (1975) reported such improvement in the domain of length and weight conservation. Our own experiments were carried out without any knowledge of this work, and thus provide independent confirmation.

Several other investigators (D. Kuhn, 1972; Rosenthal & Zimmerman, 1972; J. P. Murray, 1974; Zimmerman & Lanaro, 1974) have also found improved conservation with a single observation of a model. Does this mean that an explanation of cognitive development based on the notion of socio-cognitive conflict is inadequate? We do not think so, because the effect of the model may well be due to the conflict it induces. When Kuhn (1972:843) writes: 'Thus, observation of a model performing a task in a manner discrepant from (but not inferior to) the child's own conceptualisation of the task may be sufficient to induce in the child an awareness of alternative conceptions and will perhaps lead to disequilibrium and reorganisation', we are in agreement but on condition that the restriction in brackets be omitted. We (Mugny & Doise, 1978a) have obtained results which show clearly that an inferior model can be a source of progress; and for their part, Ames & Murray (1982), Glachan & Light (1982) and Bearison, Magzamen & Filardo (1984) have all shown experimentally some of the characteristic effects of socio-cognitive conflict.

One area where our research should be pursued is the development of formal thinking. Laughlin (with Jaccard, 1975; with Sweeney, 1977) has shown that, at this stage of cognitive development as well, the group prevails over the individual. Using a different task, Stalder (1975) showed in addition how variables which modify social interaction in groups also modify the cognitive strategies of group members during the interaction. We need to find out if these effects persist after the interaction: Gilly & Roux (1984) have reported results pointing in this direction.

Our concept of the articulation of levels I and II in the investigation of intelligence depends on a spiral model: participation in certain interactions provides the opportunity to elaborate instruments which allow children to take part in more complex interactions. Acquisition of new abilities has been studied in the research reported. But this aspect of the process must not make us forget the other characteristic of the dynamic: participation in particular social interactions is dependent on the level of cognitive development reached by the child (Doise & Mugny, 1981). In a set of experiments on failures in verbal communication, Robinson & Robinson (1977, 1978) showed that children who had not reached a certain level of development systematically attributed the cause of failure to the receiver of a communication, the proximal cause, when in fact it was the sender who gave ambiguous messages. Such results can well explain misunderstandings between adults and children and the guilt feelings which may result. But we must remember that, according to our theory, the indispensable prerequisites for profiting from an interaction or for understanding the causes of failure of communication are themselves constructed socially (also see Doise & Palmonari, 1984).

V. Group membership, social status and cognitive development

Sociologists have clearly shown that children from different socio-economic groups do not have the same chances of success at school (Boudon, 1973; Bourdieu & Passeron, 1970). It is therefore not surprising that they also perform differently on tests designed to measure intellectual abilities: these tests, which were designed to predict school success, are in fact miniature replicas of the school examination situation. Why are there these differences?

A social explanation for sociological differences

Let us immediately set aside, with Jacquard (1978) and many other geneticists, any explanation at the level of biological determinism. Arguments which claim that differences between social groups are innately determined are in fact based on misunderstanding: 'heritability can only be defined and measured within a group, and can therefore never be used to analyse differences between groups' (Jacquard, 1978:182). In view of the nature of the instruments themselves, measures of differences between groups are in fact not really valid, and in addition, there is at the moment no method by which to estimate the proportion of the difference between socio-cultural or ethnic groups which is to be explained by genetic inheritance.

In our view, a social psychological analysis of the situation in which the test is given would give more reliable answers. Several investigators have shown that simply changing certain aspects of the situation is sufficient to reduce or eliminate differences between children of different social groups. Some of these modifications were not inspired directly by analysis of the cognitive functioning of the subjects alone. In a series of investigations, Katz (1973a, b) showed how problems of social identity interfere with test performance: in different situations of real life or symbolic encounters with

Whites, American Blacks produced different results. Motivation or self-confidence (see also Zigler & Butterfield, 1968, on this), familiarity with content and familiarity with the test situation all play an important role. But all these explanations, however important they may be, do remain to a certain extent external to any definition of the cognitive function of the test itself.

Bernstein's contribution

Theories like that of B. Bernstein (1974), though designed more specifically to explain differences at the linguistic level, can nevertheless be helpful in explaining differential performance in test situations. The thesis which emerges from his work is that individuals develop different linguistic codes in different social situations. The more the actors in a situation have characteristics or interests in common, the more they can call upon a collection of shared meanings which do not have to be made explicit at every moment. This results in a particularised or 'restricted' discourse, to the extent that it cannot be understood outside the situation. Other situations are characterised by differences between actors. In such conditions, meanings have to be made more explicit. The code here would be 'universalistic' or 'elaborated' so as to permit expression of the particularity of each individual experience. Now some types of interaction predominate in certain social groups and favour elaboration and use of specific codes, so that 'one of the effects of the class system is to limit access to elaborated codes' (Bernstein, 1974:176). This theory has frequently been misunderstood and is thought to disvalue members of the working class who are likely to find themselves more often in situations which favour the 'restricted' code. Bernstein denies this:

I must emphasize that because the code is restricted it does not mean that speakers at no time will not use elaborated speech variants; only that the use of such variants will be infrequent in the socialization of the child in his family. (1974:183)

The problem therefore is not differences in competence but differences in the influence of social situations which lead to variations in performance. Between competence and performance falls the situation.

To explain differences in performance in a test situation we therefore have no need to suppose that those who succeed less well generally have a habit of using a restricted code, nor a less decentred attitude in other areas of life. It is enough that for them, in contrast to others, the test situation is a specific situation for which they have not learned the adaptive code.

Let us therefore describe in some detail an experiment which shows the link between communication codes used in the family and efficiency of communication in a given situation. Using a questionnaire completed by the mothers of children in the experiment, Bearison & Cassel (1975: 31) defined the ways mothers controlled the behaviour of their children:

The bases upon which mothers attempt to regulate the behaviour of their children (regulatory appeal strategy) constituted the index of the families' social code orientation. This follows from Bernstein's position that regulatory activities represent a universal domain of interpersonal relations that serve to maintain the cohesiveness of the families' functions and group boundaries. A mother, for example, expresses a person orientation when her regulatory appeal strategy takes into account the particular individuating psychological characteristics of either the child, herself or other individuals affected by the child's behaviour. A position orientation is expressed in the context of a regulatory appeal strategy when the psychological properties of individuals are subordinated to general rules that govern behaviour on the basis of a person's formally ascribed status within the family or within a larger social system.

The mothers were asked to describe the way they would go about controlling their child's behaviour in five different situations. Their replies were classified as 'person orientation' or 'position orientation' and mothers were divided into two groups depending on whether or not they gave a majority of 'person orientation' replies.

The experiment in which the children took part was an elaboration of a communication task used by Flavell: they had to explain the rules of a game to two people, one who could see the elements of the game, the other who could not. Dependent variables in the experiment were measures of differences between the two communications. On five measures, decentration was greater in children whose mother had given a higher level of 'person orientation' replies.

This experiment is of course not enough to provide a solid foundation for the whole of Bernstein's theory, but it does illustrate the value of some of his analyses. Another direction of research, also inspired by Bernstein's analyses, has been explored by Cecchini, Dubs & Tonucci (1972) in Italy. Their main thesis is that increasing the number of social coordination situations at school for children from underprivileged backgrounds can diminish their handicap in relation to those from more favoured environments.

Limits of the socio-cultural handicap

Similar reasoning is the foundation for our research into the articulation of sociological and situational factors in cognitive development. If, as we have frequently found in the research cited, cognitive functioning improves in interactional settings, intervention at this level should counteract the sociological dynamic which leads to children of different social groups performing differently on cognitive tests. By reanalysing her results on quantity conservation, Perret-Clermont (1979) had found that interaction tended to overcome the large differences which existed between children from different social backgrounds. Subsequently she replicated these results in another experiment (Perret-Clermont, 1980). We continued this line of research with G. Mugny, with children from two very different backgrounds in Barcelona.

Our experiment (Mugny & Doise, 1979b) uses the interdependent motor coordination task already described. In the individual pre-test, children from the more favoured background succeeded significantly better than the others: this was true for all children from 5 to 8 years, but especially between 6 and 7 years. In addition, performances improved significantly for both groups with age. During the experimental phase, children worked with the same apparatus either alone or in groups of two or three. One week later, children were given an individual post-test. For children from both social backgrounds, the results were as follows: they all profited from a group interaction and only older children improved in individual practice. Once again, the efficacity of social coordination is confirmed; it precedes the efficacity of purely individual exercise independently of social origin. However, children from the advantaged background were able to profit from this social coordination at a relatively earlier age. Probably we must conclude that their background prepared them better to take advantage of a group interaction. But the most important result of this experiment seems to us to be that it was no longer possible to find a difference which correlated with social background between those children of 6 to 7 and 7 to 8 years who took part in a group interaction. This is a good illustration of the validity of our approach to the study of these so-called cognitive differences between children of different social classes. In another experiment carried out in Barcelona, Mugny & Doise (1978b) also observed that in a spatial transformation task a single social interaction was sufficient for children from underprivileged backgrounds to reach the level the more favoured children had reached at pretest.

By employing a definition of intelligence which does not treat it simply in terms of structures established in the individual but also in terms of structures developed during social interaction, we are led to question the validity of a large number of findings on the differences between children from different social backgrounds. In effect, what do differences which disappear after a few minutes of interaction mean? Certainly one cannot any longer invoke biological determination. Naturally these investigations must be generalisable to other age levels and other tests. But these results do illustrate the need to articulate psychological and sociological explanations. The psychological approach alone as currently practised, in particular by the

Piagetian school, masks the problem of differences in social origin. Sociological study alone, on the other hand, leads to the conclusion that social differences are irreversible. Only articulation of the different levels of explanation can lead to progress in this problematic area.

Social marking

To reposition the study of cognitive development inside a framework of personal interaction does not in itself mean one must subscribe to the thesis that progress requires the kind of cooperation between equals which permit total social reciprocity. This kind of interpretation of the passages by Piaget we have cited above would mean excluding any possibility of other ways of articulating social and cognitive rules. Many social rules imply a fundamental asymmetry, e.g. relationships of authority or differences in status. They may nonetheless be involved in the development of operational structures.

One could consider that the relative statuses of adult and child are closely related to differential placement in a system of social relationships and so require analysis at level III. We came to incorporate such status relationships in our analysis when working out plans for an experiment designed to investigate acquisition of length conservation (Doise, Dionnet & Mugny, 1978). The notion of social marking helped us carry this articulation. Social marking refers to correspondences which may exist between, on the one hand, the social relationships characteristic of an interaction between the actors in a specific situation, and on the other, the cognitive relations linking particular properties of objects which mediate the social relations. The correspondences may be a similarity, or homology, between the sets of relations.

There is social marking when the social relations established within a situation and the cognitive relations which link characteristics of relevant objects in the social situation are homologous. The specificity of social relationships in a given situation depends on a system of norms and representations which exist prior to the experimental situation. Intervention of these norms and representations is not arbitrary: a certain necessity or invariance characterises the principles and schemata which govern the development of a social interaction. This necessity is related to differences in status and power which are dealt with in analyses at level III. In addition, we know that writers like Piaget who work at level I also invoke necessity, notably that which characterises the operational structures described by the Genevan school. The notion of social marking should allow us to study the articulation of principles of social regulation and principles of logic.

To illustrate this articulation, we had to use an experimental situation where correspondence between a social norm and an intellectual notion was particularly salient. Conservation of length seemed to fulfil our requirements. In fact, the relation of length between different objects can, in the context of an exchange between adult and child, refer to physical or social characteristics of the protagonists. The correspondence between cognitive idea and social norm was established during a phase of interaction involving sharing, or allocation of one of two bracelets of different lengths to the adult and one to the child himself. In a control condition, the allocation was also made, but to cylinders of paper of different diameters.

In the two conditions, only subjects who were not conservers in tests for length were involved. After having compared the two bracelets, subjects had to fit the bigger one round the experimenter's wrist (experimental condition) or round a large cylinder, and the smaller round their own wrist or round the small cylinder. By changing the appearance of the bracelets, the experimenter confronted subjects with a contradiction: they judged as longer the one which was in fact shorter; they were incorrect in their choice and yet were able to choose and attach the correct bracelets to wrist or cylinder. The adult accentuated the contradictions by systematic counter-suggestion. The two conditions are logically identical, the only difference between them being precisely the social marking of the operations to be carried out. The hypothesis was of course that we would find more improvement in the 'wrist' condition where the socio-cognitive conflict was in close relationship with the social rules intervening in the situation, the child being already aware of the norms which attributed bigger objects to adults and smaller ones to children. The results confirmed this hypothesis and showed at the same time that interaction between individuals of different status can in itself lead to cognitive progress. This provides another way to study the articulation of factors at level III and cognitive development.

The notion of social marking has been adopted by other investigators. We shall mention here the research by Roux and Gilly (1984). They applied the notion of social marking to a task designed for 12- to 13-year-olds which called for rules to be applied according to two criteria. If several entities present were identical according to one criterion and different according to the other, priorities were set for the latter (e.g. young people should take the initiative in greeting their elders). But if differences occurred on both criteria at the same time, a rule had to be introduced which specified the relative importance of the one and the other (e.g. age precedes gender in determining who is to take the initiative in greeting the other). In the experimental phase of their experiment, Roux & Gilly used either tasks which did not call for social rules to be applied as organisational criteria, or tasks where these social rules were applied either arbitrarily or according to well-established custom. The material used at post-test was devoid of social marking, but the subjects who made most progress were those who, during the experimental phase, had had the opportunity of practising (alone or in pairs) on socially marked material using well-established customary rules. It is important to note that practising in a situation of completely arbitrary application of social rules is even more inefficient in producing progress than a situation where the criteria hold no social significance.

VI. Culture, society and cognitive development

Cognitive universals

Intelligence is constructed during inter-personal interactions, which are modulated by the different dynamic fields created by the possible relationships between the partners in the exchange who may occupy different positions in the pre-existing network of social relations. It is possible to imagine that such social conditions for the construction of intelligence could only produce forms of intelligence which vary arbitrarily as a function of different social conditions. This is not so, however, since the characteristics of the co-ordination of inter-personal actions necessarily involve invariants, e.g. coordination of front–behind, right–left, above–below. No doubt social marking can give differential meanings to different positions, evaluate differently what is high or low, what is on the right or on the left, what is in front or behind. But this does not alter the fact that each of these positions involves of necessity a complementary one, and that in the course of some concrete activity these positions cannot be coordinated arbitrarily. This is Pinxten's thesis (1973:82), which affirms that such semantic universals are largely independent of cultural contexts:

All peoples (cultural communities) on earth live in environmental conditions that vary according to the same criteria: only the specific values on the respective criteria differ from place to place. The same physical, chemical and biological laws hold for every human being. Man is universally determined by the same organic and environmental laws. Moreover, one can postulate that the perceptual, mental and motor capacities of every new-born human being are universally identical, that is, are *identical to some degree and largely independent of cultural differences*. The totality of universalities is quite impressive: each baby possesses an elaborate neurological system to perceive and process information up to a certain non-random degree; he acts upon his environment with the same movements. Most of all, the uniformity of properties of received information (though not necessarily perceived as such) must be – initially – quite extensive. This set of *invariants* in a highly variable surrounding defines two interacting systems: man (self, body) and environment. Language and mind – two human subsystems – are the results as well as the instruments of this interaction.

The task of anthropology therefore should be to investigate these universals (see also Lloyd & Gay, 1981).

But we think there is a source of universals ignored by Pinxten: those social organisational schemata, such as relations of power, hierarchy, division into groups and subgroups, which are also a source of cognitive operations.

Far from it being the case...that the social relations of men are based on logical relationships between things, in reality it is the former which have provided the prototype for the latter...The first logical categories were social categories; the first classes of things were classes of men into which these things were integrated. It was because men were grouped, and thought of themselves in the form of groups, that in their ideas they grouped other things, and in the beginning the two modes of grouping were merged to the point of being indistinct. Moieties were the first genera; clans the first species. Things were thought to be integral parts of society, and it was their place in society which determined their place in nature. (Durkheim & Mauss, 1963:82)

The work reported by Chance & Larsen (1976) is along the same lines when they relate hierarchical systems and certain mental schemata.

Cross-cultural differences

We will not attempt to arbitrate in the debate about the universality or particularity of particular cognitive functions. We simply wish to reply to an objection which claims that our concept of the articulation of different levels of analysis in the explanation of cognitive development is essentially relativistic, and a contradiction of theories of more universal foundations for cognitive operations. Of course, one does find average differences between members of different cultural groups when performance is studied at the level of learning, memory, or use of particular cognitive operations. At first sight such differences should be related to factors at our fourth level of analysis. It might be thought that different cultures conceal specific norms and representations which interfere with different modalities of cognitive functioning, or that they propagate different definitions of intelligence. While this may well be the case, hardly any trace of this is to be found in research into different 'cognitive styles' in different cultures. So that, until the eighties, investigations into the notion of intelligence itself or into the knowledge transmitted by different cultures were rarely found, either in books which invoked questions about the links between culture and intelligence, or in specialist journals like the *Journal of Cross-Cultural Psychology*. This situation is changing. The concept of intelligence, as employed in our industrialised societies, has become a topic of investigation (see Sternberg, Conway, Ketron & Bernstein, 1981) and its scientific definition has become more complex at the same time (Sternberg, 1982). On the other hand, we begin to know more about the concepts transmitted by different cultures (e.g. see Gill & Keats, 1980; Dasen, Dembele *et al.*, 1985).

However, current explanations of cross-cultural differences in intelligence still frequently invoke other psychological notions like 'field dependence or independence', 'need to achieve' or turn to factors of an ecological nature. While authors like Berry & Dasen (1974) concede that ecological factors intervene across factors of a social order, the latter have barely been studied as such. It is typical of this subject that the social variables studied are restricted to schooling, bilingualism, sex, but rarely include the social positions occupied in their society by those members of the culture who are studied. To a certain extent, other societies or cultures are treated as homogenous, without differences of power and status.

In a sense, traditional cross-cultural studies of intelligence have led to an impasse. This is in part due to the use of tests which are supposed to be 'culture free':

It appears that the effort to make some test of cognitive functioning 'culture-free' is to seriously misunderstand the nature of cognition. Cognition itself is not 'culture-free', it is not best conceived of as a set of processing rules independent of the particular circumstances and intentions of the cognizer. In fact, our efforts should be to make our measures of cognitive functioning more culturally sensitive. We should be bending our efforts toward understanding the ways in which particular abilities are brought to bear on particular areas of functioning, to provide a road map of demands and cognitive strategies in the context of those demands. (Glick, 1974:379)

And in the same place, the author adds as a footnote:

This, of course, does not deny the possibility of universal forms of cognition. Rather, our point is that these universal forms will be understood only in the context of an organismic analysis of thought forms within cultures. The analyses of Levi-Strauss bring this point out with particular clarity.

Cole & Scribner (1974) therefore made an effort to create the appropriate conditions for the emergence of particular cognitive operations in subjects in other cultures. Because of their endeavour to articulate intra-personal, situational and cultural theories, they abandoned any attempt to develop 'culture free' tests designed to capture individual processes in their pure form.

Greenfield & Bruner (1971) also provide examples of theories which incorporate our level IV. In particular, they show how general cultural concepts, which may carry values for a more personal orientation or for a more collective one, can interfere with the individual cognitive strategies of children presented with Piagetian tasks. The children studied were Senegalese, of the Wolof tribe, who had or had not been to school. Children who had not been to school responded differently from the others in a liquid conservation test: when an adult poured the liquid into glasses of different shapes, they usually claimed that quantity changed, but not when they themselves did the pouring. The authors explained this by the fact that the children had a certain control over the situation when pouring the liquid, and no longer resorted to magical explanations, or ones which attributed extraordinary powers to the adult experimenter since they knew they did not have such powers. In the context of a culture strongly based on collective values the child searched first for a social explanation, though a simple change in the situation was sufficient to direct him to one of a more physical nature. This is a good illustration of the need to articulate different levels of explanation.

Differences within a culture

Similar articulation of levels of analysis can be made equally well within our own society. One of the official institutions in our society, the school system, has in some sense a monopoly on the definition of intelligence, or, at any rate, on the selection and propagation of the 'most intelligent'. Now there is a basic contradiction in the way this institution works. On the one hand, it is based on an egalitarian ideology, which discounts social class and is concerned only with the individual's personal intellectual abilities, and on the other, it is strongly discriminatory and perpetuates the established social order (Bourdieu & Passeron, 1970; Baudelot & Establet, 1971).

How does this work in practice? There can be no doubt that children from different social groups show inequalities before they enter the school system and these continue to exercise an influence within the system, which is, in the final analysis, strongly dominated in turn by representations of particular social groups. To be convinced one has only to read the study by Bourdieu & Boltanski (1976) on teachers in the Institut d'Etudes politiques in Paris. Different biases characterise teachers at other levels of the educational system and bring in different dynamics at level III. But these sociological dynamics can only come into play because there exists a general definition of intelligence which is predominant in society and to a certain extent accepted by those who are objectively devalued by this definition.

The articulation of this 'universalist' definition and group differences is made possible by the process of category differentiation (Doise, 1978), in which differences in characteristics held to be related to differences in social groups are accentuated. This dynamic occurs in agents of the scholastic system.

Categories of judgement used by school teachers reflect in fact the multiple social divisions inside and outside the school system. Thus in France, socio-economic status and whether one comes from Paris or the provinces, or, within the school, different sub-divisions and sections, categorise individuals definitively from a practical point of view, and for the rest of their lives, by giving them diplomas of unequal value. The articulation of school assessments and sociological differences can be illustrated by an example from Bourdieu & de Saint-Martin (1975). These sociologists showed a three-way correlation in judgements by a teacher of his students: they linked social origin, scales of judgements used and marks given which determine a school career. The material used for this illustration was a set of 154 files belonging to a philosophy teacher in Paris, and which included profession of parents, home address, marks given for written work and oral tests, and supporting remarks.

First, let us report how the investigators classified the children according to their social background:

We ranked the pupils...according to the *amount of cultural capital* they had inherited from their families, or, if you prefer, according to their father's progress in the educational system, using as criterion in the absence of a more precise one profession or occupation and address of parents (in Paris or the provinces). Thus children ranged from middle class to upper class, and within these groupings, from those relatively deprived of cultural capital (industrial workers and managers) to the best endowed (university teachers), with liberal professions being in an intermediate position. (Bourdieu & de Saint-Martin, 1975:70)

With this classification, there was a corresponding scale of judgement of school work, from 'simpleminded, inane, servile, coarse, insipid, flat, heavy, dull, slow' at one end 'fine, clever, subtle, intelligent, cultivated, individual, alive, masterful, searching, philosophical mind' at the other. The work of children with less cultural capital (daughters of tradesmen, artisans, provincial civil servants) was of course more often characterised by the first set of adjectives while the work of those with the greatest amount of capital available (daughters of doctors and Parisian university lecturers) most often received attributions from the opposite pole. The marks given to their work are obviously also strongly correlated with their social origin classification.

This example can be supported by more representative statistical studies carried out by sociologists of education. Furthermore, in the same article, Bourdieu and de Saint-Martin show how, in obituary notices written by old pupils of the Ecole Normale Supérieure (training college for university teachers) about former colleagues, the social origin of the dead still played an important role: sons of peasants, artisans and provincial civil servants were most often described in obituary notices as resigned, good, ascetic, simple, modest, while sons of university or Ecole Normale teachers were described as fine, delicate, brilliant, clear-minded, intelligent, rigorous, witty, lucid, masterful, original, creative, writer, poet, essayist, great scholar, great philosopher, theoretician.

These examples clearly illustrate how judgements made by agents of the school system carry within them extra-scholastic social contrasts and can, by accentuating these differences at the level of a 'universal' social definition of intelligence, help in the continuance of social divisions through-out the school. To look on intelligence as an asocial and purely personal characteristic in fact leads to social discrimination. It is therefore not surprising that sociologists demand a redefinition of intelligence.

It is the major contention of this essay to show that the concept of 'intelligence' as manifested in Britain in the present century has been a concept which has arisen out of the nature of various aspects of the social structure of this country and has been used, educationally, both to express a certain construction of reality – arising out of the social situation and perception of certain groups – and as an instrument protecting and maintaining certain political and economic features of society. (Squibb, 1973:58)

This analysis obviously does not apply only to Great Britain, nor only to Western countries. It is equally relevant to certain socialist countries where perhaps the status of the intellectual is of even greater consequence (Konrad & Szelenyi, 1979).

School and social representations

It still remains for us to elucidate the processes by which the sociological effects operate. In the final analysis, a study like that by Bourdieu and de Saint-Martin does not permit one to conclude that there has been distortion in these scholastic judgements. Only careful analysis of how social representations and expectations function within teaching in school can show how important these factors are in modifying both teachers' pedagogic behaviour and children's performance. The research by Gilly (1980), to be described in a subsequent chapter, was dedicated to this task. But what do the children think, without whom the notion of intelligence could not function in the way described? Even if they reject the dominant concept, substantial support still remains for the social dynamic which may operate via the rejection itself. Such rejection often means effectively their reclass-ification in a different section, which prepares them for a different place in society. However, the process by which concepts of intelligence and others allied to it are established in the children themselves still needs to be investigated.

Our study began with children at the end of their obligatory schooling in a town in French-speaking Switzerland, some of whom were getting ready to enter the working world and others who were going to continue their studies in establishments which could lead to university entrance. The latter, in replying to a questionnaire, already valued more highly the role of the individual, her/his development and autonomy, whereas the former defined themselves more in positional terms, and more frequently made reference to school when asked to give a definition of intelligence. When asked for examples of things which belong to everyone, those remaining in education more frequently gave as reply, ideas, nature, life, while those leaving mentioned public things like benches, buses, streets. When questioned about power in Switzerland, those who were going to enter the working world gave replies like cantons, state, government, whereas those with a long school career ahead more often replied, the people, and produced in general more ideological representations, which they also were willing to question, as for example when they made less distinction between male and female roles. Worlds of specific representations have already been established in these students with their different scholastic careers: everything seems set for the perpetuation of social differentiation via the intervention of an institution which is founded on a 'universalist' concept of intelligence (Doise, Meyer and Perret-Clermont, 1976; Doise, 1985b).

To conclude, let us emphasise the need to articulate different levels of analysis in the domain of cognitive development. Sociologists explain differences between different social groups, at their level, by the selective and discriminating function of the school and emphasise the ideological nature of the notion of intelligence involved. But, to explain how teachers and students participate in this process, frequently with a good conscience, we need explanations of a social psychological nature, like those which use the theory of categorial differentiation. Indeed, it is only by turning to this kind of articulation that we can understand how social processes of differentiation can occur in an institution which still preaches an asocial concept of intelligence.

3 Levels of explanation in the study of social influence

Processes of social influence can be defined, in their most specific sense, as governing modifications in the perception, judgements, opinions, attitudes or behaviour of an individual which are brought about by her/his knowledge of the perceptions, judgements, opinions etc. of other individuals. Processes of influence therefore offer a particularly propitious area for the study of levels of analysis, since such research depends upon an articulation of the changes which occur at the individual level and the processes which intervene during inter-personal or symbolic social encounters. We might therefore expect that theories explaining the phenomena of social influence would spontaneously place their analyses at the level of this articulation. However, as examination of different trends in research shows, explanations are usually at one level of analysis only, the inter-personal or the intra-personal, and only rarely attempt interpretations which take account of the social positions of the protagonists or of relations between groups or of ideological concepts.

I. On the setting of norms

An individual is placed in a completely dark room and is asked to judge the extent of the apparent movement of a tiny source of light with no points of reference at his disposal. This is the kinetic effect used by Sherif (1935) in his study of how norms arise. He found that in this situation the individual rapidly reduces the variance in her/his responses around a central value: s/he establishes a framework of reference for subsequent judgements, constructs a personal norm in the absence of all objective measures, which have been made impossible by the situation. If we put several strangers together in the same situation and ask them to make judgements in turn, aloud, the results (which have been confirmed many times) show that such groups rapidly establish a norm which provides a central value and standard variation from the central point. A process of inter-personal convergence has taken place. This effect has been studied many times, and very different explanations given. We will describe some of them, which involve analyses at various levels in the psychosocial spectrum.

The subject as statistician

A first level of analysis looks for reasons for this convergence in intra-personal processes. This applies to Sherif's own interpretation, which emphasises the uncertainty of the subject who is asked to impose order on an unstructured object to which he can apply no objective measure, nor any other form of empirical verification. In default of empirical validation, the subject resorts to other criteria so as to restore some degree of certainty. To do this, he considers his first replies, establishes a median value and progressively reduces the range of his subsequent replies. In a group situation, reciprocal evaluation of the replies of each person permits establishment of a modal point and group range which are defined as the interaction proceeds. The replies of the others thus only have an informative value and are integrated cognitively in the same way as the earlier replies of the lone subject required to make judgements on his own. This interpretation is fundamentally intra-personal, since the setting of the norm of inter-personal convergence appears to be the result of cognitive mechanisms in the individual who uses as data the replies of the other individuals: 'the underlying psychological principle, in individual and group situations, is the same, namely that there is a tendency to reach a standard in either case' (Sherif, 1954:767).

Other formulations have been proposed at the same level of explanation. Flament (1959a, b) and Montmollin (1977) conceptualise the evolution of judgements in a situation leading to a norm as being determined by the logical or statistical operations carried out by subjects on the information (replies) provided by their partners in the interaction. In effect, the subject is said to establish the distribution of responses, calculate the mean, median and standard deviation, set cut-off points beyond which responses are held to be improbable. In short, the subject behaves like a rational being, a logician or statistician who, in default of other objective criteria, proceeds to calculate probabilities.

But an interpretation of norm setting in terms of intra-personal processes need not involve cognition only: it might equally be a matter of personality. This has been illustrated by an experiment by Montgomery, Hinkle & Enzie (1976) who took Jacobs & Campbell's (1961) paradigm on the perpetuation of arbitrary norms in the laboratory. At the beginning of the experiment, a naive subject was put in a Sherif-type situation with three confederates who consistently gave replies comparatively far from the spontaneous replies of the subject. Then after 20 trials, one of the confederates left and was replaced by another naive subject, and so on for ten 'generations': after four generations, all subjects were naive. How was the norm established while the confederates were present maintained? Montgomery *et al.* postulated that this could depend on the nature of the 'societies' created in this way. They studied them in terms of the authoritarian personality (Adorno, Frenkel-Brunswik, Levinson & Sanford, 1950): they divided subjects into strongly and weakly authoritarian, theorising with other writers (Crutchfield, 1955; Frenkel-Brunswik, 1949; Nadler, 1959) that a high degree of authoritarianism is associated with greater conformity, and with greater resistance to change (Mischel & Schopler, 1959; Steiner & Johnson, 1963). They were able to show that 'societies' of strongly authoritarian subjects changed the norm originally established by the confederates less overall than those weakly authoritarian. Personality factors can therefore influence the maintenance or modification of an initial norm. In conclusion, it is not uninteresting to note that the authors, who were after all attempting to model the processes of maintenance and change of social norms, came to define their 'societies' only in terms of the personality of their members.

Inter-personal relations

But convergent situations are not accounted for only by application of logico-mathematical operations or personality traits. The information provided by the replies of the others also carry value statements and meanings which call upon other levels of analysis. To begin with, convergent effects are not independent of the inter-personal relations established prior to or during the setting of a norm. The need for other levels of explanation was realised by Sherif, who noted that if there is inter-personal convergence, it does not simply lead to a mean, as asymmetries on the way to a consensus might appear. Did he not write:

> If, for the group, there is a rise or fall in the norms established in successive sessions, it is a group effect; the norms of the individual members rise or fall toward a common norm in each session. To this the objection may be raised that one subject may lead, and be uninfluenced by other members of the group; the group norm is simply the leader's norm. To this the only possible empirical reply is that in our experiments the leaders were constantly observed to be influenced by their followers – if not at the moment, then later in the series and in subsequent series. (Sherif, 1952:255)

Before accounting for such differences in convergence in members of a group, let us look at explanations in inter-personal terms for convergence itself, independently of its differential strength in different people.

A first example of explanation at level II (in fact, an articulation of levels I and II) is provided by Allport (1924) who accounted for moderation of judgements in a situation with others in terms of the insecurity arising from risk of inter-personal disagreement which is maximised by extremes in judgement. Reciprocal concessions (Allport, 1962) would therefore be necessary to establish an interaction without conflict. For French (1956), it is equality of status which ensures equal social influence for each partner, in virtue of a law of minimal concessions.

Such inter-personal negotiations are not independent of the inter-personal relations established prior to the experiment. In an experiment using judgements of ambiguous auditory stimuli, Pollis (1967) first placed subjects in a situation where they learned response criteria in different social conditions: two subjects worked together who (a) did not know each other before or (b) belonged to the same community and were known to be friends: in a control condition, subjects learned alone. In the second phase, subjects were required to carry out the same task in a group situation. On each occasion, three subjects who had learned different scales were put together. In addition, in each of these groups, one had worked with someone he knew already, another had interacted with a stranger, and the third had worked alone. Results showed that stability of scales in the second phase varied depending on how they were established: those who learned alone changed their scale most; those who learned with a stranger were intermediate.

Harvey and Consalvi (1960) created groups on the basis of sociometric status. When subjects from high, middle or lower status were put together in groups, it was found that lower status subjects converged more towards the high status than the other way round. These inter-personal relations, established prior to or during the course of the interaction and defined by their asymmetry, explain why in general a group norm does not correspond to an algebraic mean of individual judgements. These effects have been confirmed by other investigators, among them Lemaine, Desportes & Louarn (1969) who showed that the effect of hierarchical differentiation operates in fact mainly with inter-personal relations characterised by strong reciprocal attraction (cohesion).

Other processes of inter-personal differentiation can be observed in norm-setting situations. Thus, taking up an observation by Sherif (1937), Moscovici & Neve (1971) found that prolonging the interaction of a subject with an accomplice whose responses were markedly different led to reduction in the experimental subject's own convergence: but if the accomplice was removed from the situation and the subject continued alone in his judgements, he went on to reply according to a norm established jointly: those who are absent are not always wrong. The behaviour of the accomplice, because consistent, can eventually take on the same meaning as a block in inter-personal negotiations. A complex combination of attribution and social differentiation can therefore interfere with the process of convergence.

Social differences and divergent perceptions

Discrimination does not take place just in relations between individuals. It often takes its meaning from much more profound social divisions, from relationships of power or from ideological confrontations. Sampson (Sherif & Sherif, 1969: 168–70) studied convergence between dyads of monks from different positions in the hierarchy. In a first condition, he took novices newly arrived, with a more or less equal relationship. In a second condition, novices at the end of their first year, who had already had time to establish precise inter-personal relations: in each pair was an individual esteemed by his partner but who did not reciprocate, an asymmetrical relationship established previously by sociometric questionnaire. In a third condition, Sampson confronted novice and monk, between whom there existed both a hierarchical or positional difference and also a conflict of an ideological nature. Results showed that convergence was established between the new novices, and that convergence between first year novices was asymmetric, the highly esteemed subjects giving way less than the others. Finally, the novices showed a greater tendency to converge than the monks at the start of the interaction, but changed their initial judgments during a later stage: they ended with differentiation of judgements and a sort of bipolarisation (Paicheler, 1976, 1977) which expressed within the framework of the experiment the tensions existing between the two subgroups.

As to the effect of more exclusively ideological divisions in an experimental situation, this is illustrated by an experiment by Lemaine, Lasch & Ricateau (1971–72): before being introduced to the usual situation for experimental norm setting, subjects replied at the same time as an accomplice to an opinion questionnaire apparently unconnected with the subsequent experiment. Subjects were categorised as to ideological orientation, and the accomplice as having the same or opposed views. Subject and accomplice were then put in a situation similar to the autokinetic one. Accomplices gave answers which were either very remote from those of the subject, fairly remote or nearly identical. Results showed that convergence of subject with accomplice was greater when he was held to have the same views. When the accomplice gave the same replies as the subject and he held different views, the subject made his own judgements more different, so as to preserve his identity. On this point, Lemaine wrote that:

(the subject) adopts a strategy which differentiates him from the other even when it is only a question of estimating the distance covered by a luminous point. This search for *otherness*...is an expression of the subjects' concern as to their identity which is being threatened by a lack of consistency in the categorisation of the other who is very different (and rejected) and who persists in being the same. One might say along with Goffman (1959) that this search for consistency which is induced by the perceived inconsistency of the other (how can someone so different be the same as me?) is a strategy of self-presentation the aim of which is to avoid any misunderstanding on the part of the public which is here the experimenter who must share his own unfavourable opinion of the accomplice. (Lemaine, 1975:116)

We have here a good example of the complexity of an explanation which articulates analyses dealing with inter-personal relations or with social divisions which have meaning both outside and within the experimental situation, and which implicate the experimenter her/himself.

One of our experiments (Doise, 1969a) also confirms that convergence can be affected by the dynamics of inter-group relations. Subjects were asked to evaluate their own school, individually or in groups, with or without another school more prestigious than their own as comparison. Results showed that convergence among replies increased when their identity was threatened by the symbolic presence of a rival group. The convergence can be an inter-personal response to social situations which implicate wider social relationships.

Convergence and naive epistemology

If the effects of convergence can, and should, be articulated with explanations at level III when inter-group relations are made explicit, what about the original situation created by Sherif, which appears not to implicate any social relationship and especially not dominance? How can one explain convergence here? Is it because the situation is so low in motivating power that subjects agree so as not to enter into conflict, as suggested by Moscovici & Ricateau (1972)? In our view, this would be equivalent to explaining convergence as due to lack of sense instead of accounting for it by use of sense.

What is the criterion common to situations in which a norm is established? It appears to be a perceived equality of status. But why do individuals of the same status, not seeing any differences between each other (except those of perceptual judgements), without special relationships, converge instead of sticking to their initial judgements? Our hypothesis is that in the conditions of an experimental group, an inter-personal solidarity emerges which aims to verify the hypothesis that the experimenter cannot fail to have in her/his head. If we set aside all social relations determined outside the experimental situation (such as inter-personal relations or divisions of a hierarchical or ideological nature), we are still left with the fact that subjects find themselves in a specific situation, face to face with an experimenter who represents a scientific institution. Subjects as a group see themselves as charged with carrying out the task of helping to establish the truth concerning a particular phenomenon. Now the general concept of a scientific truth, as promoted by the school system, implies establishment of a consensus. This search for consensus would therefore be the goal of the experimental group, based upon a very widespread conception of science. Several experiments illustrate the plausibility of the intervention of such naive epistemology.

Some authors directly manipulated subjects' expectations about the tasks. Thus Sperling (1946) warned his subjects that it was a perceptual illusion:

60% then refused to converge; but the 40% who did said, in a post-experiment interview, that they tried to establish the truth in spite of what they had been told. This would thus imply the need for consensus.

Following Riecken (1962), Orne (1962) and Rosenthal (1966), Alexander, Zucker & Brody (1970:111) interpret convergence in terms of the demand characteristics of the experimenter:

the laboratory setting is almost without equal in creating general expectations of exactitude and regularity. The symbols of meticulous order and ritual standardization are pervasive, overwhelmingly conveying the impression of carefully planned, precisely controlled, logically executed, and systematically recorded events...Procedures specific to the autokinetic experiments serve to reinforce this image of the experimental situation.

The authors carried out an experiment where they revealed to subjects that it was an illusion, or they warned subjects, 'You will all be seeing the same point of light, but you should not expect to see it moving in the same direction or for the same distance.' (1970:113) Obviously, no effect of convergence was found in this experiment. However, in place of the experimenter effect they substituted another, as pointed out by Pollis, Montgomery & Smith (1975). One can therefore conclude nothing about a 'spontaneous tendency' in subjects since the experimenter openly showed what responses they should avoid.

Pollis *et al.* carried out a more convincing experiment where they separated the information about the nature of perception being studied (perceptual illusion) and anticipation of convergence or divergence between individuals. In a first condition, subjects were not told of the illusory nature of the situation. In a second, they repeated Alexander *et al.*'s (1970) procedure: not only did they tell subjects it was an illusion but also warned subjects not to be surprised at variations in response. In a final condition subjects were only told that it was an illusion without informing them that they did not need to establish regularity of response. In each condition, half the subjects replied together and half not. The essential result is that the last condition led to reduction in variance of responses which shows, according to the authors, 'where there are no implicit or explicit instructions suggesting either convergence and decreasing variability or divergence and increasing variability and where subjects know full well that the light does not move the tendency over trials is toward convergence and decreasing variability' (Pollis, Montgomery & Smith, 1975:370). However, we should add that these authors do not interpret this result as we do:

If this condition does in fact constitute a closer approximation of subject response to an unstructured situation in a 'pure' sense, one with a minimum of preconditioned, prepotent response tendencies, then it provides significant evidence in support of the generalization that the psychological tendency is toward the structuring or organization of experience. (1975)

Again there would have had to have been really no 'preconditioned' response tendency. One might in fact doubt this.

Let us recall another experiment which shows a 'tendency' to consensus in the perceptual domain. Allen & Levine (1968) started with Asch's (1951) demonstration of the fact that, in his paradigm on majority influence, it only needed one of the members of the said majority to change his reply, and so destroy the majority consensus, for naive subjects to recover their independence of judgement. Using Crutchfield's (1955) apparatus, these investigators systematically studied the effect of social support on non-conformity (Allen, 1975) in situations requiring expression of opinion or perceptual judgements. In a control condition, subjects were opposed to several confederates who gave unanimous deviant or improbable replies. In a condition of 'real' social support, one confederate replied normally, thus corroborating the naive subject. In a final condition a confederate broke the majority consensus but then gave an even more improbable reply than the others. Results showed that where opinions were concerned, only 'real' social support reduced the influence of the other confederates and a more extreme reply did not reduce the effect. On the other hand, for perceptual judgements, any rupture of unanimity was sufficient, whatever the answer of the dissident. This result shows that a certain expectation of consensus rules replies of subjects in a realm believed to be more 'objective'.

An explanation at level IV, which brings in general concepts belonging to a given culture, seems to us necessary here if we are to understand the processes leading to convergence. Again it must be shown that subjects do act as believers in a consensual concept of knowledge. An experiment by Pêcheux (1972–73) is useful in this respect: subjects were high school pupils, to whom the experimenter explained the psychological theory of subliminal perception which he would afterwards demonstrate with a classic experiment. To half the subjects, he showed blank slides, so subjects could see nothing: to the others, he showed slides just long enough for them to read a number distinctly: methodologically, therefore, conditions for demonstrating subliminal perception were not fulfilled. Then the experimenter made a fictitious analysis of replies and gave half the subjects a report according to which there was a strong degree of convergence between subjects, which supposedly confirmed the theory, or one according to which there was strong divergence between individuals, which was a contradiction of the theory. Results showed that subjects subsequently attested to the validity of the theory only as a function of convergence of replies between individuals, taking no account of whether methodological conditions for testing the theory were or were not fulfilled. Consensus thus is part of the 'intuitive' representation of the scientific definition of an object (here a psychological theory).

The last experiments described seem to show that subjects import into the experimental situation very general representations of knowledge, which can be reinforced by expectations attributed to the experimenter, who is seen as an expert in knowledge.

II. The Asch effect and minority influence

While studies of norm setting looked at processes of convergence of responses of diverse individuals, studies of conformity investigate the conditions which lead an individual to adopt the position of another individual or of a group (or at least to come near) frequently in the absence of any pressure or explicit persuasion by the influence source.

The experiments carried out by Asch (1951, 1956) provided the prototype of an enormous mass of empirical research. We will briefly describe the basic paradigm: an experimental subject is placed in company with others, who do not appear to differ from him but who in reality are accomplices. The task is to judge which of three lines of variable length is the same as a target line. The reply in reality poses no difficulty at all as all stimuli are unambiguous. However, the naive subject responds in last but one position and finds himself confronted by the same incorrect response given unanimously by several accomplices in a large number of trials. Results show that a little more than a third of responses by experimental subjects are affected by the group's incorrect one. In these cases, a process of influence to conformity has taken place. Numerous experiments have confirmed this 'Asch effect' and have varied the conditions in which it appears.

Interpretations proposed to account for social influence in such conditions consider that the phenomena demonstrated concerned majority influence on a minority. Is not the subject the only one to deviate from the responses given by a numerical majority who, besides, are in entire agreement? The relations usually taken into consideration in an explanation are those established in the here and now by the protagonists. As with the norm setting effect, most current explanations of the conformity effect have therefore been elaborated at levels I and II and at their articulation (see Ricateau, 1970–71a, and Mugny & Doise, 1979a, for a review). But it is more important here to describe how the work of Moscovici (1976b) has enlarged the framework of this interpretation, and how Mugny in turn (1981) has tried to place Moscovici's reinterpretation in a more sociological context.

Asch effect: majority or minority influence?

Traditional explanation of the Asch effect was therefore based on a definition in terms of inter-personal, within-situation relations. Groups numerically greater than the experimental subjects were defined as a majority: if 3, 4 or 9 accomplices reply incorrectly, are they not a majority compared to a single experimental subject? While this is plausible in numerical terms, the experimental subject defending his lone position against a number of unanimous people, it is not so plausible when one thinks of the nature of the alternative replies. In effect, in Asch's paradigm, the 'majority' oppose totally incorrect replies to the subject's correct ones: the conflict which leads to influence comes from the uncertainty of the subject who is placed between his own perceptual evidence and the majority consensus to an absurdity. From this point of view, one can consider, as does Moscovici, that the social norm recognized outside the laboratory has been put in question. Indeed, subjects arrive in the experimental situation with their usual schemata for evaluating differences in length. These norms are shared by all members of a community, at least within the limits of normality which this defines. From that point of view, the confederates, by putting in question the usual schemata for judging, schemata which are shared by the experimental subject, constitute in this way a minority and not a majority group in normative terms. In terms of norms, the influence exercised by these confederates, even though superior in numbers, gives evidence, not of a majority effect, but of the potential influence of a minority. This reinterpretation arises from the fourth level of analysis since relations within the experimental situation are linked to systems of representation in operation in a given society.

The explanation of minority influence given by Moscovici himself, using both old and new experimental results, incorporates the first two levels of analysis as well. More precisely, minority influence is said to have as its source diachronic or intra-personal consistency (repetition over time of the same response or same set of responses) and synchronic or inter-personal consistency (consensus of members of a minority). These variables lead (especially in a situation of tension created by conflict) to activation of processes of integration of information coming from the other or of processes of attribution such as have been described in classic works on social influence.

The Moscovici effect

Let us examine in more detail the novel manipulations proposed by Moscovici to illustrate the potential of minority influence, and especially the operation of the two types of consistency, diachronic and synchronic. Like the Asch paradigm, the paradigm developed by Moscovici, Lage & Naffrechoux (1969) is relatively simple: subjects begin by sitting a test together to make sure they have normal colour vision. After immediate analysis of the perceptual tests, it is explained to subjects that they will be shown slides and their task will be to name the colour. The colour usually perceived is blue. In the experimental condition, two of the six subjects are confederates and, in contrast to the experimental subjects, they name the slide colour 'green'. In a control condition, with no confederate, subjects always call the slide blue. In an experimental condition where confederates are all consistent, all giving the contradictory response 'green', 8.42 % replies by experimental subjects are 'green', showing a significant minority influence. On the other hand, when confederates are inconsistent and give only 66 % replies 'green', there is no significant influence. This demonstrates the importance of diachronic consistency in a minority. As to synchronic consistency, this depends on variations in the rate of agreement between members of the minority. While we have no direct verification of the effect of this type of consistency, we can illustrate it by numerous classic experiments on the Asch effect, on condition of course that we accept Moscovici's claim that Asch has shown the power of minority and not majority influence.

In the work which followed the first formulation of this reinterpretation (Faucheux & Moscovici, 1967; Moscovici, Lage & Naffrechoux, 1969) we find concentration of research on the processes of attribution implicated. Thus for example, Nemeth, Swedlund & Kanki (1974) show that attribution of consistency does not only depend on repetition of the same response, but that it can equally appear when different responses coincide with modifications in the stimuli, the perceived coherence in these changes leading to significant minority influence. Similarly, Nemeth & Wachtler (1973) show how choice by the minority source of a strategic position round a table ensures more influence in negotiation than if the experimenter assigns him that place. To be seen and produce influence, consistency must sometimes be salient through certain behaviour. This research, though inspired by Moscovici's reinterpretation, arises more from explanations which articulate levels I and II. In fact, most theories of attribution (notably Kelley, 1967), from which the idea of consistency itself seems to have been borrowed, only consider attribution within the framework of immediate inter-personal relations.

It is therefore not surprising that some authors have tried to reinterpret Moscovici's work in terms of the classical approaches criticised by Moscovici himself (S. Wolf, 1977; Doms, 1978; Cramer, 1975). Thus Doms hypothesises that a minority of two who reply first in a group of six can influence the first experimental subject because they are a majority: in this case, in effect, the naive subject finds himself in opposition to a greater number. The same applies to all the following naive subjects, although for them the problem increases that the 'majority' will not be unanimous since preceding naive subjects will not necessarily conform. Her own experimental results give partial support to such an interpretation.

It should be noted that Moscovici's paradigm does lay itself open to such criticism, for a good reason: Moscovici *et al.* even while investigating the influence of the normative system (cf. Lage, 1973; Moscovici & Lage, 1978), continue to define majorities and minorities in numerical terms. When they manipulate the minority or majority character of the source by introducing two or four accomplices into a group of six (as replicated by Doms and others), how has methodology really been improved? In addition, an apparent contradiction appears in the results of some experiments which manipulate consistency; it is not always a source of influence, but in some cases leads to rejection.

Schachter (1951), who was studying deviance phenomena, hypothesised that a deviant who sticks to his guns will be rejected more by a group than one who is more flexible. In his famous experiment, various forms of deviance were introduced into *ad hoc* groups. One confederate never deviated, but adjusted his behaviour to the modal behaviour of the group. To create one form of deviance, a confederate began by deviating very greatly from the group norm, then came closer to the average response. Finally, one confederate was consistent in Moscovici's terms, and maintained an extreme position for the whole session; this deviance corresponded therefore the most closely to the theoretic demands for consistency proposed by Moscovici for the production of minority influence. But the opposite appeared to occur: in this experiment, the group rejected the consistent minority. We should, however, add that Schachter did not take any measures of possible influence by this deviant on individual members of the group.

Furthermore, Moscovici himself (Doise & Moscovici, 1969–70) has demonstrated experimentally the risks of minority consistency. Subjects were required to rate as introverted or extraverted the behaviour of a student described in a booklet. In a control condition, subjects replied in pairs using a single booklet. In two experimental conditions, the booklets were supposed to be filled out by three people: the third person responded always before the others, and was supposedly in another room where the experimenter would collect his replies. These, which were faked, varied according to the conditions. The first behaviours were clearly introverted and became subsequently more and more extraverted (experimental material taken from Luchins & Luchins, 1961), but the responses by the absent person were either always 'introverted' or always 'extraverted'. In the first case, this therefore represented a belated deviance, since the responses fitted the first accounts and only got progressively more deviant as the behaviour became more extraverted. In the second case, on the other hand, the deviance showed immediately, with the third person disagreeing with the two subjects from the beginning. The results of this experiment (which implicated a variable of cohesiveness as well) are best remembered for demonstrating that while the belated deviant can influence the experimental subjects, the premature deviant can have the opposite effect, as subjects actually resisted this minority influence by giving 'introverted' responses for longer than those in the control condition. There therefore seems to be a contradiction, apparent at least, between these results and the theoretical predictions, since consistency can produce a 'boomerang' effect.

Negotiations and ideological blocks

To solve the problems of methodology presented by Moscovici's research and to explain how consistency can also lead to negative effects, Mugny (1982) suggested a sociological analysis of minority influence which we will summarise briefly.

Asch and Moscovici used tasks involving perception. In their paradigms, since there existed an objective reply, i.e. defined by everyone in terms of the same perceptual and cognitive schemata which transcend all social divisions, it is easy to distinguish between majority and minority responses. No social relationships divide this majority. Now this does not apply to opinions and attitudes which are established more often than not in an atmosphere of tension and social division, and for the most part, have some reference to some form or other of dominance (power being defined here, not as a reversible interpersonal relation, but rather as a non-reversible social relationship, at least in the context of the experiment).

Looking at conscientious objection, for example (Mugny, 1975), the opinions involved may arise in a society whose constitution imposes obligatory military service on all its citizens. Subjects studied in such a framework are not in a majority just because of their opinions, nor yet in a minority. They are above all citizens and occupy certain positions in their society. It is therefore possible to make a distinction, somewhat crude certainly but nonetheless meaningful, between the 'majority' (even if numerically a 'minority'!) which holds power and the 'silent majority' (the 'population' by analogy with the experimental population) which is subject to the power it does not share. A minority which wishes to upset an established order is, by definition, confronted simultaneously with the majority in power and the so-called silent majority, the population being the only social entity that the minority can aim to influence (or at least, only this aspect is considered). A first hypothesis is therefore that consistency will be a characteristic of the relationship the minority needs to establish with the majority in power, in terms of blocking negotiations, a style of behaviour which allows (or could allow) it to be recognized by the population as an alternative in the social field. It would not be just a straightforward case of attribution of consistency, but of recognition of new positions ('political' at some level or other) with a view to social change.

A second hypothesis is that such blocking of negotiation in relation to the potential target (the population) reduces minority influence. In effect, just by being consistent, the minority also creates a conflict in its relations with the population which submits at least partially to the ideology of the dominant group. So the minority needs to negotiate this conflict. Several experiments (Mugny, 1974, 1975) have shown that a rigid minority which sharply opposes the population (e.g. by asserting conscientious objection is a reactionary response in front of people who take it seriously) are less influential than a minority which, without reducing the consistent break with those in power, accept certain 'compromises' and thus attenuate their conflict with the population. Even though this explanation refers to cognitive mechanisms (attribution, image of the other) and to inter-personal relations (blocking of negotiation, compromise), at the theoretical level, these notions are articulated with the social divisions from which they derive their meaning. Minority influence is not just an inter-personal process: it takes place within social relationships which go far beyond the experimental situation.

A series of experiments has been carried out in this general framework. The earlier ones (Mugny, 1974, 1975: Mugny & Papastamou, 1975–76) show that a minority source which uses a flexible negotiating style has more influence than a source using a rigid style which blocks negotiation. More recent work (Papastamou, 1979) has tried to show that these different syles of presentation can have several meanings and the efficacy of their influence can be modified by other factors.

Explanations of negative effects of rigidity were first investigated at the level of the inter-personal processes of attribution implicated in the experimental situation. Essentially, an extreme position like those rigid positions taken in Mugny's experiments seemed to create a strong conflict which subjects could resolve by discrediting the source, so that they attributed some sort of bias to the source, notably in the form of categorising them as dogmatic. The work of Ricateau (1970–71a, b) had already suggested this: by making subjects use only a small number of categories to describe deviant individuals, had he not in effect shown that the dimension of negotiation blockage (or dogmatism) became salient and considerably reduced minority impact?

An experiment by Mugny & Papastamou (1980) involved confronting subjects, not just with a single minority, but with several independent individuals defending the same position. The effects were clear: while the negative effect of rigidity appears again when there is a single source, it disappears completely when the same message is shared by two sources. It might have been that the rigidity was no longer perceived; but measures showed that this was not the case. Rigidity was still seen as a characteristic of the message, but did not intervene as a determinant of social influence. It was as though the message from several sources was no longer seen as the product of an individual, but as the symbolic reflection of a reality to which subjects could subscribe, notwithstanding the dogmatic style whose significance had altered.

Let us introduce here the notion of 'naturalisation', which is a term used to describe one of the mechanisms by which a social system immunises itself against deviants by ruining their credibility: 'This naturalisation may take many forms: biological (because he is Black, because she is a woman...); psychological (it's in his character, he is paranoid...); sociological (he's a trade unionist, a politician...)' (Doise, Deschamps & Mugny, 1978:61–63). Mugny & Papastamou (1980) tried to show experimentally how 'psychologising' can ruin a potential minority influence. They gave subjects a conciliatory or dogmatically worded text, and asked them either to work out while reading it the personality traits of the writer or to extract the main lines of the text itself. Results showed a marked reduction in minority influence when reference was made to 'psychology'. The conciliatory text in these circumstances has as little influence as the dogmatic one, which showed very little influence whether subjects thought of psychology or not. In the second experiment, subjects read a minority text. Before completing a post-experiment questionnaire to test for possible influence, they were then asked to describe the source either in political terms, or in a combination of political and psychological terms. Once again, introduction of psychological judgements led to reduction in the influence of the minority. Attribution of psychological terms, i.e. of internal factors to the minority source reinforces an ideological process which leads subjects to discredit the content of the innovatory message, to disregard it as a possible alternative social position and so to reject or ignore it.

This new research has tried to articulate analyses dealing with processes of attribution and those which focus on more general functions of ideology. These include the 'psychologising' or even 'psychiatrising' of political behaviour which tries to question the dominant order.

III. Another paradigm: submission to authority

We know that Milgram's (1974) experiments showed that many people, recruited via classified small ads. to take part in a study of memory, could be transformed into torturers at the insistence of the experimenter. Results were explained by intervention of an 'agentic state'; making a parallel with cybernetics, the author describes how every organism undergoes changes as it shifts from autonomous functioning to functioning within a social organisation, in this case, a hierarchical institution in which the experimenter is one of the elements. The agentic shift defines the change from autonomy, where the subject alone is master of his actions, to a state (agentic) where the subject considers himself to be an agent or instrument for carrying out the wishes of others.

At which level is this explanation? At the level of the intra-personal and inter-personal processes which are activated in such a situation. Essentially we could say that the effects are only studied as a function of variations in inter-personal relations established in the experiment. For example, relations with the victim are important: proximity to the victim strongly increases disobedience, and especially the greater the visibility or reciprocal contact. Also social support by confederates of the same status, playing the same role of torturer, but who refuse to carry on with the experiment as soon as the victim protests, saps the authority of the experimenter. But perhaps above all, direct relationship with the experimenter plays an essential role: if he leaves and no longer directly controls the experiment, subjects obey very little, likewise when they are left free to set the rate of electric shock. It is the same when two experimenters contradict each other, one requiring the subject to continue, the other telling him to stop. Furthermore, the authority of the experimenter is indispensable for the Milgram effect, since when a subject is required to act as experimenter by proxy, there is no effect. Analyses at level III therefore seem indicated.

But then what is the explanatory status of the 'agentic state' hypothesis? We are in fact tempted to see it as a simple description of the process of obedience which itself needs to be explained. Nevertheless, elements of complementary explanations have been put forward by Milgram who, in his list of preliminary conditions for obedience, cites family, school, institutional framework as teachers of submission to authority. While he does therefore appeal to dominant ideology as an explanatory principle, the variations in his paradigm have never been explicitly linked to it.

This is an example of the frequent lack of coherence in experimental social psychology: operational procedures use within-situation variables, while theories deal with intra-personal or inter-personal processes, or even with their articulation, and ideology only gets a mention. There is therefore a great contrast between the care with which Milgram manipulated the situational variables and the speed with which he put forward an explanation in terms of ideology.

Meeus & Raaijmakers (1984), prompted by Holzkamp's (1972) theories, also took up the problem of submission to authority. They asked their subjects to give a recruitment test to an unemployed man and, for the purposes of a scientific investigation, to create so much tension in the situation that the man would fail the test and so lose any chance of getting the job applied for. As with Milgram, they found a very high level of obedience, even when they gave subjects a better means of measuring the responsibility they were assuming ahead of time, or when they took as subjects personnel managers who had already developed professional and ethical standards. Only when subjects had to sign a declaration beforehand which made them legally responsible did one find a significant reduction in obedience to the experimenter. A legal requirement often considered to be part of the ideological structure succeeded therefore in counteracting the impact of a scientific authority which was abusing its power. This is to some extent an argument in favour of separation of powers, as advocated by Montesquieu many years ago.

IV. Another attempt at articulation

Inter-group relations and social influence

To reduce the gaps between theory and experiment in the study of social influence, we propose to begin with a systematic study of factors at level III. Certainly, the investigation of variables relevant to level III, i.e. inter-group relations and positions within an existing social system outside the laboratory experimental situation, has not been totally neglected.

Hovland and Weiss (1951) attributed a message either to Oppenheimer, outstanding representative of American scientific credibility, or to *Pravda*, no less outstanding representative of political non-credibility because anti-American. Results showed that immediate influence was only strong for Oppenheimer: however, long term, *Pravda* showed an increase while Oppenheimer's influence diminished. This was one of the first experiments which demonstrated the existence of a 'sleeper effect' (for a discussion of the delayed effect, see Kapferer, 1978). Influence processes therefore arise from relations between groups and from representations forged outside the experimental situation. However, this experiment was carried out, not so much to advance the understanding of such relations, as to illustrate the psychological process which depends on credibility of the source. Group membership was only of procedural value, a means and not an end in itself.

Operational procedures involving conditions of appearance of a given process of social influence across group categories appear even more clearly in the work of Kelman (1958). We remember that the author proposed to distinguish several processes of influence. First, compliance, which occurs in situations where conformity is only apparent and plays an essentially instrumental role. The subject desires to obtain approval of the group or to avoid disagreements which could result from obviously deviant behaviour. Beliefs of subjects are not touched. This process appears in conditions where the influential relationship is grafted on to existing coercive power (French & Raven, 1959) and where conditions make the subject visible to the source. Identification arises from a desire to maintain or establish positive relations with the influence source. This would be the case when the group is attractive to the subject and at the same time, visible or salient for the subject. Finally, internalisation leads to real change in the beliefs of the subject apart from any direct or symbolic relationship with the influence source. This is the case when credibility of source is high and subject is led to consider the message as endowed with the intrinsic values of objectivity and truth.

Kelman's subjects were Black students at a Black college at the time of the inauguration of desegregation laws in American public schools. The students had to listen to a radio message advocating maintenance of certain Black institutions so as to preserve the tradition, culture and history of Blacks, a segregationist position at that time and in opposition to the strongly anti-segregationist views of the majority of subjects. The person interviewed on the radio broadcast varied in different conditions. In one, he was 'president of the National Foundation for Colleges for Blacks' who announced his intention to cut off funds for colleges whose students expressed opposition to his proposal. In a second condition, it was not power but attraction or identity of the group which was the foundation for influence: the speaker was presented as president of a representative student organisation which had played an important role in the evolution of anti-segregation laws in education. In the third condition, the speaker was a White teacher of history whose scientific 'respectability' was recognised.

Several measures of influence were taken in each condition. A first measure was taken straight after the message had been heard, replies being accompanied by names: in addition, there was control by the source as replies were to be communicated to him. Following this, an anonymous measure was taken but still with group salience, relations with the source being still strong due to recency of both message and the first measure. A third measure was made several weeks later, without control or group salience.

Results showed that all speakers had influence in the first measure, whoever they were. In the second, the speaker who had made great play with his power had no influence on opinions, but the other two speakers did. Several weeks later, only one source showed any marked influence, the White teacher with scientific status. These results were analysed by the author in terms of processes activated in different conditions. A process of compliance occurs when the relationship is based on control or power, identification ensures influence when the relationship with the group is salient, and interiorisation leads to change in belief, which is then no longer contingent.

This work lies thus at the very heart of an articulation of the psychological and the sociological, for these processes are activated by an experimental situation which implicates inter-group relations. When the speaker belongs to the in-group but tries to impose control in a dominance relation, he brings about compliance, or change only on the surface. When subjects are reminded of their group membership (Black students), identification takes place, leading to change so long as their identification is psychologically salient. A lasting change finally appears when the message goes beyond group membership: this applies to the teacher whose scientific discourse supplants all individual biases to offer a discourse of universal because scientific value. We have seen in relation to norm setting how such a representation depends on a naive universalist epistemology which can, in other circumstances, overcome relationships between groups.

Other research implicates an articulation of group membership and processes of influence. For example, in studies of social support, we have seen a minor dispute between, on the one hand, Malof & Lott (1962) who claim to have shown that, with visual stimuli, strongly racist Whites will accept support even from a dissident Black (which appears to support the ideas of Rokeach, Smith & Evans (1966) on the nature of racist attitudes, which are said to be based on difference in beliefs); and on the other, Boyanowsky & Allen (1973) who showed that this is so only for visual items. Malof & Lott's results are therefore said to be due, not to non-racist attitudes, but to the implicit hypothesis of unanimity or consensus in the perceptual domain, since no such hypothesis holds for opinion items which directly involve the social identity of the White subject. These investigators show in addition how salience of the White in-group and direct visibility of the subject to the group have an impact on the influence obtained.

These few experiments show that articulation of influence processes and inter-group relations is possible and necessary; elements for such analysis are already available, but the relevant conceptualisation has not yet been developed as such. An older current of research however seems to offer a more systematic framework for studying the articulation of inter-group relations and social influence: this is the work on reference groups, which shows how processes of identification (belonging or not belonging) lead to changes in beliefs in the individual (Hyman, 1942; Merton, 1957; Merton & Kitt, 1950; M. Sherif, 1948; Kelley, 1952; etc). Thus Newcomb (1943) showed that the majority of students from conservative backgrounds progressively adopted the typically more liberal attitude of their college. While explanatory factors were numerous, one of them could be linked to the establishment of processes of inter-group influence, especially for students who chose their friends but not their families as their essential frame of reference. Thus opinions expressed on a questionnaire also depended on the salience of the reference group (Charters & Newcomb, 1958): Roman Catholics expressed more orthodox opinions when told they were with other Catholics and that they would have to work together on the basis of Catholic opinion than when they had to reply in a large room without any reference to their religious affiliation.

Other examples could be developed. We have proposed an explanation in terms of category membership to take account of phenomena of group polarisation:

These results offer preliminary support for the hypothesis that variations in salience of a categorisation are related to variations in polarisation. When, by invoking a second group, a symbolic confrontation is created between the two groups, or when, in a real encounter, two members of a group are in the presence of two from another, polarisation of judgements is intensified. Is it not likely that group polarisation is a product of the process of categorisation? For a given problem, the divergent position of members of a group would be first translated into conflict of opinion. Then the group would pronounce in favour of one opinion – a distinctive notion because opposed to the other opinion – which would lead to new responses being more polarised than the first. Subsequent experiments should investigate this hypothesis. (Doise, 1972:314)

Social identity and social influence

Turner (1982) also plans to get involved in research which articulates the study of social influence and the study of social identity, as determined by the category memberships of the individual. His hypothesis is that cognitive processes relating to self-stereotyping are the source of a particular form of social influence which he calls 'Referent Informational Influence'.

The notion of Referent Informational Influence is, in our opinion, especially important for understanding uniformity of behaviour and attitude in members of wide-spread social groups. It takes place in three stages:

1. Individuals define themselves as members of a distinct social category.
2. Individuals form or learn the stereotypic norm of that category. They ascertain that certain ways of behaving are criterial attributes of category membership. Certain appropriate, expected or desirable behaviours are used to define the category as different from other categories.
3. Individuals assign these norms to themselves in the same way that they assign other stereotypic characteristics of the category to themselves when their category membership becomes psychologically salient. Thus their

behaviour becomes more normative (conformist) as their category membership becomes salient. (Turner, 1982:31)

Two experiments reported by Mugny (1982: experiments 13 & 14) do
already articulate the study of processes linked to social identity and those
related to minority consistency. More especially, one of these experiments
shows that stronger identification with an influence source can mean that
even a dogmatically worded message will influence subjects. However, the
other experiment confirms that risk of public identification with an
unpopular influence source can also weaken the impact of this source. This
research shows that introduction of our level III into the study of influence
allows us to make a connection between this classic area of social psychology
and more recent studies of social identity and inter-group relations. It
therefore provides a transition towards the next chapter.

But before closing this chapter, we must emphasise the fact that the study
of influence phenomena cannot be reduced to the study of inter-group effects
and, more particularly, to the study of the effects of identification with a
source of influence. In fact, many recent experimental results show that it
is necessary to distinguish between, on the one hand, direct and immediate
influence, and on the other, indirect or belated influence (see e.g. Moscovici
& Personnaz, 1980; Moscovici, Mugny & Papastamou, 1981; Mugny, 1982;
Mugny, Kaiser & Papastamou, 1983; Personnaz, 1981). If it were all a
matter of identity, we would then need to distinguish between different sorts
of identity which can operate in opposing directions. In any case, it seems to
us that articulation with analyses at level IV is required to solve the problem.
In fact it is just such an articulation that Moscovici (1980) proposed in his
chapter on conversion, which deals with the distinction between majority
and minority influence. Subjects confronted with a majority source offering
an unusual response watch very carefully to see what others reply, and may
join in their response. But once freed of this majority pressure, they continue
to see properties of stimuli as they always have seen them. This is not,
however, the attitude of subjects faced with a deviant minority. For them,
there is no pressure to conformity at first. Nevertheless, consistency and
firmness in this minority make them look further for objective reasons which
might justify the minority response. In our opinion, similar dynamics
operate when there is identification with the source and when this identification is made difficult. In the first case, subjects may often adopt their
replies for purely relational reasons; in the latter case, they will usually
invest more in examining reality. It is as though certain social relationships
make it easier for people to consider a different point of view, to appeal to
a concept they can consider more objective because independent of their
immediate relationship with the influence source. Beyond questions of

identity and social differentiation, there may be belief in truths or values of wider significance. It is such a process that we saw at work when Mugny, Kaiser & Papastamou (1983) showed that young Swiss were influenced more lastingly by a foreign minority source who invoked humanitarian arguments to defend the rights of immigrant workers than by a Swiss minority source using the same arguments.

4 Levels of explanation in the study of inter-group relations

Intelligence and social influence are research areas which are ideal for analyses at our levels I and II, while at the same time being relevant to the two other levels. Investigation of the relations between the social classes and social groups maintained in a given society is principally concerned with analysis at levels III and IV, and belongs more especially to the domain of sociology. Nevertheless, the dynamics studied by sociology actually take place via individual dynamics and inter-personal dynamics, and require studies which articulate levels just as much as the areas looked at in our two previous chapters.

In this chapter, however, we will change our approach: up to now our principal aim has been to show how analysis at levels I and II are not fully adequate, whereas now we will need to show that analysis at these levels is nonetheless indispensable for the investigation of more specifically social processes. To a certain extent, we are talking to different people: earlier, we wanted to convince psychologists and social psychologists of the limitations of traditional intra- and inter-personal analyses, and now we need to show sociologists of the 'Durkheimian' tradition that more psychological analyses could usefully complement their own analyses. Naturally this does not mean that we subscribe to the theory that every analysis of social phenomena is, in the final analysis, personal or inter-personal in nature. Our goal remains still an articulation of levels of explanation, each of which is legitimate in its own right and will develop autonomously. We are not advocating the 'psychologising' of sociology with Tarde (1904:81) who said, 'just as progress in physics requires more and more mechanisation so progress in sociology requires more and more psychologising'. It is nevertheless a fact that a social psychology has recently been developed in the field of inter-group relations which complements the work of sociology proper.

More specifically, in this chapter we will present work whose psychological origin is obvious but where the possibility of articulation with sociological analysis is no less so.

I. Contrasts in judgements and social differentiation

Categorisation and accentuation of differences

Tajfel and Wilkes (1963) would certainly not have disagreed with the statement that their theory, which was the foundation stone of their research into the effects of categorisation on judgements of stimuli of different lengths, is psychological in nature: the theory predicts that in certain conditions, judgements will accentuate resemblances between stimuli which belong to the same category and differences between stimuli belonging to different categories. The origins of this theory are to be found in the Gestalt tradition of psychology which studied the organisation of perception in the individual. More directly, Tajfel's theory was based on Bruner (1957) who established links between perception and cognition, both operations having in common a procedure of verifying hypotheses and, more especially, of being guided by categorial membership of the object perceived or known.

We shall briefly summarise Tajfel & Wilkes' (1963) experiment: subjects had to estimate lengths of eight lines presented several times in random order. The lines were of unequal lengths: the longest was 229 mm and the shortest 162 mm, with each line approximately 5 % longer than its neighbour when ranged in ascending order. In one experimental condition, the four shorter were always accompanied by the letter A and the four longer by the letter B. There was therefore perfect correspondence between class membership and length of lines. In two other conditions, this correspondence did not exist: either the labelling A and B varied randomly in each presentation, or there were no letters. Two main predictions were: (1) accentuation of differences between categories and of resemblances within categories would occur when the classification superimposed on stimuli systematically linked physical dimensions to category membership (condition 1); (2) such accentuation would not occur when there was no systematic link between category membership and the physical characteristics to be judged (conditions 2 and 3).

In the first condition, differences between stimuli belonging to categories A and B were overestimated, and when stimuli were repeatedly shown, a tendency to overestimate resemblances within categories was found also. These effects were absent in judgements by subjects in the two other conditions.

Tajfel & Wilkes (1963) related this effect of classification to the formal aspect of social stereotypes. In their introduction, they gave the example of a possible stereotype which might link belonging to the group 'Swedes' with tall stature, and belonging to the group 'Italians' with short stature, and in their conclusion they wrote:

These findings may possibly have some fairly wide implications for a variety of judgement situations they represent, in a sense, a simplified exercise in stereotyping. An essential feature of stereotyping is that of exaggerating *some* differences between groups classified in a certain way, and of minimizing the same differences within such groups. It may be important to note that these effects were shown to exist in the present experiments despite the relative ease and simplicity of judgements, the minimal amount of experience with the classification and its minimal significance to the subject. The drastic effects of a small but consistent and direct increase in the amount of experience with the classification can be seen when one considers the results of the additional trials in one of the experiments. There is therefore the possibility that the phenomenon of stereotyping, occurring in situations where judgements are usually neither easy nor simple and where classifications have been built through long and continuously repeated past experience is no more than an exaggeration of the effects found in the present experiments. (Tajfel & Wilkes, 1963:113)

Effects of classification on social stereotypes

Tajfel did not stop at this single connection between characteristics of judgements of physical stimuli and social stereotypes. He directly applied the theory of contrasts in judgements to accentuation of differences and of resemblances in certain social stereotypes. Thus the theory predicts that contrasts will be more accentuated when a value dimension is related to the category. In this way he explains why French Canadians accentuate more than do English speakers differences between their respective accents; the relative differences in terms of socio-economic status in Canada are 'more salient, worrying, and relevant to the French than to the English subjects, especially as the French subjects were all college students, future direct competitors of the English group' (Tajfel, 1959b:89). According to this theory, members of a group should also be seen as resembling each other more in traits which form part of the group stereotype than in traits which do not: Tajfel, Sheikh & Gardner (1964) found this accentuation of resemblances for stereotypic traits when their subjects described two Indians and two Canadians.

Does this mean that explanation of social representations can be reduced to that which accounts for individual organisation of judgements of physical stimuli? It is true that the research cited here, and other we have reported elsewhere (Doise, 1978, 1979), permit the conclusion that social psychologists have been usefully inspired by theories developed in a different area in their explanations of some characteristics of social stereotypes. However, it should not be forgotten that Tajfel carried out his research into perceptual judgements because he was interested in problems of a social nature. The legitimacy of using a psychophysical model in social psychology is, in our opinion, not a real problem if put in general terms. Every theory is a special case, whose utility in the particular domain one wishes to apply it to must be proved. Reductionism does not consist so much borrowing from a different level of analysis as in the exclusivity accorded to analyses at a particular level. Thus Tajfel & Wilkes (1963) were right to claim, at the end of their paper, that the introduction of a theory of classification processes into social psychology constituted a net gain for a social psychology supposed only to deal with individual differences. On the other hand, while there certainly are general processes involved in both judgements of physical objects and judgements of social objects, one can only account for their function in a social context by incorporating analyses at other levels as well. This is just what Tajfel (1959b) proceeds to do in the quotation given above dealing with differences in socio-economic status between French- and English-speaking Canadians.

Extension of the theory of category differentiation

In order to facilitate articulation of levels of analysis we propose an extension of the definition of the categorisation process. We distinguish three aspects of relations between groups: behaviour, value judgements, representations. These distinctions, which are classically used in psychology, do not imply that we are dealing with different realities. There is no inter-group behaviour which is not also accompanied by value judgements or more objective judgements. On the other hand, a judgement is already a behaviour, it is a stance taken in relation to another group and often a justification or anticipation of some act in relation to it. The hypothesis we propose is that differentiations at the levels of cognitive representation, evaluative discrimination and behavioural discrimination are all linked. As regards Tajfel's theory (1959a) which links evaluative and representative discriminations, extension of the theory is related more precisely to explanation of the behavioural aspect of inter-group relations. This is a fundamental dimension which governs the entire setting in process of the category differentiation dynamic. If there are discrimination and contrasts in representations and evaluations, this is because they facilitate differentiated behaviour in terms of category membership between members of different groups. Discriminations between groups operate in a vicious spiral: behavioural discrimination as a function of category membership leads to evaluative and representative discrimination, which in turn facilitate further behavioural discrimination.

The process of categorisation, which allows the individual to organise her/his subjective experience of the social environment, thus also takes account of the structuring of a system of social interactions. Behaviour, as a function of shared or opposed memberships, structures and transforms social reality. The process now describes, not just a fundamental way of understanding reality, but also a form of articulation of collective behaviours, which transform reality as a function of social cleavages of the most diverse origins. Percepts, feelings and individual actions are thus oriented along collective lines of force.

Illustration by experiment

Elsewhere (Doise, 1978a) we have reported in detail several experiments carried out in the general framework of this extension of the theory of category differentiation. Here we will summarise a few of them.

One experiment was designed to test the effect of behavioural factors on value judgements and representational discriminations. Subjects were divided into two groups, apparently according to their previous choices in an aesthetic judgement task but in fact at random, and anticipated either a cooperative or a competitive interaction with members of the other group. In a control situation, no interaction was expected. All subjects rated members of their own group and of the other on evaluative scales, e.g. friendly–hostile, generous–mean, and on more objective scales, namely fair–dark, tall–short, fat–thin, active–quiet. In fact, since they did not know who was in their group or the other, they had to guess their characteristics in a situation where they did or did not anticipate future interaction. As predicted, anticipated competition with an important stake led to more differentiated descriptions than in the control condition, both on evaluative and on the more objective scales. This experiment therefore succeeded in reproducing experimentally the accentuation of differences of a physical nature observed in racist cultures (Pettigrew, Allport & Barnett, 1958; Secord, Bevan & Katz, 1956).

Another experiment also studied the effects of convergence or divergence at a behavioural level on discriminations at the level of representation. The representations were those which boys have about girls in our society, and thus relate to analysis at levels III or IV. But in our experiment we wanted to show how variables relating to the level of interactional analysis modified these representations. Male students anticipated a cooperative or a competitive interaction with female students. When their anticipation was competitive, they displayed a greater evaluative discrimination in relation to female students than when their anticipation was cooperative. In the competitive condition, they also attributed more feminine characteristics to the other than in the cooperative. This stronger differentiation was only found where competition between two males and two females was anticipated, and not where competition was to involve only one male and one female. We relate this difference between collective and inter-personal interactions to the functioning of the categorisation process itself: in a group interaction, convergence in respect to another member of one's own category is possible, which also leads to the opposite aspect of the process, divergence in relation to the other group. During an inter-personal interaction, one aspect at least of the process, convergence in relation to a member of one's own group, is impeded, which weakens the effect. The same difference between personal encounter and group encounter was demonstrated in an experiment studying the evaluative representations which members of two groups of different social positions (apprentices and high school boys) held about themselves and about the others.

Confrontation of one group with another can in certain conditions lead to tightening of links within the group and an effect of 'sacred union'. Two of our experiments showed that evocation of another group or of another category is sufficient to lead to accentuation of within-category resemblances in social representations. In one experiment, we again looked at the notions men have about women: all subjects described six photographs, three girls and three boys, according to a list of traits relating to feminine and masculine stereotypes, the only difference between the two experimental conditions being that in one, subjects first described the three photographs of one sex without knowing they would have three more of the opposite sex to describe, while in the second all six photographs were presented together. The categorisation process should operate in a stronger fashion in the second condition where both categories were available from the start. This is what the results showed: in the second condition, descriptions revealed a greater differentiation between categories and a greater resemblance between photographs of the same category. Another experiment looked at the same process of accentuation of resemblances and differences, but this time using stereotypes that Genevans have about different regional groups in Switzerland (German-speaking Swiss, French-speaking Swiss, Italian-speaking Swiss). When two of these groups had to be described at the same time as a third non-Swiss group, resemblances between the two Swiss groups become more salient that when they were described with a third Swiss group and without any opposition from a foreign group. Such research illustrates well how collective representations are actualised in different situations according to a definite process.

When category memberships are crossed

Though in myths and ideologies the social world is usually divided into two opposing camps, this dualist view does not necessarily reflect the complexity of social systems. Nor is dualism always the end product of the categorisation process. The social arena is often made up of a network of affiliations which cross each other. Let us distinguish two types of situation: a situation of 'simple categories' in which opposition between one membership category and another is made very salient, and a situation of 'crossed categories' in which, for individuals, some members of their membership category and some members of a different category according to one criterion find themselves linked as members of a different group according to a second criterion. Let us suppose that the two category systems are equally salient: how will the categorisation process work in the crossed category situation? There should be increase of differences between the two categories in the first categorisation as well as increase of differences between the two categories in the second. At the same time, there should be accentuation of differences within the same category since it is, by definition, made up of members of two different groups. For the same reasons, there should be both accentuation of resemblances between members of the same and of different categories according to the first criterion since they belong to the same category according to the second. Therefore one might suppose opposed effects would weaken the operation of category differentiation.

In one experiment, we introduced a situation of simple categories and a situation of crossed categories. In each situation, six girls and six boys had to evaluate their own and the others' performances, but in one situation, only gender divided them, whereas in the other three girls and three boys also belonged to group 'blue' as distinct from the other three girls and three boys in group 'red'. Results showed that crossover of membership had the predicted effect: in simple categories, subjects made different evaluations of the performance of members of their own groups from members of the other, but this difference disappeared in the crossed condition where neither gender nor colour category showed any effect. Deschamps and Doise (1979) found effects in the same direction by using two natural categories (men–women, young–adult) crossed or not.

Results reported by Arcuri (1982) and Vanbeselaere (1984) confirm that crossed membership weakens discrimination between groups. The results of Brown and Turner (1979) are similar when the four groups resulting from crossover of two different categories are present in the experimental situation: when only two groups are present, they once again find the usual effects of inter-group differentiation.

Deschamps (1977) also studied the effect of crossed membership in judgements of physical stimuli: he again found disappearance of the effect of category when crossed membership was introduced. We have thus gone full circle: a theory applied first to quantitative judgements has enriched analysis of social phenomena and has returned to its original field to test properties of the theory revealed in social psychology.

Certain ethnologists also use the notion of crossed membership (LeVine

& Campbell, 1972; Jaulin, 1973), and Lorwin (1972) explains survival of nations marked by linguistic and ideological conflict by turning to a passage by the sociologist Ross (1920:165):

A society, therefore, which is riven by a dozen oppositions along lines running in every direction, may actually be in less danger of being torn with violence or falling to pieces than one split along just one line. For each new cleavage contributes to narrow the cross clefts, so that one might say that society is *sewn together* by its inner conflicts.

This is the approach taken by ethnologists, sociologists and political analysts to those dynamics which activate crossed categorisations at the level of their operation in the individual.

II. Group interaction

Mechanisms which relate to analysis at level I, such as those described by the categorisation process, can therefore be integrated with analyses at other levels. We will now give an account of two bodies of research, one initiated by Sherif and the other by Rabbie, which have in common that they principally relate to our second level of analysis since they deal with interaction between individuals belonging to different groups but not necessarily occupying different positions in the social hierarchy.

Sherif's experiments

Let us briefly summarise the procedure and results of Sherif's most famous experiment on inter-group relations: the Robber's Cave. Two groups of children of around 12 years were occupied with enjoyable activities which required active participation from each child. During this phase of group formation, each group was unaware of the existence of the other, but each developed a strong group structure with its own norms and hierarchy. When the two groups were well formed, they were put in contact and a tournament was suggested. Competitive games put the two groups in conflict for several days. Very rapidly a strong hostility developed, insults and brawls became the order of the day. Appropriate measures showed that the competition greatly influenced the representations and evaluations of the antagonists. The image of the other group became unfavourable compared to one's own group, performance of one's own team members was rated higher than that of the others. Structure of the groups changed also: solidarity increased and in one group a leader seen as too soft was replaced by a member more active in the fight with the other group.

How was this conflict ended? If competition or incompatibility of aims of the two groups led to their hostility, would their compatibility lead to reconciliation? Introduction in a third phase of the experiment of a series of joint, non-competitive activities – eating meals, cinema shows – did not reduce the animosity. Peace was not brought about until both groups had to solve a number of problems of great importance to everyone and requiring the efforts of every one of their members on several occasions. Such supraordinate goals were introduced in a fourth phase in the experiment when members of both groups had to work together to find a way of restoring their water supply, pool resources to rent a film, and rescue the lorry which brought their food and which had broken down. While these supraordinate goals were being achieved, hostility between the groups gradually decreased. The image of the other group became nearly as favourable as the image of one's own and choice of best friends began to be made across the boundaries between groups.

Let us summarise the results of this experiment, putting them in the theoretic framework proposed by Sherif (1966): individuals, led to realise a goal by interdependent actions, become a group. When two groups need to realise incompatible goals, one of them being able to fulfill its aim only on condition the other does not, an unfavourable representation of the other group develops and members of a group can only envisage and experience hostile contact with members of the other group, at the same time increasing solidarity within their own group. Only realisation of supraordinate goals which require the united effort of all members of both groups can reduce hostility, improve the representation of the other group and lead to friendly contacts between members of the two groups. Understanding of the psychological relations between groups, according to Sherif, can only be achieved by studying the relations between the goals of the different groups in the interaction.

This explanation in terms of relations between goals is typically at level II: it relates to the dynamic of an interaction between individuals, who are treated at the outset as occupying interchangeable positions but whose subsequent relations are linked to the shared or opposed affiliations which the experimenter introduces into the situation. However it also seems to us possible to integrate these explanations with the theory of categorial differentiation: if we accept that the creation of incompatibility at the level of goals means differentiation at the behavioural level, the theory predicts that such differentiation will lead to differentiations at the level of representations and evaluations. Introduction of convergence at the level of behaviour, such as that realised with a supraordinate goal, will on the contrary diminish the other differentiations. This is exactly what happened in the Robber's Cave.

After Sherif

This perspective can be extended to other experiments which followed on from Sherif's approach, such as the work of Diab (1970) in Lebanon: the experimental procedures are similar to those of Sherif, here for groups composed of Christians and of Muslims. The results show many similarities with Sherif's. But there are also differences: only the winning group evaluated its performance as better than that of the other group, and at the end of the third phase, four members of the losing group wanted to quit the camp, having not only developed a strong aggression towards the members of the victorious group but also towards one member of their own group. It is tempting to invoke the cultural context to explain these differences; but this would mean forgetting that Sherif, in an earlier experiment prior to the Robber's Cave, got similar results:

The victorious Bull Dogs were elated, happy, self-content, and full of pride. The losing Red Devils were dejected. Chiefly because their leader became vindictive, blaming defeat on low-status members of his own group, their loss was conducive to signs of disorganisation. Low-status Red Devils resented the accusations, and there was conflict within the group until later the Red Devils faced broadside attacks from the Bull Dogs. (Sherif & Sherif, 1969:241)

On the other hand, if the Lebanese context did have an influence in Diab's experiment, we still need to define the mechanisms which might have been operating. In this connection we should recall the existence of crossed memberships, in so far as the two competitive groups were each made up of Christians and Muslims. This could explain that at a given moment sociometric choices took less account of group boundaries than with Sherif. It has been claimed also that, for the losing group, the cleavage between religious affiliations became salient: the four boys who wanted to quit the camp were all of the same faith, the definite failure in the tournament having eliminated all meaning from membership of the competitive group. Furthermore, it is a usual observation among ethnologists (Beals, 1962; Chance, 1962) that groups which do not succeed in achieving a goal fragment into subgroups along prior demarcation lines. Such behaviour can also be interpreted in the framework of Tajfel & Turner's social identity theory, which we will describe below.

To show that these results are not applicable only to children's games, Sherif recalled the experiments by Blake & Mouton (1962a, b). Their research was with adult trainees in management or research institutions. The groups studied in every case were composed of eight to ten members. A competition was organised between two, three or four groups in the following manner: after a period of group formation over about ten hours, each group was required to discuss a problem of human relations for three hours. The experimenter announced in advance that one group would be designated the winner and another the loser, and that there was no possibility of an *ex aequo* outcome. After the groups had worked out their solutions, these were reproduced and distributed to all members of the groups present, who were required to evaluate them. Out of 48 groups studied, the solution of the membership group was judged superior to the solution of the other groups in 46 groups, members of the two other groups giving on average the same value to their own group's solution and that of the other. Once again, divergence between introduced goals leads to evaluative differentiations. The same authors (Blake & Mouton, 1962a) also showed that such divergence leads to bias in judgements of a more objective nature, specifically when it was a matter of reconstituting the elements of solution common to both groups.

Blake, Shepard & Mouton (1964) posed the problem of resolution of conflicts between groups whose goals remain fundamentally antagonistic. Their book describes three interventions in industrial conflicts. The success of such interventions depended on the prior sensitisation of a majority of the members of the hostile groups to the perceptual and evaluative distortion phenomena which accompany a conflictual interaction. Intervention itself consisted of organising several meetings alternatively between members of the same group and between representatives of the two groups in conflict. Several members of each group first discussed the representations and attitudes they had with regard to their own group and the other. Then the first encounter took place between representatives of the two groups, accompanied by observers. The only aim of this meeting was for representatives to describe exactly the representations they had of their own and of the other group. Returning to their own group, the representatives and their partners tried to understand the differences between the images presented by their group and those presented by the opposing group. Other meetings between groups were then supposed to permit correction of distortions and take account of principal divergences between the positions of the two parties. It is at this point that negotiations can begin, starting from positions defined together. The social psychologists followed the development of the negotiations, and if unsuccessful, they would intervene with both parties, with each providing a list of those solutions they would accept so as to avoid polarisation of the two opposing positions. The notion of supraordinate goal is absent with Blake *et al*: their intervention consists of making groups which have fundamentally opposed goals understand they can have compatible aims in the short term.

The problem posed by such interventions is related to differences between levels of analysis. This attempt seems to imply that opposing parties in an industrial dispute can be persuaded to put themselves in the place of the other and that they occupy interchangeable positions. By neglecting analyses at level III, it seems to us, the book by Blake, Shepard & Mouton proposes too optimistic a view of social relations. It is not impossible that a social psychological intervention might, on the contrary, exacerbate a conflict: the technique of inversion of role, for example, where each antagonist has to defend the point of view of his adversary, can lead to exacerbation of the conflict where there is real incompatibility of positions (Johnson, 1967).

Rabbie and 'common fate'

We should not conclude at this point that the work by Sherif, Blake and Mouton dealt with all the possibilities in situational analysis of relations between groups. A number of important investigations by Rabbie and his colleagues in the Netherlands show that many things still remained to be looked at following the work of these American researchers. Rabbie & Horwitz (1969) introduced the notion of 'common fate' into the experimental study of inter-group relations. In fact, in Sherif's research, the fate of individuals, whether they won or lost during a competition, depended on their membership of a given group. Rabbie & Horwitz simply examined the effect of sharing a common fate, separate from any active involvement by members of a group in a competitive interaction. In their experiment, eight people who came to the laboratory were divided into two equal groups, one 'blue', one 'green', apparently for administrative purposes. The experiment was presented to them as dealing with elaboration of first impressions. The subjects in the two groups individually described two photographs. The experimenter then announced that payment for participation in the experiment unfortunately consisted of only four transistors, which would be given to members of just one group, either (depending on experimental conditions) at random, or according to the experimenter's decision, or following a vote by members of just one group. Then one of the groups was given the four transistors. In a control condition, the experimenter did not speak of payment. At this point the subjects were introduced briefly to one another and gave their first impressions of all participants, using the same scales they had previously used to describe the photographs. They also described the general characteristics of the two groups. While there were no differences between the descriptions of their own group and its members and those of the other in the control condition (absence of payment), the differences were significant for the experimental groups. Those who had received payment as well as those who had been frustrated described the members of their own group and the characteristics of this group in general more favourably than the members and atmosphere of the other. The mere fact of sharing the same fate, independently of the way in which this was inflicted, was thus sufficient to bring about an evaluative discrimination in favour of one's own group. But why should sharing a common fate have this effect? Subjects are said to anticipate easy interaction after the experiment with those who have experienced a similar fate and a more difficult interaction with the others: 'Our reading of the present evidence is that they were reacting to the perceived emotional changes in themselves and others and to the consequent change in ease or difficulty of face-to-face interaction' (Rabbie & Horwitz, 1969:277).

A series of experiments was then carried out by Rabbie and his colleagues on the effects of simple anticipation of intergroup interaction. Let us summarise some of the salient results. Several experiments (reported by Rabbie, 1974) showed that members of a group, who were to be required to carry out a task together in the presence of another group, already showed a bias favouring members of their own group before the task was undertaken, and independently of the competitive or cooperative nature of the anticipated group relations.

As regards over-evaluation of the products of one's own group, this bias was rare in the judgements of individual members, who appeared to protect themselves in this way from possible future disappointment in some future objective comparison of outcomes. A competitive situation only led to overevaluation of the products relative to a cooperative situation where members of a group were required to come to an agreement via collective discussion on the respective merits of the product of their group and of the other. There were also certain very specific conditions which produced an accentuation of hierarchical relations, increase in conformity or in hostility towards the other group.

But these results were practically all obtained in anticipation of real confrontation with members of the other group which was to take place after measures of dependent variables had been taken. The effects of frustration or of cooperation, of victory or of defeat, were not studied as such. Thus a second series of experiments was undertaken to look at the consequences of competition and cooperation which actually occurred. Once again, only the most salient results will be presented here, Rabbie (1979) having published an extensive review of this research.

Competition and cooperation between groups

A first result concerns the effect of the presence of the 'base group' during negotiations between representatives of two groups: when other members of the group are present, representatives of the groups in a competitive interaction become more competitive and representatives of cooperative groups become more cooperative. These results are related to the polarisation phenomena which arise when several members of a group have to decide what position to defend when confronted by the other group. Such polarisation has been observed by Rabbie & Visser (1972) in the Netherlands, and independently by Louche (1974–75a, b) in France. Discussion within a group also has the consequence that its representatives are invested with more restricted mandates (Rabbie, Visser & Tils, 1976). Elsewhere, other research (Lamm, 1973) showed that negotiators can give themselves a greater margin for manoeuvre if they enjoy a higher status in their group.

Several investigations deal with interactions which occur during mixed motivation games. Cooperative orientation or competitive orientation are induced in the following manner: the players are informed that they will encounter members of the other group at the end of the game (cooperative orientation) or that they will not meet them (competitive), that they can listen to the discussion of the other group (cooperation) or that they cannot listen (competition). In these game situations, and before introduction of any experimental variables, members of the same group are once again evaluated more favourably than members of the other group. In one of these experiments, Rabbie also confirmed that after the interaction the members of one's own group are perceived as relatively more differentiated and members of the opposing group as relatively more similar to each other than before the experiment. We would relate this result with a property of impression formation proposed by Bruner & Perlmutter (1957:253): 'the more widespread one's experience with diverse members of the category the less will this category membership affect the impression formed of the person encountered'.

In such mixed motivation games, the differentiation between in-group and out-group is in general greater along dimensions which have to do with confidence and loyalty, the in-group being perceived in a more favourable light. Thus bias is stronger when the group is confronted with a competitive opponent, which fits in with our concept of categorial differentiation, which should intervene more strongly where there are behavioural differences. Furthermore an important contribution of the game paradigm is that it illustrates a dynamic development in spiral: simple anticipation of a competitive interaction generates representations which in turn cannot fail to influence behaviour towards the other group. The fact that the two opposing parties tend to develop similar representations leads to a cumulative effect, and what ensues ends by corresponding to the representations which preceded it.

Attribution of different intentions can of course also correspond to a real difference between the behaviour of the two groups. Situations have thus been created where a group with cooperative orientation is in fact confronted by a group practising a competitive strategy. The cooperative groups are thus in a sense exploited and lose the game, but do not give themselves up to defeatism: on the contrary they consider themselves as 'moral victors'. They have respected the experimenter's instructions, which the others have not. They feel their conduct is less blameworthy than that of individualist or competitive groups and they affirm more often that the game also implies moral issues, that it is a serious matter and not just a "game".' (Rabbie, 1979:216). By introducing considerations of a more general order, the subjects themselves produce an articulation of levels of analysis to explain their behaviour.

In other situations, defeat can lead to lowering of morale in the group, 'a greater sense of dissatisfaction, weak cohesion and a tendency to attribute responsibility for defeat to each other' (Rabbie, 1979). We know elsewhere (Bass & Dunteman, 1963) that such weakness can be temporary, especially when it is possible to attribute responsibility for failure to another allied group. On the other hand, like many others (Blake & Mouton, 1962b; Diab, 1970; Lott & Lott, 1965; M. Sherif, 1966) Rabbie observed that in winning groups 'cohesion and mutual understanding are high, the hierarchical structure which led the group to victory is reinforced. Overevaluation in relation to the losing group is accentuated: the better group has won. Members become more tolerant toward differences of opinion within the group because there is nothing any longer at stake' (1979:214).

Games between two dyads or two triads do not produce the same results: the latter are less competitive than the former. We explain this difference by a facilitation of in-group convergence with couples, where it operates with regard to a particular individual. Research by Gerard & Hoyt (1974) also shows that members of dyads, differentiated from other members of a group of ten persons according to a criterion apparently not important to the experimental task, have a stronger bias towards the other member of their category than have members of groups of five or eight members to another in-group member. Gerard & Hoyt also explain this difference as an effect of categorisation: membership of a category with relatively few members leads to greater visibility and greater possibility of differentiation.

Threats to the leader and inter-group conflict

Rabbie (1979) also reported that during real interaction between groups, hierarchical roles seemed to be more easily differentiated when the interaction was competitive than when it was cooperative. But on the other hand, the leaders of groups could also use inter-group competition to ensure or reinforce their status in the group. The degree of competition induced by the leader was therefore studied as a dependent variable as a function of the stability of his status (Rabbie & Bekkers, 1976). Leaders who could be deposed by a majority vote by members of the group had a greater tendency to introduce competition between groups, especially when members of their group were divided and when their group occupied a comparatively strong position relative to the other group. But when their status was more strongly threatened, they tried to introduce inter-group competition nevertheless, even when they had little chance of winning. Rabbie and Bekkers (1976:282ff) report the results of a field study which attempted to confirm these experimental results. In 29 Dutch trade unions, members of the ruling committee and grass roots militants were questioned as to their degree of satisfaction about the way in which their respective leaders conducted the affairs of the union. A positive correlation was found between their discontent with the leader and hostility towards opponents of the union as expressed by the leader in his speeches to the militants. Experimental research showed that it is the discontent of the members which could be the source of the leader's aggressivity towards opposing groups.

The various investigations by Rabbie and his colleagues show that one must define the conditions which lead to the occurrence of the different effects of competition and cooperation described by Sherif and others. Certain mechanisms have been determined by which the dynamics invoked by competitive or interdependent goals come into operation. It thus becomes possible to explain with more rigour why certain effects occur or do not occur, how they are reinforced or counteracted by different dynamics. At first sight, the diversity of results obtained by Rabbie could give the impression that scientific knowledge bursts into fragments on contact with reality. This is not so: it becomes differentiated, and calls for articulation of theories both at different levels of analysis and at the same level. However the research by Rabbie and his team cited above, like Sherif's, uses explanatory models which most frequently operate at level II. Relations between groups are thus studied via the interactions of individuals. In this regard, it is revealing that Sherif used the same notion of goal as an explanatory principle for both relations within the group and relations between groups.

III. Differentiation and social identity

In their experiment on common fate, Rabbie & Horwitz (1969) used a control condition where the fate of individuals did not depend on their membership category and where members of a group did not have to take decisions with regard to members of the other group. No bias in favour of the membership group was found. This research in a way set in motion research into the minimal conditions necessary for the appearance of a bias in favour of the membership group. The recent work by Tajfel and his team in Bristol was, at least in the first stages, concerned with this problem.

Tajfel and the pursuit of difference

The aim of the experiment by Tajfel *et al.* (1971) was precisely to determine the minimal conditions for the appearance of discrimination in favour of the membership group. The subjects in their experiment were pupils in the same school who all knew each other well. They began the experiment with a perceptual task or a task of aesthetic judgement. Then subjects were told they would be divided into two groups, depending on the nature of the preceding task, either into a group of overestimators or underestimators, or into a group of 'Klee fanciers' and a group of 'Kandinsky fanciers'. It is the latter procedure which has been used in subsequent uses of the paradigm. The subjects think that the division is made according to their performance on the first task but in fact it is made at random, and each is informed individually of his membership in one or other category. No one knows which category his friends belong to. The experiment continues with a study of decision taking. Using several matrices, subjects decide on the financial remuneration their comrades will receive for participating in the experiment. Each matrix gives the payment to be given to two pupils; these may be members of the same group or two different groups. Subjects never know the name of the pupil they are rewarding: they only know which group the pupil is in and a code number. They never reward themselves. Therefore their decision cannot affect their own interests and cannot be affected by individual characteristics of those who will profit, since they are anonymous. Therefore any differential treatment of the others can only be determined by membership of different groups.

The most surprising result of this experiment is the following: when subjects can choose between a strategy which gives, in absolute value, a maximum gain to members of their own group and to members of the other group at the same time, and a strategy which, while giving less in absolute value to their own group, nevertheless gives more to members of one's own than to members of the other, they reduce the absolute value for members of their own group so that they get relatively more than members of the other. Since then, these results, which demonstrate pursuit of differentiation, have been replicated several times by members of Tajfel's team (1978), and also by ourselves (Dann & Doise, 1974). The first interpretation that Tajfel (1970) gave for these results was formulated in terms of a 'generic norm of behaviour towards out-groups' (Tajfel, 1970:99).

A later investigation by Billig and Tajfel (1973) showed that it is membership of different groups which is the foundation for discrimination and not similarity or dissimilarity between individuals, which in the first experiment covaried with membership of the groups. Indeed, when individuals are divided into two groups by tossing a coin, discrimination again appears; it is, on the other hand, absent or much less strong when subjects are not explicitly divided into two groups, and when the only possible criterion for their decision is similarity or dissimilarity of prior aesthetic choices.

As to the minimal condition for the appearance of inter-group discrimination, a limit does seem to have been reached in these experiments. Induction of membership of two different groups is sufficient to arouse discrimination in rewarding behaviour, even if the subjects have to reduce the absolute overall gain for members of their group. On the other hand, we have found (Dann & Doise, 1974) that it is not just anticipation of differential treatment on the part of others which is the foundation for evaluative discrimination because subjects in our control situation, who were only divided into two groups on the basis of their aesthetic judgements and did not have to take any decisions, also showed an evaluative bias with regard to their own group. Subjects in Rabbie and Horwitz's (1969) control situation did not show such a bias. Turner (1975:26) remarks in this regard that the characteristics of this situation prevented the appearance of a bias:

although it might seem that classification was thus accomplished, other aspects of the situation and the rating procedure seem designed to weaken both the salience of this classification and of the subject's location within it. Thus they were told that division into groups was for 'administrative reasons only', that the 'subjects would not work together in any way' and that members must not talk with one another 'since this would interfere with your task later on – to give *unbiased* impressions of the *personality* characteristics of the other subjects in this room'. (italics Turner's)

Simple evocation of group membership is therefore held to be sufficient to produce inter-group effects, on condition they are not counteracted by other aspects of the situation. This is an extreme situation, and sensitive to the introduction of the least variation.

Experimenter effect and subject effect

But if a situation is so sensitive to the least influence, can one not explain the behaviour of subjects in terms of 'experimenter effect' (Orne, 1962; Rosenthal, 1966)? Subjects behave in a given manner because they perceive the expectations of the experimenter. According to Tajfel (1978:36) such an explanation only displaces the problem:

The problem then must be restated once again in terms of the need to specify why a certain *kind* of intergroup behaviour can be elicited so much more easily than other kinds; and this specification is certainly not made if we rest content with the explanation that the behaviour occurred because it was very easy for the experimenters to make it occur.

Tajfel *et al.* (1971:174) invoke a 'subject effect':

What does seem theoretically important is the fact that a few references to 'groupness' in the instruction were sufficient to release the kind of behaviour that was observed despite its 'non-rational', 'non-instrumental' and 'non-utilitarian' character, despite the flimsy criteria for social categorization that were employed, and despite the possibility of using alternative and in some ways 'better' strategies. The experimenter effect cannot, by definition, be considered here without its collateral, the 'subject effect'. The former effect could have worked within our experimental procedures only through the salience for the Ss of the relevant normative background and of the expectations consequent to it.

Tajfel's first explanation therefore was based on the existence of 'a "generic" social norm of ingroup-outgroup behaviour which guided the Ss' (subjects') choices' (1971). If we accept this explanation at level IV, we nevertheless need to explain why this type of norm intervenes more or less strongly in certain situations, sometimes even contrary to the expectations of the experimenters (Tajfel & Billig, 1974). For this we must examine the psychological meaning, or more precisely, the social psychological meaning that a particular norm may carry. This is exactly what Tajfel and his team have tried to do in their subsequent work. The result of this attempt is, in our opinion, a theory which introduces articulations with analyses at level III dealing explicitly with differences in status between groups.

Tajfel's theory

The origins of Tajfel's new theory are to be found in Festinger's (1954) theory of social comparison. This theory postulated in the individual a need for self-evaluation, which in certain conditions could only be achieved by comparisons with other individuals similar to himself as to the characteristic evaluated. A certain asymmetry showed in these comparisons, as the individual had a tendency always towards self-improvement and to prefer to compare himself with others who were slightly superior for a given ability. This is only an incomplete summary of Festinger's theory, but gives the nub which is relevant to the development of Tajfel's theory (1972, 1974, 1978, 1981).

While, according to Festinger's theory, social comparison is essentially inter-personal, Tajfel's theory deals with comparisons between membership categories, and with that aspect of social identity which relates to individuals' membership of social categories. According to Tajfel, the need for positive evaluation in an individual can be satisfied by membership of social categories positively evaluated by the individual. This evaluation is relative and is carried out in relation to other pertinent categories. The individual does not limit himself to evaluating the balance of these comparisons, he tries to make the balance positive. Individually, he can try to change his category affiliation or, on the other hand, to make his category affiliation more positive on a given dimension. In our first chapter, we have already pointed out that Tajfel (1975) sees a relation between these two strategies and the ideologies of individual mobility and collective change. But, in order to achieve a positive categorial identity, other strategies are also possible according to Tajfel's theory, such as those that Turner and Brown (1978:204) describe by the term 'social creativity'. They consist principally of introducing new dimensions of comparison, reversing certain value judgements and changing the categories with which one makes comparison.

Turner's experiments as illustration

Where experimentation is concerned, it is Turner's research which best illustrates the different dynamics of intercategorial comparison. In one of his first experiments (Turner, 1978a, experiment II), he studied inter-personal and inter-group comparisons, using the Klee-Kandisky paradigm. In Tajfel's first experiment, subjects never took decisions for themselves, which facili-tated the intervention of a strategy designed to create differences between groups as such. Turner therefore brought important modifications to the paradigm. Half the subjects use the matrices to share out money, but the other half to share out points, which should increase pursuit of relative value rather than absolute gain. On the other hand, and as in the first experiment, all subjects for a part of the experiment only take decisions for others, while in another part, they also take decisions for themselves and for someone else, this other being either a member of their own group or of the other group. Half the subjects began with decisions which only concerned other individuals and subsequently took decisions which concerned themselves and certain others; the other half began with decisions which directly concerned themselves. The principal aim of introducing decisions directly concerning the subjects themselves was precisely to create a situation where they could differentiate in their own favour without necessarily having recourse to differentiation between groups.

These modifications had an effect. In general, subjects who only decided on attribution of points without monetary value differentiated more between themselves and others or between members of their own group and the other. On the other hand, subjects who began with decisions which concerned themselves personally differentiated between themselves and others without taking account of the latter's membership of their own or the other group. Identification with a group only intervened to the extent that it was the only way of arriving at a positive evaluation of self; it did not intervene when the positive differentiation could be obtained more directly by establishing differences between self and others. Other results of the experiment modify this conclusion: when subjects began by deciding for others and thus used the criterion of affiliation, this criterion continued to operate when decisions involved them directly. Then they made less differentiation between themselves and members of the in-group than between themselves and members of the out-group. Division into two groups appears to be a necessary but not sufficient condition for appearance of discrimination between groups; discrimination only appears if there has been prior identification with the membership group.

However, let us remember that it is always a question of minimal conditions and, more especially, that the instructions for the decision between self and another told subjects that they were to choose 'for yourself and someone else' (Turner, 1978:125). Another division has thus been created in the experimental situation which seems stronger than division into two groups when the latter has not yet been used by the subjects. Let us apply an analysis at level II to such a situation: on the one hand there is the subject and on the other there are anonymous people about whom the subject only knows that they are divided into two groups; but this division does not seem to be so important since it is a question always of choosing for 'yourself and someone else'. What would happen in such a situation if the others were no longer anonymous? At first sight, one might think that their identification should weaken group membership even further, but strong reasons suggest an opposite effect. In such a situation, the subject could feel a greater need to justify his decision, as it would be difficult to justify 'selfish' behaviour towards someone who knows they both belong to the same group, and much easier with regard to someone who belongs to another group. It could be therefore that in Turner's situation there was an effect of deindividuation (Zimbardo, 1970) which favoured egocentric behaviour, whereas individuation could lead to reinforcement of group norms. Deschamps (1976), in a replication of Turner's experiment, added a condition where the others were identified, and found indeed that, in this new condition, subjects who began with choices for themselves and for others treated these others (whose identity they knew) differently depending on whether they did or did not belong to their own group. Furthermore, in general terms, discrimination between groups was stronger in this experiment when individuals for whom one was taking decisions were identified.

The nature of inter-group relations and social identity

Other investigations by Turner lead more directly to analyses of social identity theory at level III, since they deal with the relations of given categories within a social domain. According to the theory of intercategorial comparison, the tendency to establish a positive identity in relation to another category should become stronger when comparison with the other category becomes more relevant. An experiment by Turner, Brown & Tajfel (1979) manipulated this relevance: after participation in a task of aesthetic judgement, subjects were divided into four groups of equal numbers, division apparently made as a function of expressed preferences: 'shape' people were said to focus on shape and pattern, and were further subdivided into 'triangle group' and 'circle group'; 'colour' people were said to focus on colours, and were subdivided into 'dichromats' and 'polychromats'. The experimenter emphasised the differences and incomparability between 'shape' people and 'colour' people, and led them to expect a test which would measure typical 'shape' or 'colour' abilities, though a comparison between the two categories could not be made as their aptitudes were too different. But before taking part in this test, subjects were asked to decide on remuneration for each other using traditional matrices. In reality all subjects were told that they belonged to the 'triangle' group and had to take decisions which affected other members, not identified, of their own group, of the 'circle' (relevant) group and of the 'dichromat' (irrelevant) group. As predicted, results showed that there was a greater discrimination with regard to members of the relevant out-group than with regard to members of the out-group with which no comparison was anticipated.

Another experiment (Turner, 1978b) used natural categories (Arts and Science students) to manipulate relevance and importance of the comparison in a task presented as measuring verbal intelligence. As predicted, Arts students differentiated their performance more from others than Science students. Differentiation is also stronger when it is a question of comparing the performance of similar university groups rather than different ones, on condition however that subjects have been made to believe that the test can measure relatively stable aptitudes in students in the same faculty. In accordance with the theory of social identity and with the result of the previous experiment, the bias in favour of one's own group is thus stronger when the attribute to be evaluated is more important for one's own identity and when the out-group is more comparable to the in-group.

Arts and Science students also took part in an experiment by Turner & Brown (1978): they carried out a task which related to their reasoning abilities, then evaluated the results of their group and finally were asked to give suggestions about other possible measures of reasoning ability and other intellectual capacities which might be measured. These last dependent variables were to measure creativity of invention of new forms of comparison. The variables manipulated dealt with: (1) difference of status: it was predicted to members of the groups that they would do better or less well than the other group; (2) legitimacy of this status: the experimenter affirmed that the experimental task was a valid instrument or that it included a disturbing bias; (3) stability of this status: the experimenter expected to find or did not expect to find differences generally observed between the two categories. Results showed that overall the groups with superior status showed a stronger bias than lower-status groups, that the illegitimacy of the status increased the inter-group bias, that instability of respective status increased the bias within superior groups with legitimate status and within inferior groups with illegitimate status, but diminished this bias in the superior group with illegitimate status. In certain conditions, an uncertain social identity may lead to a more active search for some other means of comparison.

Turner's is not the only research to illustrate the pertinence of Tajfel's theory for analyses at level III. Some research deals more directly with social categories occupying different positions in a given social context. Thus in the experiment by Branthwaite & Jones (1975), English and Welsh students interacted with one another using Tajfel's matrices. The Welsh, more in need of a social identity than the English, showed more discrimination in their own favour than reciprocally. Research by Brown (1978) was carried out in a large English factory: one category of workers whose relative superiority in relation to another category had been put in jeopardy by wage reforms also showed more discrimination with regard to this other category than inversely. The effects of such asymmetry are modified by situation charac-teristics: Deschamps & Personnaz (1979) showed that a dominant group (boys) valued themselves more in the presence of a less dominant group (girls) than in their absence, but when it came to behaviour, absence of the dominant group favoured discrimination against them in members of the less dominant group.

IV. Articulations with ideology

Intervention of general values

Let us look again at a number of investigations to see how they turn to analyses at level IV. When Turner & Brown (1978) deal with the instability that can threaten a group which, in other respects, has a superior status, they first invoke the action of a group with inferior status, then members of the group with superior status who may perceive a conflict between their own system of values (their social and political morality) and the bases of their dominance; the latter 'threat' is based on a conflict of values. Van der Berghe (1967), for instance, argues that the physical segregation of the races in the southern U.S.A. was in part a response by the Whites to the loss of social distance between them and their 'inferiors' in the post-bellum period (threat from the L.S. [low status] group). Also, both he and Milner (1975) suggest that the burgeoning of racist theories in European and American societies may derive from the contradiction between the official Christian or democratic ideals of equality and the institutions of colonialism and slavery. (Turner & Brown, 1978:208)

What is important here is, not the historical validity of these considerations, but the fact that Turner & Brown need to invoke the existence of value systems, both during the development of the experiment and in discussion of their results (1978:223). In the same vein, we have already reported that Rabbie (1979:216), as well as the participants in his experiments, invoked the existence of more general values which permitted the losers to transform their defeat into moral victory. Van Knippenberg (1978:197ff) also turns to analyses at level IV to account for results which show that, for certain characteristics, members of a group with superior status give a more favourable description of the group with inferior status than to their own group:

If the L.S. group were to adopt the perceptions and evaluations of the H.S. [high status] group, they would not be completely deprived of a positive self-image. They would, for instance, be aware of being more sociable and friendly than the other group. These are highly valuable traits, although their professional relevance would not be very high. It should be noted that in certain circumstances L.S. groups adopt evaluations, associated with their relative status, which are essentially in agreement with evaluations given by the H.S. group.

In fact, in the more general system of which both groups form a part, evaluative dimensions would be developed which would permit the dominant group to justify its advantages, while at the same time allowing the dominated group a positive evaluation of itself, but as regards characteristics which do not justify economic privileges. It is thus not surprising that Van Knippenberg refers in this passage to the Marxist notion of the dominant ideology.

Complementary positions

Complementary dimensions which allow groups occupying different socio-economic positions each to have a positive identity appear to be a fairly widespread phenomenon. A questionnaire developed by Peabody (1968) permits investigation of these systems of inter-group representations. It presents a number of groups of four traits in which two always deal with the same objective characteristic, such as 'generous' and 'extravagant' which both denote a certain ease in spending, and the two others an opposing characteristic, such as 'thrifty' and 'stingy' which both describe a more calculating attitude. At the same time, two of the four traits always have a positive connotation ('generous' and 'thrifty') and the two others a negative connotation ('extravagant' and 'stingy'). When he asked Chinese living in the Philippines and Filipinos to describe themselves and each other, Peabody found a certain consensus in the descriptions: the description of the Chinese group was situated towards the 'tense' pole (self mastery, economical, serious) and that of the Filipino group towards the 'relaxed' pole (spontaneous, generous, lighthearted). Such differences accord with the economic positions which the two groups occupy in relation to one another. We should also note that evaluative bias showed in the descriptions obtained by Peabody. Thus the Chinese who described themselves as more masters of themselves, economical, serious, were perceived by the Filipinos as rigid, stingy and gloomy, while conversely, the Filipinos who described themselves as spontaneous, generous, lighthearted, were seen by the Chinese as unstable, extravagant and frivolous. The dynamic described by Peabody seems therefore more complex than that described by Van Knippenberg; it may be that a set of representations allows each group to find a positive social identity relative to its socio-economic status without at the same time needing to evaluate any other group positively. In a sense, the groups may systematically invert value signs for objective characteristics which they attribute to each other.

Personality factors and ideological relations

One important line of research has explicitly aimed at studying the links between certain aspects of belief systems, and more especially, between more or less rigid adherence to an established order (authoritarianism) or to a cause (dogmatism), and certain characteristics of attitudes and representations in the domain of inter-group relations. We have participated in this research (Doise, 1969b), which is closer to the study of personality than the study of ideology itself. Deconchy's current research (1980) approaches the problems of authoritarianism and of dogmatism at a more social level, as we have already indicated in our first chapter. This research into orthodoxy is important for the study of inter-group relations. Deconchy (1976–77) has also made a preliminary incursion into this area by showing experimentally that members of an orthodox group (priests) see more compatibility between their own doctrine and theoretical analyses proposed by members of other non-orthodox group (leftists) than with the same analyses proposed by members of another orthodox group (Communist party). Conversely, practical choices which carry a certain social risk would be relatively more easily accepted by priests when they come from members of a group with strong social control (Communist party) than when they come from members of groups with weak control (leftists).

Ideology and perception

We will now give a few examples of more explicit articulations between levels which involve value systems directly. Experiments have studied support for a particular ideology, e.g. racism, and its effects on processes at level I, such as changes in perception. Here let us cite the research by Secord, Bevan & Katz (1956) which starts with the presupposition that belonging to the category of Whites or Blacks is emotionally more important for segregationists than for 'neutrals'. It follows that the former will accentuate differences between pictures of Blacks and pictures of Whites on traits held to represent the negroid type (black skin, thick lips, wide nose, crinkly hair, etc). This is in fact what the three investigators found when they asked their subjects to describe on different scales the physiognomic characteristics of 15 photographs: 10 of these photographs showed people with more or less negroid features, the 5 others showed Whites. Segregationist subjects in effect perceived more negroid features in the photographs than 'neutral' subjects, and accentuated the differences between the 10 photographs considered to represent Blacks and the 5 of Whites. While on this subject, it is also interesting to note that other subjects belonging to a strongly anti-segregationist group gave intermediate results between segregationists and neutral subjects; one might think that those who fight segregation do so precisely because they have become conscious of the unjustified importance given to membership of different races. Similarly, Pettigrew, Allport & Barnett (1958) were able to find a perceptual difference in South Africa between Afrikaners belonging to a strongly discriminatory culture and more recent English-speaking immigrants who did not speak Afrikaans and were less committed to a culture of racial discrimination. The Afrikaner tended much more to attribute to perceptually opposed categories (Blacks or Whites) than to intermediate categories (Coloureds or Indians) images which in fact were the result of simultaneous projection of two photographs, frequently of individuals of different races.

Power and equity in inter-group relations

The difficulties of inter-group relations, and especially the spiral of mistrust which tends to develop, may be well known by those who participate in such relations. But what guarantees can there be that this spiral can be broken?

Ng (1981) created a situation where members of two groups had to share out payments between groups and observed the usual discrimination for such a condition. On the other hand, in another situation, the experimenter led subjects to believe that they were the only ones to decide the payments to be given to members of their own and of the other group. Discrimination in favour of the membership group was practically absent in this condition, subjects not being able to expect discriminatory behaviour on the part of members of the other group. So it appears to be in order to counter possible discrimination on the part of the other group that a group becomes unfair towards it. More recent research by the same author (Ng, 1984) shows that better integration of investigations into specific inter-group processes and the effects of a general belief in equity is needed, since these new results demonstrate that the effects of equity and the effects of categorisation are, in certain conditions, of equal importance. Similar results have often been obtained in inter-group experiments by the Bristol team (see Billig, 1973; Bornstein *et al*, 1983; Branthwaite, Doyle & Lightbown, 1979; Turner, 1980, 1983) but have barely been taken into consideration at the theoretical level by Tajfel and his colleagues, as a methodological discussion appears to have replaced debate about ideas.

V. Further articulations between levels

Articulation with individual development

An interesting way of articulating levels of analysis is offered by developmental social psychology. Kohlberg has thus put forward the hypothesis that differentiations corresponding to social categories occupying specific positions occur according to a definite order. A differentiation essentially based on size and strength is the first to be established in children and then a corresponding differentiation between the sexes:

It appears likely, then, that children's stereotypes of masculine dominance or social power develop largely out of this body-stereotyping of size–age and competence. Children agree earliest and most completely that fathers are bigger and stronger than mothers, next that they are smarter than mothers, and next that they have more social power or are the boss in the family. (Kohlberg, 1966:102)

This is how one can explain why 'the 6-year-old boy is a full-fledged male chauvinist, much more so than his parents, and he is that way regardless of how he is brought up in a society that fosters role differentiation. Fortunately, later phases of cognitive growth qualify, moderate or undo this male chauvinism' (Kohlberg & Ullian, 1974:213).

But it could be that male chauvinism even at this age is only one side of the coin. In fact we have studied the evaluative aspect of intersex representations in girls and boys of 7 to 13 years (Deschamps & Doise, 1975). Girls as well as boys value their own sex more than the other. But while for boys this bias remains constant for all the ages studied, girls show a reduction in bias as a function of age. After 8 to 10 years, they begin to attribute to themselves a greater number of negative traits than before. These results suggest that sexual differentiations are established in several stages; girls progressively modify their evaluation of their own group so as to integrate differences of positions occupied by sexual categories in our society.

An interesting example of articulation of levels is given by Vaughan (1978) who links historical changes, in New Zealand, in relations between the Caucasian majority (the Pakeha) and the indigenous minority (the Maori) with the ontogenetic development of a bias in favour of one's own group. In recent decades, this bias has become relatively greater in Maori children and has diminished somewhat in Pakeha children; but at any time it is the relatively older children who first show this change, and so would appear to be more aware of the historical changes which are taking place.

Negotiations between groups

The articulation of individual dynamic and inter-group processes may appear to be an abstract problem since the concrete reality of social relations always combines these processes. However, for a specialist in negotiation between groups (Stephenson, 1981) an explanation for both sorts of dynamic must be found if we are to understand the very complex phenomena which occur when representatives of a group meet the representatives of another group, usually in a situation of conflict, to work out how relations between their groups are to be conducted in future. When negotiators thus enter into contact, it involves not only relations between groups but also individuals who interact with other individuals. Stephenson therefore emphasises the need for appropriate articulation of inter-personal and collective elements if a negotiation is to succeed. It is important that the position of the group be expressed very clearly, but also that the more personal endeavours to interpret opposed points of view and to integrate them may intervene in the process of negotiation. The same author reports the results of observation of real negotiations, which seem to confirm an alternation between collective and inter-personal dynamics. Study of negotiations between groups as well as the interactions in these negotiations therefore requires articulation of analyses at levels II and III.

Universalist beliefs also intervene in the process of negotiations between groups, especially during mediation by a third party. Touzard (1977) analysed the role of mediation in the resolution of inter-group conflicts. To a certain extent, in a conflict situation the mediator must represent the values of society which show the direction the negotiations should take. It is therefore very important that the mediator should have a concept of his role and a manner of intervening which accords with the nature of the conflict, as an overly technical mediation could neglect the ideological and symbolic aspects of a conflict or vice versa. An ill-adapted mediation style can exacerbate a conflict and make a solution even more difficult. In other words, it is essential that the mediator take account of the general ideas which are actualised in the situation. To analyses at levels II and III must be added analyses at level IV for a more complete study of inter-group negotiations.

Inter-group effects of belief

Here we will add other examples of articulation of three levels of explanation. We have already mentioned the research by Lerner (1971) on the innocent victim, which constitutes the prototype for articulation of levels II and IV; depending on the situation (victim paid or not paid, involvement of the observer, intervention which is to continue or stop) the ideology of the 'just world' intervenes differently. But some research also explicitly brings in category membership, shared or not shared with the victim. Thus Katz, Glass & Cohen (1973) confronted White subjects with a victim who was either White or Black, and the shocks to be administered were either strong or weak. In accordance with their prediction, which was based on the ambivalence of the situation, they found that the Black victim to whom one was to give strong shocks was the most depreciated: a significant interaction showed the factors of shock intensity and race of the victim.

Projections of self image

The dominant ideology prefers heterosexuality to homosexuality. Nevertheless certain aspects of a situation may lead subjects to attribute an unfavourable characteristic to members of their own category. Bramel (1963) made some students believe they had homosexual tendencies. These subjects then found more homosexual themes in analysis of a TAT (Thematic Apperception Test) protocol attributed to another student (someone like themselves) than when the protocol was attributed to a prisoner. Attributing a little-liked trait possessed by oneself to those similar to oneself permits one to maintain a good self image, whereas they hesitated to attribute their own characteristic to representatives of a social group which does not enjoy the same prestige as members of their own group. Edlow & Kiesler (1966) obtained similar results for another characteristic generally evaluated negatively: 'indecisiveness'. The attribution of a little-valued characteristic is thus made both as a function of a group membership and as a function of a specific evaluation received by the subjects in a given situation. To understand such attributions, it is essential to articulate analyses at levels II, III and IV.

Several writers (Billig, 1976; Doise, 1978a; Tajfel, 1972; H. E. Wolf, 1979) have criticised in different ways the reductionism which often characterises the psychological study of inter-group relations. In this chapter we have not wished to deal yet again with this problem. Our claim is that psychology has already developed analytical instruments which permit articulation of analyses which then transcend psychological reductionism even in the study of inter-group relations. The reader may judge whether this claim is justified.

5 Articulation of levels and experimental methodology

We have seen that experimental research can link the investigation of intra-personal processes, inter-personal relations, sociological position and collective representations in domains as different as cognitive development, social influence and inter-group relations. We have thus shown the heuristic value of using several levels of analysis: in domains which each correspond in a preferred manner to a different level of analysis, applying analyses at the three other levels can enrich our understanding of complex problems and at the same time resolve certain apparent contradictions. A beginning has therefore been made in replying, with supporting evidence, to the questions posed at the beginning of the first chapter. Social psychology is not necessarily reductionist and blind to ideological determinism; on the contrary, it explicates and demystifies certain ideological processes. The dichotomy between a more individualistic and a more collective approach can be overcome by articulation of explanations. The subject matter peculiar to social psychology is precisely the study of this articulation of levels. However, there seems little point in stressing again the role experiment can have in studying the articulation of the psychological and the social. Nor do we wish to start a technical argument about experimentation, but rather to illustrate the flexibility of experimental or quasi-experimental methodology, as it has already been demonstrated in different studies dealing with articulations.

It should not be supposed that we overestimate the contribution that experimental research can make, especially when it remains isolated. Here we support the conclusion of Campbell & Stanley (1966:34) who, after listing all the criteria of validity which an ideal experiment should satisfy, gave this wise advice:

From the standpoint of the final interpretation of an experiment and the attempt to fit it into the developing science, every experiment is imperfect. What a check list of validity criteria can do is to make an experimenter more aware of the residual imperfections in his design so that on the relevant points he can be aware of competing interpretations of his data. He should, of course, design the very best experiment which the situation makes possible. He should deliberately seek out those artificial and natural laboratories which provide the best opportunities for control. But beyond that he should go ahead with experiment and interpretation, fully aware of the points on which the results are equivocal.

Every experiment described in the rest of this chapter must in some sense be considered as a statement which only makes sense when taken in the context of the whole discourse. A discourse only develops through a chain of statements which modify, transform or even mutually contradict each other. Experimental discourse develops in the same way. No experiment is ever definitive and self-sufficient. But some experiments are to be found at the centre of a development, just as certain statements are at the centre of a discussion. It is such experiments that we wish to describe below, for they are at the very heart of articulated explanations, development of which may take many forms. But before describing examples of such experiments or of transformation of groups of experiments, we must first make clear our concept of social psychological experimentation.

I. Social psychological experimentation

The revelatory effect of the experimental situation

What happens in an experimental situation? Individuals meet in reality or symbolically, often through the mediation of questionnaires and other experimental tools. These individuals have a history and social affiliations: they have acquired schemata or regulatory principles for their representations and social behaviour in different situations. In creating particular conditions for relating in a real situation, however transitory, the experimenter primarily aims to throw light on these schemata or principles, which we will call processes. The experiment is thus essentially a condition for the reproduction of processes developed previously by the experimental subjects; in this way, it becomes a situation which reveals regulatory processes.

Science develops by actively transforming reality. Social psychological experimentation also brings about transformations of reality. The processes which organise the individual's participation in social relations are not brought to light simply by reproducing typical situations. It is more a case of creating situations which transform these processes by reinforcing or by counteracting, at least fleetingly, the dynamics of the process. The experimental situation constitutes a condition for the reproduction of certain processes, a condition more or less homologous to conditions believed to constitute these processes. The characteristics of some experimental conditions intensify the dynamics of the processes which have been set in action, whereas other conditions interfere with the unfolding of the same processes.

Let us take as example the process of category differentiation: it accounts for the accentuation of differences between two social categories and of resemblances between members of the same category at the level of behaviour, of representation and of evaluations. What does experimentation do? It can create situations of conflict of interest between groups, for example, which intensify the differential effect of the process, and compare these situations with others, for example, those of convergence of interest, which attenuate the differentiation. In a sense, these conditions may appear artificial: in fact they have been constructed to increase or diminish the probability of intervention of a particular process. In addition, it is clear that the historic reality which produced and constantly brings about the intervention of such processes is very much more complex than the manipulations of an experimenter. But this is precisely because experiment permits one to ensure, within the limits of the possible, that only a single process varies, whereas outside the model situations produced, several processes interact and modify each other constantly. Subsequently it could aim to grasp the dynamic of this interaction of processes.

Moreover, is the experimental approach thus defined so very different from other attempts to explain social reality? With Lemaine & Lemaine (1969:99) we believe that there is no case for singling out experimentation:

The psychologist willingly thinks of himself as a physician, but it is not impossible that he might think of himself as an astronomer as well. In the one case, he manipulates conditions and variables in the true sense of the word; in the other he waits for nature to furnish him with the factors of variation, and any manipulation can only be symbolic. The differences between what Claude Bernard called provoked experience and what he called invoked experience corresponds to the distinction between physician and astronomer, *but does not imply a fundamental difference in the experimental reasoning* which underlies both.

Every theory of social knowledge necessarily involves a limited number of variables, and looks for events which reveal the intervention of these variables. A science of the social proceeds necessarily by the construction of models which filter out certain aspects of social reality. The experimental approach tries to inscribe these models in a concrete situation. In this it is no more complex and no more elementary, no more real and no more artificial than any other scientific construction, and above all it is not closer to or further from what we call experience.

Grisez (1975:87) describes an important consequence of this concept of the experimental situation:

it is not a question of reproducing in the laboratory the exact conditions of real situations, but on a smaller scale. The relationship between experimental situations and real ones is not provided by comparisons with the latter, it is created by the experimenter, and this is done by a dual process, starting from a theoretical model..., which leads to construction of the experimental material on the one hand and to interpretation of results on the other. What is simulated is therefore not social reality but a theory of this reality, so that when confronted by an experiment one should not ask: is it a good representation of reality, but rather, what theory is it intended to represent and is it a good representation of this theory?

Subjects are citizens

We must therefore delimit the object of the social psychological experiment. It cannot pretend, in the limited and fleeting situations that it produces, to grasp all the complexity of a historic situation. Its *raison d'être* is to study, on the one hand, the specific processes which permit individuals to participate in dynamics of social relations, and on the other, the effects that modification of social relations have at the level of the operation of individual processes. Further, social relations never occur between individuals who are isolated from a sociological context. Individuals occupy specific positions in a social group and these positions influence the relations they establish among themselves. Experimentation is the way to create, at least fleetingly, situations which reinforce or weaken these sociologically-determined relations, and so help us discern better their function and how changes might occur in the processes which link individual and social dynamics.

Such a concept of experimentation can only be made effective through an appropriate experimental approach. Far from eliminating from the experimental situation all external influences on experimental subjects, on the contrary, the approach we advocate is to work on the primary material constituted by the norms of behaviour and representations that the subjects bring with them into the experimental situation.

Our approach differs profoundly from that which attempts to build up a theory of social functioning from situations of so-called minimal interaction and which takes no account of the prior social relations which have already fashioned the subjects. The fleeting and limited variations we introduce into a given situation will change, sometimes very weakly, the pre-existing dynamics and so give us information about their nature. So that, in every experiment, the existing links between the specific situation created experimentally and the general social conditions considered to produce the processes under study must be defined. The experimental situation never occurs in a vacuum devoid of social relations (Tajfel, 1972); on the contrary, multiple links connect the particular situation under study to a very dense tissue of relations which enclose it. In this sense also, to use Moscovici's image (Moscovici, 1970: 58), social reality would be both 'upstream' and 'downstream' in relation to the experiment. To understand what is happening within an experimental situation, we need to know which among the relations that enclose it reinforce and which counteract the processes operating in the particular situation.

Towards an experimental psychosociology

Experimental social psychology therefore does not aim to construct a model of social reality simply by starting with an analysis of what happens within a limited situation. What happens in an experimental situation is always only a modification of a set of forces which goes beyond that situation and which must be analysed as such. It is in this sense that we speak of experimental psychosociology: articulated theories must be developed to account for theories of sociological processes that are not created experimentally but which nevertheless must be brought into the analysis, and for theories of the processes by which the individual participates in these sociological dynamics. The social psychological experiment thus cannot be based purely on theories dealing with individual differences nor on theories dealing exclusively with the interaction of individuals treated as though deprived of any previous social experience. Therefore theories which deal with the individual as an abstraction, without specific social experience or position, must be considered inadequate. The type of experiment that we advocate takes the experience and social position of subjects explicitly into account at the level of experimental reasoning. In a sense, we could be said to give experimental subjects back their status as citizens.

The relationships characteristic of a society are never definitively established, subject as they are to incessant battles over material and symbolic spoils: experimental psychosociology is thus by definition a science in a state of becoming. Investigations into the articulation of individual and social dynamics will always remain incomplete. Does this mean it is impossible ever to discover truths of a general import in this field? We do not think so, or at least, we do not exclude *a priori* the possibility that relatively stable and general processes underly the individual's participation in the complexity and variety of changing social relationships. The complexity of these relationships would be in fact the consequence of an overlapping of the various processes going on in the social field, which produce their own norms of behaviour and evaluation, and are the targets of continual battle.

This conception of social psychology allows us to reply to the two principle objections most often made to experimentation in social psychology: that of its artificiality and that of its ideological overdetermination. In so far as experiments really succeed in shedding light on the processes which articulate the individual and the collective they cannot be accused of artificiality, even if, to achieve this aim, they make use of conditions which do not occur as such outside the experimental situation: the best way of understanding the phenomenon of lightning may well be to produce a weak electrical discharge in a weatherproof laboratory; it is not necessary to produce dark clouds.

As far as the putative ideological role of experimental practice is concerned, just as experimentation does not occur in a sociological vacuum, nor does the scientific activity of social psychologists occur in an ideological vacuum. On the contrary, it should continually question ready-made ideological truths, and seek to reveal their origins and functions. In so far as social psychological experiment includes an analysis of the social relations in which the experimental situation is inserted, it does not necessarily reproduce as such the current representations of these relations, but it does show how these representations reflect a particular type of relationship. Experiments thus become a source of demystification; they show how characteristics, believed to be universal and part of the nature of groups and of people, are in fact only the expression of certain relationships which exist between these groups and people, and that they change when these relationships change. There is therefore no *a priori* reason why experimental social psychological experiment should be condemned to be a prisoner of the dominant ideology for ever.

Linking the experimental situation to the social context

We have already pointed out, in relation to Milgram's (1974) experiments on obedience to authority, that only critical reflection on the role of science itself in our society can in the final analysis account for the results. This is just one example of the demystifying dynamic which may originate in social psychological experiment. If then it is true that the model of man incorporated in numerous social psychological experiments is in fact just a blind reformulation of certain ideological prejudices, one of the causes is, in our opinion, that until now too little effort has been made to place experimental practice in the wider context of an analysis of society itself. The experimental situation is too often treated as a controlled situation dominated by the experimenter while the control society itself has on the experimental situation is forgotten; indeed, there are 'systems of control at different levels' (Pagès, 1973).

The rest of this chapter will now show that this concept of experiment is not utopian, as it is already incorporated into the reality of experimental practice. Articulations of different levels of analysis have in fact succeeded in integrating experimentation into the web of social relations which extend beyond the experimental situation. To show this we will present more detailed descriptions of certain experimental procedures, some of which may have already been cited in preceding chapters. In particular we will show how experimentation has led to the further development of certain too exclusively psychological notions, such as that of attitude, how it has included the level of physiological functioning in its articulation of explanations, and how, at the opposite extreme, it illustrates the inadequacy of an exclusively 'cultural' concept of social norms. Moreover, the experimenter has at his disposal numerous ways of linking experiment and social context, among them, experimenter effect itself and the reinjection of experimental results into the population under investigation. But in the final analysis, it is theoretical models which allow links to be made between experimental situation and social context.

II. Attitudes: personal or collective?

The beginnings

When Thomas & Znaniecki (1918–1920) published their study of the Polish peasant in Europe and the United States, their problems arose from a need to articulate different levels of analysis. As Jaspars & Fraser (1984) remind us, they linked 'objective' elements of a collective, social way of life, which they called social values, to other objective characteristics observed in members of a social group and which are given the name attitudes. A food, a coin, a diploma may constitute a social value: thus there exists in individuals a tendency to act, an attitude towards these values. These attitudes are the psychological side of a reality of which the reverse, sociological, side is the value: 'An attitude is a psychological process treated as primarily manifested in its reference to the social world and taken first of all in connection with some value' (Thomas & Znaniecki, 1974: 22). The disturbances and changes in attitude of Polish immigrants are therefore studied in the framework of a confrontation, not to say a clash, between two cultures and not at all as a problem of individual differences.

Subsequently, however, individual differences in attitudes have most interested the inventors of paradigms, much more than their aspects as reflection of a cultural or social reality. This applies to the method of measuring attitudes proposed by Thurstone & Chave (1929). Let us recall that this method involves, in the first instance, submitting to individuals who act as judges a varied sample of statements about the domain to be studied. These judges are asked to classify the different statements according to their content, as more or less favourable towards the attitude object under investigation. They do this by placing the statement in a determined number of categories, e.g. 11, so that the statements in each group are all equally favourable or unfavourable to the attitude object, and so that between the groupings there is approximately the same distance of degree of favourability. The judges are expressly asked not to take their own attitude into account, and to judge the amount of favourability towards an attitude object on the basis of the content of each statement only. The mean or median of the rank attributed by the different judges to each item thus produces a scale, which then allows evaluation of the attitude of other individuals according to the favourability level of the items with which they say they agree. The argument underlying this procedure is therefore that the judges can objectively classify the different statements, independently of their own attitudes, and that variations between judges correspond in fact to the hesitations and fluctuations that an individual may demonstrate in her or his own judgements.

We know now that this fundamental postulate is not supported, and that Eiser's (1971a, 1973) research shows that judges who support opposed positions class statements differently on the judgement scales they are required to use. However, belief in the postulated interchangeability of judges was so strong in Thurstone and Chave (1929) that they advised excluding judges who placed a large proportion of statements (30%) in a single category, on the grounds that they were not carrying out instructions. Such a decision would have the effect of eliminating judges with extreme views (Eiser, 1971b); in a sense, for several decades, investigators created conditions which could not falsify the fundamental hypothesis. It was a rival theory, that of assimilation and contrast, which was used to demonstrate the invalidity of the basic hypothesis of the interchangeability of judges.

Hovland & Sherif's redefinition

Sherif & Hovland (1961) turned to the theory of assimilation and contrast while engaged in a programme of research into attitude change. A first investigation (Sherif, Taub & Hovland, 1958) dealt once again with estimates of physical quantities. When a target stimulus was the same as one stimulus in a series to be judged, there was an effect of assimilation, with the values estimated for the other stimuli approaching the value of the target. When the target stimulus was very different from the series to be judged, there was an effect of contrast: compared to a control condition, the values estimated for the series were at a greater distance from the target stimulus. Sherif & Hovland (1961) hypothesised that the phenomena of assimilation and contrast also intervened in subjects' judgements of different opinions and attitudes: subjects would accentuate the similarity between their own opinion and others which were not very different, and would accentuate the difference between their own opinion and those which were very different.

Let us report a first experiment by Hovland, Harvey & Sherif (1957) on the phenomena of assimilation and contrast in judgement of a series of opinions. The study was made in the context of a campaign about prohibition in Oklahoma. Three statements were recorded: one was strongly in favour of abolition of prohibition laws, another against abolition and a third mildly in favour of abolition. Subjects were recruited from groups known for their militant activity in favour of abolition of prohibition laws, groups militant against such abolition, and finally from a group which was only moderately in favour of abolition.

Subjects were required, among other things, to show on a scale from 'strongly for abolition' to 'strongly against abolition' how they judged the position defended by each of these three statements. It is important to remember that subjects were not asked to express their own agreement or disagreement with these statements: they indicated only whether in their opinion the positions defended by the messages expressed an attitude more or less favourable or more or less unfavourable towards a given social object.

In the judgements of subjects on the three statements effects of contrast should be seen: compared to intermediate subjects, 'abolitionist' subjects should judge as 'more prohibitionist' the statement opposed to their own attitudes, and inversely, 'prohibitionist' subjects should judge as more 'abolitionist' the statement opposed to their own attitude. Results supported this prediction. They are less clear as to the effect of assimilation: only moderate subjects tended to consider the moderate statement as nearer to their own opinion than it was in fact.

The model of assimilation and contrast suggests then that identical properties characterise judgements made by individuals who defend opposed points of view. But the prediction of these similar effects no longer arises from a postulated equally shared objectivity; the polarisation in group one is predicted to arise through an effect of assimilation and in the other through an effect of contrast, and vice versa. Nevertheless other results do not support this prediction; it constantly appears that subjects who defend points of view do not react in the same way when required to judge the same opinions and attitudes. This asymmetry has been demonstrated particularly in judgements relating to attitudes towards Blacks in the United States.

One investigation by Hovland & Sherif (1952) examined ratings made by members of different groups of statements of opinion expressing more or less favourable attitudes towards Blacks. In this experiment, it was shown that Blacks and Whites who had been active in anti-segregationist movements considered a very large number of the items to be judged as very unfavourable to Blacks. 'Neutral' Whites or frankly 'anti-Black' subjects, on the other hand, gave quite similar judgements, with the 'anti-Blacks' not rejecting more of the statements in the category extremely favourable to Blacks. So the effect of contrast does not seem to operate in the same way in extremists on both sides of an issue.

Several interpretations of these results are possible: perhaps the two groups of Whites, 'neutral' and 'anti-Blacks', were not so very different.

Other investigators have however found similar results (Zavalloni & Cook, 1965) even though they had a wider spread of groups of subjects: these were Black students (group I), White students (group II), both militant in anti-segregationist organisations, subjects with egalitarian opinions but not active in militant organisations (group III), subjects with segregationist opinions but not active in militant organisations (group IV), and finally, segregationists known for their membership of groups campaigning against admission of Black students to the university (group V).

The authors supposed that the different groups were situated at irregular intervals along a continuum from favourable to unfavourable attitude towards Blacks. Subjects were required principally to arrange the same 114 statements already used by Hovland & Sherif into 12 categories ranging from 'very favourable' to 'very unfavourable' towards Blacks. For the analysis, the statements were regrouped into the three categories, favourable, neutral, unfavourable statements according to ratings by subjects in another experiment.

Results were very clear for unfavourable and neutral statements: the more the subjects were favourably disposed towards Blacks, the more they judged the statements as unfavourable towards Blacks. This result may thus reflect an effect of contrast. On the other hand, no significant tendency was found for the average judgements of favourable statements. Does this mean that the contrast effect does not operate in subjects unfavourably disposed towards Blacks? Looking in more detail at the results, we see that groups I to V gave respectively an average 10, 8, 8, 2 or 3 statements the highest rating of 11 (extremely favourable). There is therefore no trace of an effect of contrast for the groups unfavourably disposed towards Blacks (IV and V), all the more so as one can see an effect of assimilation: the favourably disposed subjects consider more statements as extremely favourable to Blacks than the subjects who are ill-disposed. The symmetrical effect however is not found in groups IV and V for judgements of unfavourable statements. Once again subjects in favour of racial segregation do not react like the anti-segregationist subjects, who much more frequently use extreme categories of judgement.

Zavalloni (1964) and Eiser (1973) explain this asymmetry by taking into consideration the connotations of value carried by the rating scales: subjects favourable to Blacks could rate as very favourable statements with which they agreed and as very unfavourable those which they rejected. But segregationists hesitated to judge as very favourable statements they rejected and as very unfavourable statements they approved.

Sherif & Hovland, as well as Zavalloni and Eiser, therefore proposed an approach which links positions and judgements, and reintroduced a more social perspective into the study of attitudes. This approach finally led to a new paradigm for the study of attitudes: the technique of Own Categories.

A new paradigm

In this procedure, as in the first phase of Thurstone & Chave's, subjects were not asked to express their own attitudes directly, but simply to distribute statements dealing with a given problem into as many categories as they thought necessary, in such a way that the statements in each category went together, expressed the same attitude, and different categories were arranged according to the degree of favour or disfavour expressed towards the attitude object. The crux of the method is not to tell subjects the number of categories they should use.

Two measures are obtained with this method:

1. Number of categories used: The more highly involved the person, the fewer the categories he uses to categorize a range of items from one extreme to the other.
2. Category widths of designated categories: The person with some involvement in the object domain distributes his judgements bimodally, the largest mode indicating objectionable items and the smaller the most acceptable items. (Sherif & Sherif, 1969:351)

The theory underlying this procedure is clearly that of assimilation and contrast, with people involved in a cause tending to reject the statements which seem to them unacceptable, and therefore including intermediate statements, and to assimilate to their position the acceptable statements.

The utility of this procedure has been demonstrated empirically, more as regards differentiation between groups of subjects than between individuals. Thus in research by Hovland and Sherif (1952) on ratings of different opinions about Blacks, cited earlier, two methods were used: one asked subjects to range statements into 11 categories, the other asked them to use as many categories as they judged necessary. This is Sherif and Sherif's (1969:352) summary of results for use of Own Categories:

The less involved moderate subjects used, on the average, about five categories with the Own Categories Procedure and...distributed their judgments about as equally as they had using imposed categories. Highly involved pro-Negro subjects, on the other hand, used fewer categories than the less-involved moderates. Their tendency to distribute judgments bimodally was greatly accentuated as a result. In fact, the most militant Negro subjects used, on the average, fewer than four categories – placing 65 of the 114 statements in a single category highly objectionable to them and 27 in a category acceptable to them.

Since then, similar results have been obtained in several other studies dealing with names of ethnic groups, behaviour of young people, price of clothing

(C. W. Sherif, 1961), opinions about political involvement (Reich & Sherif, 1963), and opinions on racial problems (La Fave & Sherif, 1968). Each time subjects who were more involved in these different domains used fewer categories and this was not because they lacked information: those groups who were better informed but more involved used fewer categories than those less involved and less well informed (Reich & Sherif, 1963).

In view of the importance of this paradigm, we will briefly describe an experiment (C. W. Sherif, 1973) carried out in a large American university during the years 1966 and 1967, an era when about one student in 200 was Black and there was no unified Black movement on the campus. Here we will simply look at the results for Black students. The material to be arranged by each subject consisted of 50 descriptions of situations of encounters between Blacks and Whites, of the following type: a Black student who has achieved academic success is invited to his tutor's house, to celebrate his success; he knows he will be the only Black at this celebration. A Black student is contacted at the end of his studies about a position in the secondary school in his home town; the head of the school tells him that he sincerely hopes to engage a Black teacher, but so as to avoid starting rumours he prefers to meet the candidate in another town. The student wonders whether he should go to the rendezvous.

The assignment given to subjects was to classify the 50 situations in as many categories as they found necessary according to whether they would recommend, and to what extent, that the Black student take part in the described encounter with Whites. At the same time they were invited to give a name to the different categories they created. In fact, previous research had shown that some less involved subjects often found it difficult to give a name to certain categories of statements.

The principle variable which should influence such a classification was the probability of contacts with Whites among subjects: the greater the probability, the more the subjects would be involved in the task and the fewer categories they would use. Two variables were used to classify the Black students as a function of such probability of contact: their status as independent students living for the most part with Whites or their membership of a Black student association, which nearly always implied that they lived with other Blacks; and sex, men in general having more contacts, especially heterosexual, with Whites than women.

Results supported the hypothesis that the number of categories used was a function of the probability of contact with Whites; the greater the probability, the fewer the categories used, and also the fewer the statements which students were unable to categorise.

To conclude: when they took into account the different positions of groups of individuals in relation to a social problem, investigators had to abandon the paradigm which treated individuals as interchangeable. Social divisions are reflected in the judgements made by subjects. It is therefore not surprising that sociologists (Bourdieu & de Saint-Martin, 1976) more and more turn to techniques like that of analysis of correspondences to study the homologies between social structures and structure of tastes and preferences.

III. Articulations with physiology

We have frequently seen, in particular in the previous pages, that social psychologists have combined the study of cognitive processes with the study of social factors. But these are not the only links between the intra-personal and the social to have been studied. The well-known research by Schachter & Singer (1962) which we have described in detail elsewhere (Doise, Deschamps & Mugny, 1978) articulates physiological states and social interaction. Their two-factor theory postulates that in man the same physiological state may have different emotional significance depending on the social context. Several writers have been inspired by this theory in their studies of aggression.

Physical exercise and aggression

Strong or weak physiological arousal caused independently of any frustrating or irritating factor may bring about different aggressive reactions when elements in the social situation lead to different meanings for this arousal. This hypothesis is the foundation for an experiment by Zillmann & Bryant (1974). A state of strong arousal was produced by demanding physical exercise, with subjects exercising for a minute on a training cycle; weak arousal on the other hand was produced by a task of threading concealed tokens with holes in. Just after the first phase of the experiment, some subjects were insulted by a confederate whom they were able to subject to an unpleasant noise as reprisal, while other subjects who were not insulted could also subject him to noise. Only those subjects who were both highly aroused and insulted became more aggressive than the others.

Zillmann, Johnson & Day (1974) also studied the interaction of neuro-physiological excitation and the social situation in the triggering of aggression. Subjects who took part in this experiment were divided into three groups according to their speed in recuperating after a physical effort. They took part in a demanding task and afterwards were given the opportunity to give electric shocks to a confederate who had previously given some to them. Only subjects who recovered least quickly became more aggressive towards the confederate so long as a sufficiently long delay separated the physical exercise from the opportunity to 'punish' the confederate. No differences were found between subjects able to 'punish' immediately after physical exercise; in effect they were able to explain their state of arousal by their participation in this exercise.

Social context and aggression

These two experiments by Zillman and his colleagues show then how certain physiological factors are involved in an individual's aggressivity; their effects depend to a great extent on the nature, or even the timing, of other factors of a social nature. The two-factor theory, applied to the study of aggression, shows extremely well the value of articulating levels of analysis in a domain in which, following Lorenz (1966), the ethological approach has been dominant but inadequate. Thus Da Gloria & de Ridder (1977, 1979) are right to emphasise the fact that it is only by explicitly taking into consideration the relevant norms for a situation that the aggressive nature of a given behaviour can be defined. By experimentally manipulating these norms, they were also able to confirm the hypothesis that women respond more aggressively to the aggressive behaviour of other women than do men to identical behaviour by other men; different norms control the expression of aggression in the two sexes, which has the consequence that infraction of these norms by a woman is both evaluated and penalised more severely. These results show very well the inadequacy of approaches based only on differences of biological characteristics or on social norms without bringing in more specific situational considerations.

We will not however deny the interest of ethological studies of human aggression like those recently published by Montagner (1978), which show that different types of aggression in children are linked to different kinds of family life. These are important studies for a better understanding of how aggressive behaviour develops, of its hormonal correlations and social causes. Nevertheless, experiments based on the two-factor theory offer a richer theoretical model because more articulated and more likely eventually to lead to understanding of the nature of human aggression.

IV. Swiss compromise and minority behaviour

Experimentation can show that social norms are far from being ready-made entities, but are transformed by the situations which bring them into play. Too often cross-cultural research sticks to comparative methodology, and does not analyse adequately the multiple transformations undergone by the norms of a given culture; the articulation of situational dynamics and more general cultural values is ignored. But this problem of articulation does not just arise in cross-cultural research: it is relevant to every body of research in experimental social psychology. Let us take as example the research into minority influence: Moscovici in France emphasises the importance of consistency, Mugny in Switzerland shows that this consistency must be accompanied by a negotiating diplomatic style to be more effective, and Doms in Flemish-speaking Belgium in fact does not find the same results as Moscovici in Paris: the differences between majority and minority effects are less pronounced there.

National differences

In the face of such disparity, one feels strongly tempted to invoke cultural differences: could one not say, the French are used to a political struggle between majority and opposition and refuse compromise; Switzerland is the land of the social contract, of compromise, where governmental responsibilities are jointly shared by elected representatives of opposed political camps; Flemish students have seen that the ideas of a minority national movement have been taken up by practically all the political parties? Even if such interpretations are a little more serious than the jokes about Belgians and Swiss currently in vogue in Paris, they are not much more convincing: Faucheux and Moscovici began their research in Paris with the help of American students; the Swiss can become intransigent, so that a commentator on Radio Suisse Romande said in April 1979, about the Jurassian movement and its relations with Berne: 'Only inflexibility can bring success to the Jura which is so small, and to the Jurassian movement which is so short of numbers.' And if one looks more closely, the results obtained in Paris (Moscovici & Personnaz, 1980) and in Louvain (Doms, 1978) may well reflect identical processes if one accepts that the parameters manipulated did not necessarily have the same strength in the two experiments.

Within-culture variations

Fortunately there are more direct methods for studying the links between influence process and culture than those which just look at a single cross-cultural comparison: these methods are in fact indispensable for truly cross-cultural investigations. They consist of showing how, even within a culture, the behaviour styles of an influence source do not have a single meaning as such, given once for all, but that this meaning is modulated as a function of the specific representations activated in a given situation. This is the approach taken by G. Mugny in his research into minority influence. In a first phase, this work demonstrated that the effect of consistency of a minority influence source could depend on other aspects of that source's behaviour style. Mugny, Pierrehumbert & Zubel (1972–73:790) proposed a distinction between, on the one hand, firmness and consistency as regards the content of a message put out by the influence source, and on the other, behaviour style at the level of inter-personal relations; while remaining firm in his position, the agent of influence (confederate) could make concessions as to the formulation of this position:

A dogmatic confederate is seen as blocking the discussion (or the negotiations), that is to say he creates an interpersonal conflict (rather than a cognitive one); resolution of the conflict is then focussed on change in social attitude to the detriment of underlying opinions. While in contrast, a confederate (or a minority) with a negotiating approach does not evoke images of blockage (or very slightly) and places the conflict in the cognitive field and may obtain changes in the underlying level.

In the experiment carried out by these writers, a source of influence who made no concessions as regards his fundamental attitude towards the army, but who modified the degree of extremity of his replies, exercised a greater influence than a source who did not demonstrate such flexibility. Several other experiments have confirmed the role of flexibility: when there is a strong divergence between the opinions defended by the source and the target of influence, a flexible source is more effective than a dogmatic one. This is no longer so when divergence between source and target is reduced: in this case, whether flexible or dogmatic, the influence source obtains an impact as great as when it showed evidence of flexibility in the situation of strong disagreement (Mugny & Papastamou, 1975–76). In other words, the negotiating style modifies the social interaction in a differentiated manner, as a function of the differences of opinion which exist between the different social agents present.

But rigidity and flexibility must not be considered only in a context of inter-personal relations. They may be manifest in a conflict between two minorities when each is trying to influence a population. Mugny & Papastamou (1980), in an experiment cited above, compared a situation where a message was attributed to a single minority group and a situation where two distinct minorities were each originators of a part of the message. Results were clearcut: when there was a single minority source, flexibility led to a stronger impact. In contrast, when there were several influence sources, the dogmatic minorities had an influence as great as the flexible. The greater effectiveness of flexibility disappeared, even though all subjects belonged to the same Swiss culture. The same investigators then studied other mechanisms which can prevent a flexible discourse from being necessarily more efficient than a non-flexible one. One need only 'psychologise' the situation, that is, ask subjects to judge the personality traits of the source while reading the message. This manipulation is the recreation of a mechanism whereby a social system immunises itself against a disturbing message by attributing the content to personal and idiosyncratic properties of the author. For our purpose it is therefore important to show that, depending on elements in the situation, it is possible to increase the efficiency of a rigid style as well as to reduce that of a negotiating style. This should be an incitement not to study the effect of a behaviour style as such, but to articulate its study with an investigation of inter-group dynamics or ideological mechanisms, still within a single culture.

V. Turning experimenter effect to account

Equality and equity in the sharing of certain resources are currently the focus of numerous investigations which articulate the studies of such inter-personal conduct and of the cognitive development of children (Damon, 1977; Mikula, 1972; Moessinger, 1975). Van Avermaet, McClintock & Moskowitz (1978) were more interested, on the other hand, in articulating specific situational elements and the more general values which can modify individuals' sharing behaviour.

Equity and motivation

Van Avermaet and his colleagues contrast their approach with that of others, who develop motivational theories invoking primarily intra-personal or interiorised processes in their explanation of equity behaviour. Thus Adams's (1965) theory invokes principles of cognitive dissonance: inequity is said to produce a psychological tension; in an attempt to reduce this the individual tries to create an equitable situation. The desire for equity is thus looked on more as a way of escaping an unpleasant situation than as the result of valuing equity for itself. Walster, Berscheid & Walster (1976) studied equity behaviour as the end-product of a process of socialisation; they started from the axiom that individuals seek their own self-interest in the first place, but that society teaches them to limit this so as to ensure survival of the group. However, for these writers as well, desire for equity does not arise in the first place from a positive motive, but rather from the feelings of guilt and fear aroused in the individual when faced with a situation of inequity he has learned is socially undesirable. These motivational investigations have in common that they do not directly study the strategies adopted in different social conditions to escape this state of tension. In our opinion, the same problem is posed by the model of 'biosocial' compromise between 'egoism' and 'altruism' proposed by Campbell (1975) in his famous paper on 'the conflicts between biological and social evolution and between psychology and moral tradition'.

Equity and situation

The interest of Van Avermaet's approach is that he decided to study equity behaviour principally as interdependent behaviour in which the actions of the different actors mutually influence one another, not only at the time but also in anticipation of future interactions. Such a perspective may indeed appear elementary, but social psychological experiments which bring in such a perspective are rather rare. Let us recount how Van Avermaet (1975) went about operationalising this approach. Sharing behaviour is not always explicable within the temporal limits of an interaction: the subject in an experiment on sharing knows that his act is evaluated by the experimenter or by his possible partner; he is therefore aware of the effects his behaviour at the time of the interaction could have on possible future relations afterwards, with the experimenter or partner. Van Avermaet constructed experimental situations in which, for the same task, the respective contributions of the two individuals varied on two dimensions: investment of time and amount of work done. Several criteria could then be applied to the sharing of payments which was entrusted to a single subject. The subject had to send the share due to the other individual in a stamped addressed envelope; he could think that the experimenter would not be able to know how the sharing had been done and that his partner could not identify him. These anonymous conditions thus gave information on sharing behaviour in situations where no future interaction with the other actors could be anticipated. In addition, one group of subjects took part in a 'public' condition which did make such anticipation possible, and where the subject only worked half the time invested by the partner, who also completed twice as many tasks.

This is how the authors summarised the most important results in this experiment (Van Avermaet *et al*, 1978:433), results which have incidentally been confirmed by other research:

we found that actors who had performed less than another person and who, in terms of equity, deserved less than 50 per cent of an outcome, systematically *did not* provide themselves with less than half of the reward (a) when subjects had not met the other person they would share the reward with, (b) there was no possibility for future interaction, (c) they believed the other did not know the relative inputs between the actor and themselves and (d) when they expected that the experimenter would not be able to determine what distribution of outcomes they had made (Van Avermaet, 1975; Van Avermaet & Swerts, 1977). To the extent that equity is a strongly internalized value, equity would still be expected under these conditions. We observed however that they took half of the outcome, i.e. they used an equality rule. In contrast, when actors had performed less, but had personally interacted with the other who had knowledge of their relative inputs, and they were aware the experimenter would be able to determine how they distributed outcomes to self and other, they systematically afforded themselves less than half, using the specific outcome/input ratios prescribed by equity as a distributional rule. In other words, we observed that people use either the rule of equality or equity, selecting that one which is strategically most optimal in terms of one's own relative long term gains.

Equality or equity are therefore rules of inter-personal conduct chosen by subjects as a function of elements in the situation: if what is at stake is only a limited interest in the current situation, they choose the rule which is to their greatest immediate advantage, or at the most, find a compromise between the two rules. But if their conduct is likely to have more long term consequences, they probably choose the rule of equity which goes counter to their immediate interest but ensures gain in esteem in the more long term. This is a further illustration of the need to place the experimental situation in a wider social context. Such experiments demonstrate at the same time that the experimenter effect is not a necessary evil, as we have already seen in the description of Tajfel's experiments on inter-group relations. The experimenter is in a pivotal position between experimental situation and the social context which encloses it. The work of Van Avermaet shows even more directly how taking this pivotal position into account in the planning of an experiment can lead to the creation of a more articulated social psychology.

VI. Orthodoxy and experimental criticism

To take experiment out of the laboratory and place it directly in a 'natural' context is a procedure more and more widely used by social psychologists. This in itself does not guarantee better articulation of explanations since, to achieve this end, analysis of the function of the social dynamics into which the experiment is inserted is indispensable. Because Deconchy's research into religious orthodoxy is founded on this type of analysis we will return to it to look in more detail at the methodology.

An impossible dream?

A paper by Batson (1977) questioned the possibility of any psychological experiment on religion, suggesting that it was perhaps an impossible dream. Deconchy (1978:178) replied to this paper by widening the problem area:

One can summarise rapidly Daniel Batson's line of argument: (1) today there is practically no experimental work dealing with religion; (2) one should not find this too surprising, since such work is impossible. The formal validity of this argument stems from a theoretical analysis which articulates the two items, whereby he first establishes a factual state of affairs and then moves on to affirm its necessity.

Now the link between the two statements should be sought in the fact that there is no theory:

Absence of theory, and even more strongly, absence of motivation or of desire for a theory, demonstrates even more convincingly the non-existence of a discipline and the little chance it has of ever seeing the light of day. (1978)

Everything appears to support the idea that research into religion should be restricted to correlational studies or monographs, which would mean

one need not take the risk of questioning the intrinsic relevance of a system of beliefs and religious representations which still form part of the global consensus and the dominant ideology, though it is true in diffuse form, and which remain a strongly integrative social instrument. (1978:186)

And if desire for a theory does exist, too often it attempts to develop an 'absolutely original theoretical structure' which would be one more way of attributing an uncommon status to religious phenomena. While on this subject, it is interesting to note that social psychological theories have rarely been applied to the study of religious phenomena, though some of them, notably the theory of cognitive dissonance (Festinger, Riecken & Schachter, 1956) have proved their relevance in the study of these phenomena.

   Besides, rarity of experimental studies is not in fact a characteristic of the religious domain alone: Deconchy observes that such studies are also rare in such important domains as the function of politics, teaching understood as 'initiation into reading and into ways of tackling a global social situation', or the study of ideological processes. The problem thus should be posed in these terms:

can one envisage, however tendentiously, if not a basic science of history (which could only be an ideology), at least an experimental practice which would constantly be on guard not to leave out the historicity (social and individual) of the phenomena being studied, which would watch for historic circumstances favourable to its introduction into natural social groups and which at the very least would reinforce by design the effects of historic forces as they burgeon? Practically, this question becomes a simple problem to express but difficult to resolve: is it possible to experiment on and in complex cultural and institutional social systems? (1978:187)

It is because Deconchy's research into religious orthodoxy gives an affirmative reply to this question that we have mentioned it again here, and this leads us to comment more especially on a procedure which succeeded in reinjecting experimental results into the social system being studied.

Reinjection of experimental results

This methodological approach corresponds to a theoretical analysis of orthodoxy, one important characteristic of which is that it produces its own criteria of rationality. What would happen then if we showed believers that they resort to social regulation when the rational weakness of their beliefs is subjected to analysis? (Deconchy, 1980:293):

What happens when orthodox subjects...seek to enrich their beliefs and their pastoral strategies by 'bringing in the Human Sciences', and in so doing, are faced with evidence...which scientifically establishes certain laws relating to their own religious behaviour? (Deconchy, 1980:293)

Deconchy informed believers taking part in an introductory course in human sciences of the results of his first investigations, which demonstrated the function of orthodoxy, and observed that this demystification aroused defences of a utopian or eschatological type ('future times' were perceived as likely to bring about better understanding of belief) and of a mystical type (attribution of a more important role for mystics in the understanding of belief). Many other defences were observed: subjects assigned important roles in education to the use of nonmetaphorical pictorial examples, gesture and mimicry, and audiovisual methods, to liturgy, emotion, prayer, and unconscious factors in understanding belief, to action, to the psychological and natural environment, to grass-roots communities. These are so many 'artificial syntheses' (1980:130) of contemporary religious manifestations about which the author writes in passing: 'so many of these apparently innovatory and liberated fashions in reality provide a form of personal and social defence which aims to maintain, come what may, a system which is at risk from any internal or external criticism' (1980:190).

Scientific understanding of one's own behaviour does not of itself lead to questioning religious orthodoxy. Deconchy demonstrates this once again by inserting an experimental intervention into a natural situation. In the experiments we have just cited, he reported to members of the clergy or to seminarists information in direct conflict with the theoretical system implicit in their theology. In a new experiment, he compared the effect of this type of information with another type of scientific information:

Scientific information of a descriptive and monographic nature (it could be termed 'empirico-positivist') does not embody the same element of conflict. It studies facts (historical, social ethnological, psychological) but cannot, indeed does not seek to provoke them. Its latent epistemology does not make it compelling: 'elsewhere', 'in other circumstances', 'under different influences', facts have been, are or will be different...Even if an attempt is made to generalise the monographic evidence, the extrapolation seems sufficiently uncertain not to appear inevitable and necessary. In a way, such scientific information can be laid alongside any other system of knowledge...such as theology, for example, which lays sole claim to the ultimate understanding of a type of behaviour, such as religious behaviour. Inversely, the theological system can without much danger become exposed to this type of knowledge, since it does not lay claim to excessive cognitive pretensions. The system of knowledge supported by the orthodox system and 'theoretico-experimental' scientific knowledge concerned with religious behaviour (including the natural conditions of production of such a theological system of knowledge) could be said to lay conflicting claims to knowledge, and consequently to power. (1980:299)

The first stage of the experiment was like the earlier ones: subjects were students of a Theology Faculty who participated for three weeks in an introductory course on the social psychology of religion. First they were shown a number of 'truths of faith' to measure the separations they perceived between these 'doxemes' and the norms of rationality, as well as to measure the importance they attributed to them in relation to the doctrinal corpus and in relation to regulation of membership of a religious group. Subjects also gave their opinions as to the role 'future times' would play in the understanding of these beliefs. Three days after the first measurements, subjects were told the results of an enquiry: it dealt with correlations between age, socio-economic level, degree of schooling of a sample of adults and their acceptance of the beliefs presented the first time. The subjects studied the effects of the different variables and their crossover. The following day, the measures taken earlier were repeated. They were also repeated following a third phase which took place five days later. During this last phase, subjects were presented with scientific information of the 'theoretico-experimental' type: based on his theory of orthodoxy, the investigator formulated a certain number of hypotheses and reported their experimental confirmation, to demonstrate that 'in an orthodox system, the rational fragility of information is functionally counterbalanced by strictness of social control' (Deconchy, 1980).

These were the experimental predictions of the author:

The first set of scientific information – which we think is not functionally in conflict with the accredited theoretical system of the orthodox group – should neither disturb the action of the parameters of the first development (separation between reason and doctrinal corpus, control of membership), nor consequently force the orthodox subject to evoke some more or less exciting social 'ineffable' (here, utopian); he does not need to immunise himself against scientific information which does not in itself contain anything which could shake the formal defences of the orthodox system. (1980:195)

Therefore no change was predicted between the first and second measures. 'By contrast, the second set of information brings with it the problem of being functionally in conflict with the accredited theoretical system of the group' (1980:195). There should therefore be an increase in the separation perceived between specific beliefs on the one hand, and 'reason' and the doctrinal corpus on the other, as well as a utopianisation of beliefs. Results supported the prediction that 'empirico-positivist' and 'theoretico-experimental' scientific information would have different effects.

Other social psychologists, among them Holzkamp (1972) have advocated a critical and interventionist conception of their science. Deconchy has shown, in the research we have described and in other investigations, that it is possible to work out methods which allow this science to remain 'theoretico-experimental'. Reinjection of the experimental results into the population under study, still of course in their theoretical framework, is a too-little-used way of linking the experimental instrument to the relevant social context.

VII. Laboratory research and field studies

Experiments provide many ways of comprehending the links between experimental situation and the wider social context. Nevertheless, a complaint frequently made of social psychological experiment is of its artificiality. We have already challenged the distinction between 'artificial' and 'natural' situations:

The experimental situation is a real situation with real social actors. Indeed, we should hesitate to say that a 'laboratory' situation is less complex or simpler than a 'natural' situation. It is true that the experimental situation is designed to compare situations which vary only in certain respects, but one must equally simplify when one is concerned with situations outside the laboratory. Understanding inevitably must be in terms of a limited number of variables, and, as we have seen at a specific level of analysis. Thus, it represents the simplified reconstruction of a complex and overdetermined aspect of reality. (Doise, 1978a:160)

We should like to illustrate this position in the rest of this chapter, first by showing how experimentation can be implanted more directly into a more 'natural' context while using the same models as in the laboratory, and how non-experimental investigations aim to verify theories tested in the laboratory.

Inter-group relations in the laboratory and in the field

The research into inter-group relations carried out in Bristol offers a good example of give and take between laboratory and field. Thus Brown (1978) used the theoretical framework tested in the laboratory by his colleagues for an experiment carried out in a factory for aeronautical construction. Two categories of workers were studied: members of the Development group (whose job was the development and trial of prototype aeroplanes), who at the time of the study were earning 20p an hour more than the others, and members of the Production group (those who produced aeroplanes on line). At the time of the study, the small wage advantage of the Development group members was being threatened. Brown then asked members of each of the two groups to decide how much members of each group should earn, using matrices adapted from those used by Tajfel *et al.* in the laboratory (1971). We know already that a characteristic of these matrices is that they can evaluate the relative attraction of maximisation of gain in absolute terms or in terms of relative value; in other words, we can see whether those questioned attach more importance to their group's earning the maximum possible or to their gaining more than members of the other group even if, to obtain this end, they have to reduce the absolute value of their own gain. Brown found that this last strategy was the most frequently adopted by members of the Development group, one representative of which commented:

The top one would give me more money, but the difference there between D and P is all wrong...on the differential side you should go for the bottom, to protect your job. The status of the job is more important than the actual wage. (Brown, 1978:421)

What do such results mean? Several interpretations are possible, and in particular, one might conclude that management has learned how to apply the maxim 'Divide and rule', and that the replies by the workers reflect an alienation, as one of them elsewhere clearly suggests: 'Your sectarian point of view is going to cost *you* money and *save* the company money' (1978:423). But then we still need to explain why this alienation can be produced so easily. In itself, Brown's research cannot provide an explanation. But we have seen that this explanation can be found in the whole body of research into inter-group relations carried out by the team in Bristol; all of it supports in a converging manner the theory that it is in order to create a positive identity that members of one category (according to an important dimension in a given situation) seek to establish a positive difference between their own category and another relevant category. Elsewhere, Turner & Brown (1978) show experimentally that this dynamic occurs above all in members of a category whose social identity is threatened, which was the case for members of the Development group in the field study. The same theory is thus helpful in accounting for phenomena produced experimentally and phenomena found in the field. This is only possible because the experimental situation has captured a dynamic which exists independently of it. Let us give another example of give and take between laboratory and field research.

Lemaine and the pursuit of incomparability

Lemaine (1974, 1984) has developed, independently of Tajfel's theory, a theoretic framework which can account for an important asymmetry in social systems and which permits articulation with analyses at level III. The work of this researcher is different from most of the research by the Bristol team because it deals essentially with the creation of new dimensions for comparison. In a situation of relative handicap, groups and individuals attempt to make themselves incomparable with others (groups or individuals) by actively seeking to place themselves on new dimensions in the social field which the others have not yet been able to use. They then try to impose on the others this new definition of social reality. Frequently this results in a certain secretiveness at the beginning in groups which do not wish to reveal their innovatory strategy until they can be sure of imposing it as a redefinition of the situation.

Lemaine's first research (1966) was carried out in holiday camps, with groups in competition, and with one given fewer means of carrying out a task. Two groups were required, for example, to build a cabin, one being given rope, the other not. The second group's cabin naturally was less successful, but, after a period of disarray, members of this group decided to arrange a garden and fence around their construction, and then attempted to get the garden accepted as forming part of the construction for the judging by the camp leaders. Other experiments (Lemaine *et al.*, 1978) dealt with situations of inter-personal comparison and used very varied tasks, such as: writing a letter in reply to an offer of employment by students informed of the existence of other candidates, whose abilities varied depending on the experimental conditions; use of colour in the presence of another who introduced himself as being or not being 'good with colour'; judging a picture in the presence of an expert or non-expert. On each occasion, those who suffered a relative handicap sought most frequently to redefine the situation by placing themselves on new dimensions and so in a sense making themselves 'incomparable' with the other social agent.

Once again, ideas developed in experimental research have been used in research in the field. Lemaine, Matalon & Provansal (1969) began with the idea, shared by many other writers, that there exists in the scientific community a system of recompense based on recognition of the work carried out by its members (or some of its members). This recognition may take different forms, such as citations, allocation of funds for research, invitations to meetings, positions on certain committees, etc. It would be members of the scientific community who had first made public something new, whether it be at a theoretical, empirical or methodological level, who would benefit from this recognition. Investigators in a particular field (because working on associated problems) would thus always be in competition to become 'visible', which is what they become by producing original work. The writers decided to investigate decisions about research: why does a researcher choose to work on a given subject, why does s/he try to solve one problem rather than another? Their study concluded that one could explain choice of research by appealing to certain variables: first would be the estimate by the investigator of his likelihood of achieving a result in a given domain, or in other words, a comparison with others; evaluation of his own aptitudes obviously plays a large part, and also evaluation of his chances of success as a function of the means at the disposal of others, of the progress by his competitors in the field. Another factor of importance is ambition (what Lemaine *et al.* prefer to call 'level of aspiration'): is the researcher content with modest success (and therefore modest recognition and visibility) but without risk, or does he prefer big success and recognition, which are not without risk? The writers cite the example of a young chemist whose laboratory was not well enough equipped for him to be in the mainstream of his discipline. His level of aspiration was high and he estimated he had a chance of success in an unexplored area of biology: he made his research choice in this new area, that is, by diverging from what was being done he was able to escape the competition which handicapped him in chemistry. It is however obvious that there are different degrees of success, and that recognition is also given to those who produce research of 'average' importance, or even of 'very average' importance, but who in general produce a great deal. Why then do some play safe by choosing research of limited interest, but with few risks, while others take high risks? This would be due to the criteria used for the attribution of reward inside the scientific citadel: if this recognition goes to those who produce a great deal, even if their work is of no great moment in the scientific field, it is obvious that this factor will also have an influence in investigators' choices. The authors take up Kuhn's (1962) analysis of science and the notion of 'scientific revolution'. But if a scientific rupture is in a sense being prepared in the periods of 'normal' science, it is also prepared by the socially motivated changes which arise from 'social originality' (Lemaine & Kastersztein, 1971–72). In addition, the 'scientific revolution' poses certain problems for its agents.

They have to do battle to get the new point of view accepted and their work in the area legitimised. But the battle generally does not end there; the cognitive rupture is accompanied by a social schism, by creation of a school and the slow substitution of one point of view for another as the dominant view. (1971–72:679)

Lemaine's analysis however deals principally with criteria for choices in 'normal' science: the explanation brings in factors such as perceived distance from another, estimate of chances of success, the utility of success as a function of the criteria of reward.

Privilege and innovation

Let us add however that, while Lemaine studied the differentiation behaviour of agents put in an inferior social position, this inferiorisation does not seem to be a necessary condition for innovation. That is what appears to be shown by a study by Villette (1975) which deals with access to dominant positions in business. In his paper, the writer describes how certain 'heirs' of industrial families 'earn' the dominant positions in the business to which they accede. These sons of industrial families – whom we have difficulty in considering socially unfavoured – develop a 'strategy of innovation based on the permanent development of prestige and the relative weight of different functions' (Villette, 1975:98). Thus

the sons of industrial families use their capital of social relations, their intimate knowledge of the world of directors, and get themselves proposed by their father, uncle, friend for a new 'risky' experiment, in an area where very little has been happening for some time and where returns are very deficient...They make a journey abroad to study the experience of other companies, they consult specialists and they bring in a far-reaching reform...From this moment, the essential problem is solved: *their social capital has been converted into rare competence* and the most flattering promotion has become legitimate. (1975:99)

This dynamic, observed independently by a sociologist, is very similar to that which Lemaine was able to show both experimentally and in the field. Only its origin is different: in the case studied by the sociologist, it is not a matter of overcoming a handicap by developing new criteria of comparison but of justifying in some way a preconstructed advantage.

Power in the laboratory and in industry

Mulder's research (1972, 1977) into power, which we have already mentioned, also provides a good example of a theoretic model which was first developed and confirmed by experimental research mostly carried out in the laboratory, and afterwards used with success in studies in the field. In return, there is enrichment of the theory by research in the field: in his last book, Mulder (1977) distinguished several forms of power (e.g. power of sanction, formal power, power based on identification, power based on knowledge) and developed an instrument to measure them in institutions and to study the specific functioning of his model in each of these areas of power.

Several examples show that the models which are useful for understanding an experimental situation are also useful for understanding non-experimental situations. The reasons are: on the one hand, no experimental situation is a creation *ex nihilo*, but is always a real situation modified as a function of a preconceived model, and on the other, even understanding a non-experimental situation always involves explanatory schemata which use only a very limited number of variables, as is precisely the case in the construction of an experimental situation.

VIII. The specificity of experiment

An alternation between experiment and field research and the direct implanting of an experimental instrument in an institutional context are procedures which can lead to a wider application of the conclusions arrived at through experimentation. It still remains for us to make clearer the respective contributions of experimental and field research. We will do this by briefly commenting on a set of investigations presented by Gilly (1980), dealing with the role of representations in teacher–pupil relations. It will be seen that experiment has the specific task of defining the processes likely to intervene in a complex social situation, whereas only research in the field can determine the specific weight of the variables which favour or interfere with the operation of these processes.

Individual differences and social representations

In very brief outline, research into the representations teachers form of their pupils first looked at questions of inter-personal relations and later developed into investigations of a more institutional, even ideological nature. At first, the pupil was primarily perceived as endowed with specific traits and abilities which a good teacher should detect so as to adjust his pedagogic behaviour. Gilly (1980) was more interested in studying the institutional determinants of the teachers' representations of the taught: he showed that teachers represent their pupils principally as a function of goals fixed by the school system. Independently of differences related to the social origins of pupils or the ideology of the teachers, the dimensions on which pupils are judged by teachers are of great stability, and vary principally in the degree of benevolence with which the pupils are placed on these dimensions.

The Pygmalion effect

What is the effect of these representations on teaching? Since the work of Rosenthal & Jacobson (1968), the reply to this question has become the object of many debates. We know that these writers showed that induction in teachers of a positive expectation as to favourable development of certain of their pupils had as consequence that these pupils did in fact show marked progress at school. We should remember in passing that this research into teaching was an extension of more strictly methodological research into the experimenter effect. But the importance of Rosenthal & Jacobson's research into the 'Pygmalion effect' arises principally from its relevance to sociological problems: it could demonstrate the process by which sociologically determined causes are perpetuated throughout the school system. Teachers having different expectations of pupils from different social classes, the pupils consequently show differing degrees of success in school.

Gilly (1980) showed in detail the methodological deficiencies of Rosenthal & Jacobson's experiment, a major one being the prior knowledge that the teachers had of the test used subsequently to evaluate pupils. But he also puts together results of a number of other investigations into the 'Pygmalion effect', some of which confirm the results of the original experiment. The real question thus becomes: 'under what conditions and according to which mechanisms can these effects be produced and shown to have an influence on the intellectual and/or school performance of pupils' (Gilly, 1980:218). The effects expected by induction of positive expectations of certain pupils can be counteracted by many other factors: other kinds of information available to the teachers, such as their greater or lesser belief in the tests, or ideological choices which may lead them to be more interested in those children least favoured by the tests.

But the writer is rightly critical of the fact that other investigators have not adequately explained and incorporated into their paradigms the different stages of the sequential process which they suppose leads to the claimed effect:

Theoretically, investigators expect the introduction of biased information about a particular child to produce a cascade effect: the bias is supposed to modify the *representation* the teacher has of the child, this modification leading to a change in *expectations*, which in turn, should create changes in *teaching behaviour*, and one hopes these will be responsible in the final analysis for a significant evolution in *behaviour and school performance* of the pupil. (1980:221)

The paradigms used rarely allow measures of all the consequences of the implicative hypothesis. Comparing the results of different research, some of which are experiments in well-controlled conditions and others interventions in the field, Gilly concludes:

Analysis of the situation led us to think that the impact of the experimental variable had a greater chance of producing the expected effects the more the situations differed from the 'natural' institutional ones. This was confirmed. Nevertheless, whatever the situation (laboratory or institutional), the observed results are always found to be compatible with the causal model of effects in cascade. (1980:245)

This is an important conclusion for our thesis: the results of laboratory investigations for the most part confirm the different stages of the process

which account for the effect of the teacher's representation on the performance of the pupil; the results obtained in interventions in school are on
the whole less clear, but when they nevertheless permit a conclusion, they
are always compatible with the proposed model. In other words, experiment
allows one to study a single process which may be interfered with by many
factors in a 'natural' situation:

Whatever may be the underlying mechanisms, many conditions have to be fulfilled
for changes in representation to engender changes in the educational behaviour of
the teacher and the behaviour and/or school performance of the pupil. For all the
reasons analysed above, mastery of these conditions is much easier in the restricted
laboratory situation than in the institutional one. (Gilly, 1980:245)

It remains nonetheless true that significant results obtained outside the
laboratory may be plausibly interpreted using the framework of a theory
tested in the laboratory, where it is easier to determine the parameters of
the situation which facilitate appearance of the desired effects.

Theory and reality outside the laboratory

However it is possible to increase the chances that reality outside the
laboratory will validate a theory, and in a specific case, support the
hypothesis concerning the effect of teachers' representations of their pupils.
To achieve this, Gilly advocates the method of 'differential studies' of
situations where teachers 'naturally' have different expectations:

The typical situation for a differential study is that in which groups of pupils fulfil
'objective' conditions which are completely identical with regard to factors which
affect the achievement of a school goal, but differ from each other with regard to
the opinion their teachers have on this subject. If it appears that the groups in
question demonstrate different behaviour or school performance and/or are the
object of different educational behaviour on the part of their teachers, the hypothesis
of a specific effect of expectation by the latter will be confirmed. (1980:246)

Two field studies illustrate this differential procedure particularly well: one,
carried out by Palardy (1969) demonstrated the effect of a very diffused
expectation in teachers of the relative superiority of girls over boys in
learning to read, and the other, carried out by Seaver (1973) showed the
effect of expectation induced by the school results of older children in a
family on the performance of a younger brother or sister. More than
artificially induced expectations, these 'natural' expectations carry such
weight that the teacher may be led to see only what he expects to see and
to model his behaviour in consequence. Hence the conclusion:

A first lesson to learn is that, taking into account both questions of deontology and
problems of method, experimentation in a school situation is probably not the most

efficient procedure, the induced variation being unlikely to have more than a very minor influence compared to 'natural' variations and to the influence of other sources of variation. (1973:252)

We accept this conclusion, but would add that the comparative studies advocated by Gilly define their relevant variables and lead to conclusions only because they start from theories made explicit by experiment. But on the other hand, the experimenter who remains in his laboratory cannot pronounce on the respective weight that the manipulated parameters would have in the real world outside the laboratory. From this point of view he is, to borrow a very apt image from Stroebe,

in a position similar to that of the experimental psychologist studying rats in a Skinner box. He has excellent theories to account for the lever pressing in relation to the food pellets dropped into the box. But it is *he* who drops the food pellets and he has no idea about the dropping rate or dropping contingencies of pellets in a natural environment. (1979:102)

IX. Experiment: work of art and caricature

When we give up the idea that experiment can only operate with facts whose whole meaning is to be found within the spatial and temporal limits of the situation studied, and when we attempt to place experimentally produced dynamics in relation to the social reality 'upstream' and 'downstream' (Moscovici, 1970) that gives them their orientation and meaning, we are then in a better position to exploit all the potential of the experimental method, and to understand more fully what is happening in an experimental situation. Integration of experimental activity into society and treatment of experimental subjects as citizens lead to a concept of experiment with many important methodological consequences. It entails a continual readjustment of the paradigms used, as we have seen in this chapter. In contrast, not to consider the links between experimental situation and social context can only mean working in the dark, abstraction of the strongest dynamics operating in the experiment and what amounts to a rejection of the indispensable means of understanding the phenomena one produces. However, in view of the multiple links which exist between experimental dynamics and the much wider social dynamics, it would of course be vain to wish to prescribe a method which should permit the linking of these two sorts of dynamic in every case. The conclusion of this chapter is therefore that there will always be a place for methodological innovation and creativity.

Seen from this angle, the activity of the experimenter is not unlike the activity of the artist. Like the artist, and more especially like the expressionist, the experimenter does not attempt to produce a naturalistic representation of reality or a perfect correspondence between the details of the experimental situation and those of reality outside. On the contrary, as in pictures by Münch, Nolde or Permeke, an apparent disfiguring of reality in an experiment may express an aspect of the socially real more strongly. It is thus not surprising that experimentation has been compared to caricature:

An experiment might be described as a *causal caricature*. A caricature is an artificial, usually simplified, reconstruction of some natural phenomenon: it selectively emphasises essential components...A caricature is not a mirror of reality: it is an intentional distortion. Yet it may reveal reality better than a mirror, because the essential components stand out. An experiment almost always involves a caricature: one develops a simplified artificial model of some natural process. This caricature is created with a specific purpose in mind, testing one or more causal explanations. (Batson, 1977:414)

The scene setting used by the experimenter suggests yet another comparison, that which might be made with a number of works for the theatre, most especially with the plays of Brecht. When writing *The Resistible Rise of Arturo Ui* or *The Rise and Fall of the City of Mahagonny*, Brecht was not attempting a naturalistic representation of the rise of a dictator or the establishment of primitive capitalism: this would have been an impossible task in the theatre, and pointless, since it would not have led to a better understanding of historic events. On the contrary, Brecht began with a conceptualisation or schema of the historical phenomena which he used to represent them in theatrical terms. It is only in this way that the theatre can play a part in demystification.

As we have already seen when we quoted Grisez (1975:88), the procedure of the experimenter is not so very different: 'What is simulated is therefore not social reality, but a theory of this reality, so that when confronted by an experiment one should not ask: is it a good representation of reality, but rather, what theory is it intended to represent and is it a good representation of this theory?'

6   Provisional conclusions

There are many kinds of social psychology. Various theoretical approaches have been put forward at each of the levels of analysis we have examined: theories of balance or of reinforcement, theories of exchange or of social comparison, theories of power or of group identity, theories of belief in a just world or of the social definition of intelligence. These provide so many analytical grids between which numerous connections may be constructed through experiment, just as much at the same level as between different levels. By this we do not mean that all these theories can claim the same truth status, but we do not see any other way of determining such status than by making use of the perspective obtained through articulation of theories. It is not so much a question of deciding whether, for example, the theory of dissonance is more true than the theory of effect, but of deciding *in what conditions and why* a reduction in dissonance or an effect of reinforcement can be expected. No social psychological theory can exhaustively define the conditions for its application and the explanatory principles proposed always call upon others. This also applies of course to our theory of four levels and their articulation: our approach is not intended to provide a complete explanation, since it has numerous limitations.

I. The number of levels

A certain limitation is provided by the number of levels distinguished. There is no reason except practicality for not multiplying them, distinguishing sublevels or adding new levels. Thus the level of physiology could be added, since as we have seen it is directly involved in articulations with psychological and social explanations in research into the two-factor theory of the emotional state. Besides, does not Parsons (1964: 257) speak of 'the interpenetration' of physiological and social systems, and Bourdieu (1977b) of 'bodily properties which are social products'? If sociologists propose this kind of articulation, there is no reason for social psychology to reject it. It is also obvious, at the other pole of our series of levels, that general concepts of an ideological nature should be studied in the framework of a sociological analysis. When members of a traditional Arab culture value generosity and the gratuitous act and despise calculation and meanness, and when these

146

values change during their forced regrouping in camps (Bourdieu & Sayad, 1964) or after they have moved to the city (Bourdieu, 1977a), with the gratuitous act becoming stupidity and calculation reason, such changes should first be related to the kind of historical changes which usually escape social psychological analysis, even though such changes can be realised only through institutional and inter-personal dynamics. Ideological analysis is located where present trends in sociological and social psychological research intersect. Deconchy's research shows the value for social psychology in venturing into a field without worrying too much about the exact locale of an imaginary line of demarcation. Furthermore, a number of sociologists have achieved articulations with a more psychological approach, and not only those who are directly interested in the way in which individuals participate in different social dynamics. Thus Bourdieu (1972, 1980), whose basic aim is to study how society recreates itself, has developed hypotheses about individual function, habits and disposition, just as Touraine (1978a,b, 1980), who is investigating the work which every society carries out on itself, has analysed in concrete detail the interaction processes which arise between militant individuals.

II. Varieties of articulation

A more serious limitation than that which relates to the possible extension of our analytic framework concerns the definition of the notion of articulation itself. While we have cited numerous examples of articulation at a theoretical and experimental level, we do not for all that pretend we have presented a general theory of the articulation of explanations. The nature of each articulation is defined by the explanations it brings together, and just as explanations come in many varieties so too do the ways they can be articulated. While it is true that at the end of this chapter we point to certain research approaches which might perhaps lead to a certain system-atisation in the study of different articulations, we must first emphasise their great variety and the need to examine the greatest possible number of explanatory theories. To tell the truth, at the moment we are very wary, perhaps more so than in the past, of attempts to establish global links between different types of explanation in the human sciences. Let us give a few examples.

III. Some over-inclusive attempts at integration

Devereux (1972: see Doise, 1978a) is right to insist on the irreducibility of explanations in psychological and in sociological terms: they lead to two different universes of discourse and it is impossible to operate in both at the same time. Whence arises the principle of complementarity between the two sorts of explanation, which means that first each explanation should be taken to the extreme limit of its usefulness; the residue should then be explained in terms of the universe of discourse at a different level. This complementarist concept of the articulation of two levels of explanation can however take on more precise forms in psychology and sociology: what is taken to be an 'operant motive' at one level becomes an 'instrumental motive' at the other. Thus when a psychologist studies the motivations of participants in a collective movement, he studies operant motives which may vary according to different individuals but which have led them all to find in their participation in the same social movement an instrument to realise these operant motives. Conversely, for the person who studies this collective movement as a sociologist, the operant motives of the psychological level become instrumental motives.

This complementarist concept seems to us inadequate to account for the numerous articulations we have studied in this book. In what way, for example, can it account for a socio-genetic approach to cognitive development which studies the links between inter-personal and intra-personal coordinations? In what way is it helpful in accounting for the redefinition of the Asch situation proposed by Moscovici? The concept of operant motives and instrumental motives is only one kind of articulation of explanations, and it leaves untouched the problem of developing a general theory of articulations.

A very widespread way of solving the problem of articulations of psychological and sociological explanations is to postulate a certain homogeneity of nature between the individual and the collective. A number of passages by Piaget point in this direction when he traces a parallelism between the two kinds of explanation:

There are thus three systems of ideas to be distinguished in sociological explanation (just as in psychological explanation): causal actions, operations which transform them into systems and ideological factors (comparable to introspective or egocentric data in psychology) which falsify perspectives unless the properly operational mechanisms are dissociated from this sociocentric symbolism. (Piaget, 1965:60)

A structural analogy is made between the three levels of psychological attainment, sensorimotor thought, symbolic thought, operational thought, and technical, ideological and scientific activities which constitute the sociological equivalent. This analogy clarifies the question of relations between infrastructure and superstructure:

Just as psychology has come to understand that the data of consciousness explain nothing causally and that causal explanation must mount the causal chain from consciousness to behaviour, that is acts, so sociology has discovered the relativity of superstructures compared to infrastructures and turned from ideological explanations to explanations in terms of acts: activities carried out in common to ensure the life of the social group as a function of a particular material environment; concrete and technical activities, which are prolonged in collective representations rather than arising from them in the first place, as applications. (1965:21)

As with psychology, the sociological superstructure is composed of two different levels:

sooner or later, sociology introduces into the shared or differentiated modes of thought it wants to explain a distinction analogous to one made in the domain of the individual, between egocentric or subjective thought and decentred or objective thought: it recognizes that some kinds of thought reflect concerns of the limited group to which the individual belongs...; on the other hand, in other kinds of thought it discerns the possibility of true universalisation of the operations in question, as is the case for scientific thought. (1965:26)

Such global connections almost inevitably lead to the theory that individual history can be studied as a recapitulation of prior social history. Writers from a number of schools do suggest this kind of articulation, which consists in fact of consigning to a more or less distant past all explanation of current problems in their present form, and being satisfied with more or less plausible reconstructions. Certainly we should study the current development of intelligence in our children as 'the process of separate individuals' appropriation of the experience accumulated by men during the history of human society' (Leontyev, 1981:423), but investigation of the social processes which are involved today in this appropriation can also give us information about the social nature of intelligence, much better than more or less imaginary reconstructions of the historical development of the social technique of hunting (Leontyev, 1981; Ardrey, 1977; Mendel, 1977; Tran Duc Thao, 1973). To assume an identity of nature between the psychological and the sociological, between collective history and individual history is a way of avoiding the problem of the articulation of explanations in these different domains. This is the danger which threatens those who, like Piaget, start with the study of ontogenetic development in order to explain the historical development of knowledge, and of which Gréco warned:

If we accept (and why should we not?) that the evolution of scientific notions is the product of abstractions of thought and of successive equilibrations, it still remains for us to define the sociological and historical conditions which permit (or impede) this evolution. This problem in itself merits a long debate. Let us say that the Piagetian thesis, by offering an answer to *one* aspect of this problem, leads us to question more than ever what some call 'the logic of history', and henceforth it will be essential for the psychologist – particularly when claiming to avoid all 'psychologism' – to make explicit the reasons (and the analytical instruments) which authorise him to extrapolate from ontogenesis to history, from cognitive psychology to epistemology in general. (Gréco: comment in a symposium, published by Inhelder, Garcia & Vonéche, 1977:69)

IV. Role theory

Other attempts to articulate the individual and the collective take a more synchronic perspective by employing the notion of role. The usefulness of such a notion is obvious, but its limitations in studying the articulations of social and personal dynamics are no less real and may be reduced to two kinds of consideration. The point of departure for the analysis is either the question of the social determination of roles, or belief in a more 'interactionist' approach. If the aspect of social determination of roles is emphasised, then not only how they are learned, not to say interiorised by the individual in all their complexity, must be explained, but also how the same individual learns to distance himself in relation to the different roles so as to be able to evaluate their relative weight in different situations. These operations are even more complex in that, as Habermas (1973) remarked, the expectations induced by roles are often ambiguous; there is hardly any consensus between different social actors as to these expectations, and furthermore, the conformity demanded with respect to these expectations oscillates between enormous margins. In this sense, to explain the socialisation of the individual by the existence of roles is to project a dynamic of level III onto a dynamic of level I without examining the inter-personal dynamics which specify each time the relations to be maintained by the actors in connection with the different roles they are supposed to play. Or else one might believe in an interactionist approach, of which Goffman is the best known representative, and in contrast to the more structuralist and functionalist concept generally attributed to Parsons. But the 'interactionist' approach, precisely because it insists on the numerous situational transformations and continual redefinitions which roles undergo, cannot offer a general definition of the articulation of norms, social positions, situations and individual activities. It is precisely the numerous variations in the different combinations which interest the supporters of the 'interactionist' approach; taken to its logical extreme, for some ethnomethodologists or ethnogenists or con-textualists, there could be as many articulations of the individual and the collective as there are situations to study. This may be so, but does suggest to us that at any event it will not be in theories based on the concept of role alone that a more precise definition of social psychological articulation will be found.

V. Situational analyses

The psychological study of situations carried out by Argyle and his colleagues (Argyle, Furnham & Graham, 1981; Furnham & Argyle, 1981) shows that the notion of role alone cannot be enough to understand a social situation. These writers propose a componential model which includes behaviour elements, goals of the participant, rules of behaviour, formal roles, salient cognitive concepts, relevant skills and physical setting. Only an approach which attempts to integrate all these elements is truly situational. Argyle, Furnham & Graham (1981) try to achieve this by integrating research in eight different areas of investigation: aggression, altruism, assertiveness, attraction, gaze, conformity, leadership and self disclosure. But integration of the elements from each area arises much more from a taxonomic classification of variables than a true articulation of explanations. It is however in studying the definition of the goal of a situation by the participants themselves in that situation that Argyle *et al.* think they should find the key which would allow them to articulate the different elements of their componential model. But for the moment we will make our own the conclusion that Furnham & Argyle (1981:xxii) present with regard to the current state of affairs in the research they tried to integrate into a componential model:

This review revealed that whereas researchers in some areas had taken cognizance of numerous situational determinants such as social rules, roles, norms, and physical props, others had done much less to investigate the immediate physical and psychological situations in which these processes occur. It also seemed that where social situational variables had been considered, these were not selected or studied in any consistent, systematic or theoretical way.

The situational approach also can be seen to be fruitful in so far as it succeeds in articulating different theories and levels of analysis. At the moment it can hardly be said to be committed to this task, and it is difficult to see how it will be possible to produce theories which can articulate as many as seven components in a single unified explanation.

VI. Three promising approaches

Must we resign ourselves to abandoning for ever any attempt to produce a more constrained theory of the articulation of levels of analysis? We do not think so because three current research trends seem to us to introduce a certain systematicity into the study of articulations of levels of analysis: a first is research into the establishment of knowledge and competence in children, a second the study of goal-directed action, and a third the renewed interest in the Durkheimian notion of collective representation.

The work by Waller (1973, 1978) already cited is a part of the first trend: it examined the establishment of social competence in children, and showed that it is the most visible social differentiations, related to sex and age, which principally determine expectations of behaviour in young children, while more situational elements in expectations only intervene later. Such results are important from several points of view: they suggest principally that the opposition between structural-functionalist theory and interactionist theory could well give way to an articulation of both interpretations of role theory coming out of developmental research: what Waller shows is that situational elements modify general expectations, which are linked to social position and status, as a function of the age of children. But Parsons (1964) himself was not reluctant to introduce this developmental link in his paper on the symbol of the father, which in fact deals with the articulation, or to use his terminology, the interpenetration of personality, family and social systems. Parsons begins his analysis with a description of the dyadic mother–child system, which is predominant at the start of the child's life but which must give way to the constraints of the pre-existing family system where relations between father and mother prevail. By leaving his narrow dependence on the mother, the child acquires a functional autonomy which will be useful for the family and enters into a system of authority relations with the father. Up to this moment, the social development of girl and boy have been identical. Thus even inside the family the child meets a bipolarity which characterises a dynamic of many social interactions: the pole of security or solidarity, symbolised by the 'paradise' of his interdependence with the mother, and the pole of efficacity, opening toward the exterior, symbolised by the father who not only tears the child from his dependence on the mother but also stands where the family system and the wider social system intersect. Sexual differentiation, transcending the differentiation inside the family to link it with a general differentiation in the whole of society, is thus in direct relation with this bipolarity: efficacity and universalism opposed to affectivity and particularity. In sum, the child learns in the family to live the authority relations and the bipolarity of the life of groups. These are held to be essential components of the different social roles individuals may occupy in different societies. The article by Parsons offers therefore much more than a sociological analysis of certain Freudian notions, and more than an explanation of the different place the symbol of the father may occupy in different cultures as a function of the relative weight of the family system: it demonstrates the possibility of an approach articulating investigation of the evolution of the child's status within the family and of her/his entry into general social dynamics. Certainly the study by Parsons, and doubtless the summary we have made of it, may appear schematic, but it is precisely research like that of Waller or that of Kohlberg (1966, 1974) which shows the empirical way to enrich the conjectures of the sociologist. This way necessarily entails a social psychological study of the child which has scarcely even been started; in this area too often procedures use hazardous reconstructions of the social development of the child, instead of studying it in a 'theoretico-experimental' manner.

We have seen above how situational analysis proposes the idea of goal as an integrating notion. But it is above all the work of von Cranach and his team in Berne which has best illustrated the integrating power of this idea and its utility in articulating different levels of analysis (see von Cranach & Harré, 1972; von Cranach, Kalbermatten, Indermühle & Gugler, 1982). The basic concepts of the theory of goal-directed action may be grouped into three classes:

> Behaviour (class I) comprises various kinds of concepts which refer to characteristics of the manifest course of action (starting and end points, action steps, nodes and their characteristics, environmental factors, levels of organisation, etc.)
> (Conscious) cognition (class II) comprises constructs referring to functionally and/or qualitatively different (conscious) action-related cognitions (like goals, plans, strategies, values, norms, decisions, emotions, etc.)
> Social meaning (class III) comprises action-related social representations (norms, rules, conventions, knowledge) which refer to individual cognitions (like goals or values) and/or behaviour (like action steps or levels of organisation).

It is assumed that social meaning operates through social cognition (social control); this presupposes that the concepts of (conscious) cognition are at least partly socially represented, and vice versa. (von Cranach, 1982:46)

One of the basic statements of the theory deals precisely with articulation of the concepts from the three classes: 'Goal-directed action theory is derived by conceptual and empirical integration of concepts from the three classes and by descriptive and predictive validation of the resulting statements' (1982:48). This conceptual integration is of two sorts: 'Concepts in the three classes tend to be interrelated in a twofold way: any particular concept in a class is related to one or more concepts of its own class and/or to one or more concepts in one or both of the other classes' (1982:47), which is not without analogy with our own concept of articulations within and between levels. Empirical integration consists of the formulation and operationalising of hypotheses whch should once again establish links between the concepts in different classes.

Up to now, the method used has been mostly observational. Thus the actions of individuals or of groups of individuals are recorded audio-visually and then interpreted by the actors themselves as well as by observers. This is the only way that the psychosociological meaning of an action can be fully understood by the investigator. In effect the social meaning as given by the interpretation of another is part of the meaning of an action:

Goal-directedness and social meaning are particularly important aspects of goal-directed action. On each level of analysis, the goal not only directs the behaviour, but also shapes it into its specific form (selective function of goal instrumentality). This could still result in more or less isolated, idiosyncratic activities; it is the social meaning of the goal which links it to the actor's system of socially meaningful cognitions (culminating in his 'self'), and gives to goal-directed action its social quality (which again reinforces its individual significance). Socially meaningful goals define the goal-directed action unit of the act. (von Cranach, 1982:51)

However, goal-directed actions are only a part of human behaviour. This behaviour is furthermore only studied by von Cranach and his team in so far as it becomes cognitively conscious. And in order to grasp this awareness, expectations and social values, indeed all manner of social representations, must necessarily be taken into account.

The current work on social representations, carried out mostly in France following the work of Moscovici (1961, 1976a; see also Farr & Moscovici, 1984) perhaps offers an even better outlook for the articulation of levels of explanation. Indeed, what else are general beliefs, which can be modified and transformed depending on social position, aspects of interpersonal relations and individual development, if not social representations? And they can be looked on as preferentially located at the point of articulation of the individual and the collective, or, in other words, as those private manifestations of social phenomena of which Durkheim wrote (1982:55).

As regards their private manifestations, these do indeed have something social about them, since in part they reproduce the collective model. But to a large extent each one depends also upon the psychical and organic constitution of the individual, and on the particular circumstances in which he is placed. Therefore they are not phenomena which are in the strict sense sociological. They depend on both domains at the same time, and could be termed socio-psychical. (1982:55)

Today we would say social psychological, but the term still implies the belonging to two domains, even if the two domains themselves exist primarily in social representations, as opposite and complementary poles, each with different values and endowed with unequal power, depending on historical and social contexts. An important task incumbent on social psychologists is therefore to explain the multiple transformations which the field of representations undergoes. Many have devoted themselves to this task without using the term representation, and have nevertheless uncovered a good number of transformational rules for social representations. These rules do not as yet lend themselves to incorporation into a single system, so that at the moment the investigations look like so much do-it-yourself odd-jobbery. But, according to Jacob (1977), it is just this sort of unsystematic tinkering that is likely to have led both to natural evolution and to scientific understanding of this evolution.

Bibliography

Aboud, F. E. (1976). Self-evaluation, *Journal of Cross-Cultural Psychology*, 7, 289–300.

Abric, J.-C. (1976). Jeux, conflits et représentations sociales. Doctoral thesis, Université de Provence, Aix.

  (1984). A theoretical and experimental approach to the study of social representations in a situation of interaction, in R. M. Farr & S. Moscovici, *Social representations*. Cambridge: Cambridge University Press.

Abric, J.-C., Faucheux, C., Moscovici, S. & Plon, M. (1967). Rôle de l'image du partenaire sur la coopération en situation de jeu, *Psychologie française*, 12, 267–75.

Adams, J. S. (1965). Inequity in social exchange, in L. Berkowitz, *Advances in experimental social psychology*, vol. 2. New York: Academic Press.

Adorno, T. W., Frenkel-Brunswik, E., Levinson, D. J. & Sanford, R. N. (1950). *The authoritarian personality*. New York: Harper.

Alexander, C. N., Zucker, L. G. & Brody, C. L. (1970). Experimental expectations and autokinetic experiences: consistency theories and judgemental convergence, *Sociometry*, 33, 108–22.

Allen, V. L. (1975). Social support for nonconformity, in L. Berkowitz, *Advances in experimental social psychology*, vol. 8. New York: Academic Press.

Allen, V. L. & Levine, J. M. (1968). Social support, dissent and conformity, *Sociometry*, 31, 138–49.

Allport, F. H. (1924). *Social psychology*. New York: Houghton Mifflin.

  (1962). A structuronomic conception of behaviour: individual and collective, *Journal of Abnormal and Social Psychology*, 64, 3–30.

Ames, G. J. & Murray, F. B. (1982). When two wrongs make a right: promoting cognitive change by social conflict, *Developmental Psychology*, 18, 894–7.

Anderson, N. H. (1965). Averaging versus adding as a stimulus-combination rule in impression formation, *Journal of Experimental Social Psychology*, 70, 394–400.

  (1971). Integration theory and attitude change, *Psychological Review*, 78, 171–206.

Arcuri, L. (1982). Three patterns of social categorization in attribution memory, *European Journal of Social Psychology*, 12, 271–82.

Ardrey, R. (1977). *The hunting hypothesis*. Des Plaines, Illinois: Bantam Books.

Argyle, M., Furnham, A. & Graham, J. A. (1981). *Social situations*. Cambridge: Cambridge University Press.

Armistead, N. (1974). *Reconstructing social psychology*. Harmondsworth: Penguin Books.

Asch, S. E. (1951). Effects of group pressure upon the modification and distortion of judgements, in H. Guetzkow, *Groups, leadership and men*. Pittsburgh: Carnegie Press.

(1956). Studies on independence and conformity: a minority of one against an unanimous majority, *Psychological Monographs*, 70, 1–70.

Ball, P., Giles, H. & Hewstone, M. (1984). Second language acquisition: the intergroup theory with catastrophic dimensions, in H. Tajfel, ed., *The social dimension*, vol. 2. Cambridge: Cambridge University Press.

Bass, B. M. & Dunteman, G. (1963). Biases in the evaluation of one's own group, its allies and opponents, *Journal of Conflict Resolution*, 7, 16–20.

Batson, C. D. (1977). Experimentation in psychology of religion: an impossible dream. *Journal for the Scientific Study of Religion*, 16, 413–18.

Baudelot, C. & Establet, R. (1971). *L'école capitaliste en France*. Paris: François Maspero.

Bavelas, A. (1950). Communication patterns in task-oriented groups, *Journal of the Acoustical Society of America*, 22, 725–30.

Beals, A. R. (1962). Pervasive factionalism in a South Indian village, in M. Sherif, *Intergroup relations and leadership*. New York: Wiley & Sons.

Bearison D. J. & Cassel, T. Z. (1975). Cognitive decentration and social codes: communicative effectiveness in young children from differing family contexts, *Developmental Psychology*, 11, 29–36.

Bearison, D. J., Magzamen, S. & Filardo, K. E. (1984). *Socio-cognitive conflict and cognitive growth in young children*. New York: The Graduate Center, City University of New York.

Beauvois, J. L. & Joule, R. (1981). *Soumission et idéologies*. Paris: Presses Universitaires de France.

Bennett, E. (1955). Discussion, decision, commitment and consensus in 'group decision', *Human Relations*, 8, 251–74.

Berkowitz, L. (1962). *Aggression: a social psychological analysis*. New York: McGraw-Hill.

Bernstein, B. (1974, revised edition). *Class, codes and control*, (vol. 1, *Theoretical studies towards a sociology of language*). London: Routledge & Kegan Paul.

Berry, J. W. (1967). Independence and conformity in subsistence-level societies, *Journal of Personality and Social Psychology*, 7, 415–18.

Berry, J. W. & Dasen, P. R. (1974). *Culture and cognition*. London: Methuen & Co.

Billig, M. (1973). Normative communication in a minimal intergroup situation, *European Journal of Social Psychology*, 3, 339–43.

(1976). *Social psychology and intergroup relations*. London: Academic Press.

(1982). *Ideology and social psychology*. Oxford: Blackwell.

Billig, M. & Tajfel, H. (1973). Social categorization and similarity in intergroup behaviour, *European Journal of Social Psychology*, 3, 27–52.

Blake, R. R. & Mouton, J. S. (1962a). Comprehension of points of communality in competing solutions, *Sociometry*, 25, 56–63.

(1962b). Overevaluation of own group's product in intergroup competitions, *Journal of Abnormal and Social Psychology*, 64, 237–38.

Blake, R. R., Shepard, H. A. & Mouton, J. S. (1964). *Managing intergroup conflict in industry*. Houston, Texas: Gulf Publishing Co.

Bornstein, G., Crum, L., Wittenbraker, J., Harring, K., Insko, C. A. & Thibaut, J.

(1983). On the measurement of social orientations in the minimal group paradigm, *European Journal of Social Psychology*, **13**, 231–50.

Boudon, R. (1973). *L'inégalité des chances*. Paris: A. Colin.

(1977). *Effets pervers et ordre social*. Paris: Presses Universitaires de France.

(1979). *La logique du social*. Paris: Hachette.

Bourdieu, P. (1972). *Esquisse d'une théorie de la pratique*. Geneva: Librairie Droz.

(1977a). *Algérie 60*. Paris: Editions de Minuit.

(1977b). Remarques provisoires sur la perception sociale du corps, *Actes de la Recherche en sciences sociales*, no. 14, 51–4.

(1980). *Le sens pratique*. Paris: Editions de Minuit.

Bourdieu, P. & Boltanski, L. (1976). La production de l'idéologie dominante. *Actes de la Recherche en sciences sociales*, no. 2–3, 4–73.

Bourdieu, P. & de Saint-Martin, M. (1975a). Les catégories de l'entendement professoral, *Actes de la Recherche en sciences sociales*, **3**, 68–93.

(1975b). Anatomie du goût, *Actes de la Recherche en sciences sociales*, no. 5, 5–112.

Bourdieu, P. & Passeron, J. C. (1970). *La reproduction*. Paris: Editions de Minuit.

Bourdieu, P. & Sayad, A. (1964). *Le déracinement*. Paris: Editions de Minuit.

Bourhis, R. Y., Giles, H., Leyens, J. P. & Tajfel, H. (1978). Psycho-linguistic distinctiveness: language divergence in Belgium, in H. Giles & R. Saint-Clair, *Language and social psychology*. Oxford: Blackwell.

Boyanowsky, E. O. & Allen, V. L. (1973). Ingroup norms and self-identity as determinants of discriminatory behaviour, *Journal of Personality and Social Psychology*, **25**, 408–18.

Bramel, D. (1963). Selection of a target for defensive projection, *Journal of Abnormal and Social Psychology*, **66**, 318–24.

Branthwaite, A., Doyle, S. & Lightbown, N. (1979). The balance between fairness and discrimination, *European Journal of Social Psychology*, **9**, 149–63.

Branthwaite, A. & Jones, J. E. (1975). Fairness and discrimination: English versus Welsh, *European Journal of Social Psychology*, **5**, 323–38.

Breakwell, G. M. & Rowett, C. (1982). *Social work: the social psychological approach*. Wokingham: Van Nostrand Reinhold.

Brown, R. (1965). *Social psychology*. New York: Free Press.

Brown, R. J. (1978). Divided we fall: an analysis of relations between sections of a factory workforce, in H. Tajfel, *Differentiation between social groups*. London: Academic Press.

Brown, R. J. & Turner, J. C. (1979). The criss-cross categorization effect in intergroup discrimination, *British Journal of Social and Clinical Psychology*, **18**, 371–83.

Bruner, J. S. (1957). On perceptual readiness, *Psychological Review*, **64**, 123–52.

Bruner, J. S. & Perlmutter, H. V. (1957). Compatriot and foreigner: a study of impression formation in three countries, *Journal of Abnormal and Social Psychology*, **55**, 253–60.

Campbell, D. T. (1975). On the conflicts between biological and social evolution and between psychology and moral tradition, *American Psychologist*, **30**, 1103–26.

Campbell, D. T. & Stanley, J. C. (1966). *Experimental and quasi-experimental designs for research*. Reprint from Gage, N. L., ed. (1963), *Handbook of research on training*. Chicago: Rand McNally.

Cartwright, D. & Harary, F. (1956). Structural balance: a generalization of Heider's theory, *Psychological Review*, **63**, 277–93.

Cecchini, M., Dubs, E. & Tonucci, F. (1972). *Teacher training, pedagogical method and intellectual development*. Rome: Instituto di Psicologia (CNR).

Chance, M. & Larsen, R. R. (1976). *The social structure of attention*. London: Wiley.

Chance, N. A. (1962). Factionalism as a process of social and cultural change, in M. Sherif, ed., *Intergroup relations and leadership*. New York: Wiley.

Charters, W. W. & Newcomb, T. M. (1958). Some attitudinal effects of experimentally increased salience of a membership group, in E. E. Maccoby, T. M. Newcomb & E. L. Hartley, eds., *Readings, in social psychology*. New York: Holt.

Codol, J.-P. (1972). Représentations et comportement dans les groupes restreints. Aix: Université de Provence. Thèse de 3ᵉ cycle.

(1984). On the system of representations in an artificial social situation, in R. M. Farr & S. Moscovici, eds., *Social representations*. Cambridge: Cambridge University Press.

Cole, M., Gay, J., Glick, J. & Sharp, D. (1971). *The cultural context of learning and thinking*. New York: Basic Books.

Cole, M. & Scribner, S. (1974). *Culture and thought*. New York: Wiley.

Cooper, J. & Mackie, D. (1983). Cognitive dissonance in an intergroup context, *Journal of Personality and Social Psychology*, **44**, 536–44.

Cramer, D. (1975). A critical note on two studies of minority influence, *European Journal of Social Psychology*, **5**, 257–60.

Cranach, M. von (1982). The psychological study of goal-directed action: basic issues, in M. von Cranach & R. Harré, eds., *The analysis of action*. Cambridge: Cambridge University Press.

Cranach, M. von & Harré, R. (1982). *The analysis of action*. Cambridge: Cambridge University Press.

Cranach, M. von, Kalbermatten, U., Indermühle, K. & Gugler, B. (1982). *Goal-directed action*. London: Academic Press.

Crutchfield, R. S. (1955). Conformity and character, *American Psychologist*, **10**, 191–8.

Da Gloria, J. & de Ridder, R. (1977). Aggression in dyadic interaction, *European Journal of Social Psychology*, **7**, 189–219.

(1979). Sex differences in aggression: are current notions misleading? *European Journal of Social Psychology*, **9**, 49–66.

Dami, C. (1975). *Stratégies cognitives dans les jeux compétitifs à deux*. Geneva: Editions de Médecine et Hygiène.

Damon, W. (1977). *The social world of the child*. San Francisco: Jossey-Bass.

Dann, H. D. & Doise, W. (1974). Ein neuer methodologischer Ansatz sur experimentellen Erforschung von Intergruppen-Beziehungen, *Zeitschrift fur Sozialpsychologie*, **5**, 2–15.

Dasen, P., Dembele, B., Kan, E., Kovamé, K., Daouda, K., Adjei, K. K. & Assande, N. (1985). L'intelligence chez les Baoulé, *Archives de Psychologie*, **53**, 293–324.

Deconchy, J. P. (1973). Systèmes de croyances et comportements orthodoxes, *La Recherche*, **4**, 35–42.

(1976–77). Régulation et signification dans un cas de 'compromis' idéologique, *Bulletin de Psychologie*, **30**, 436–50.

(1978). L'expérimentation en psychologie de la religion: pourquoi ne pas rêver? *Archives de Sciences sociales des religions*, **46**, 176–92.

(1980). *Orthodoxie religieuse et sciences humaines.* Followed by (*Religious*) *orthodoxy, rationality and scientific knowledge.* The Hague: Mouton.

(1984). Rationality and social control in orthodox systems, in H. Tajfel, ed., *The social dimension*, vol. 2. Cambridge: Cambridge University Press.

Deschamps, J. C. (1976). Différenciation catégorielle et différenciation de soi par rapport à autrui, premiers résultats. Geneva: Université de Genève, Département de Sociologie.

(1977). Effect of crossing category memberships on quantitative judgement, *European Journal of Social Psychology*, **7**, 517–21.

(1983). Social attribution, in J. Jaspars, M. Hewstone & F. D. Fincham, eds., *Attribution theory and research.* London: Academic Press.

Deschamps, J. C. & Doise, W. (1975). Evolution des représentations intersexes entre 7 et 13 ans, *Revue suisse de Sociologie*, **1**, 107–28.

(1979). L'effet du croisement des appartenances catégorielles, in W. Doise, ed., *Experiences entre groupes.* Paris: Mouton.

Deschamps, J. C. & Personnaz, B. (1979). Etudes entre groupes 'dominants' et 'dominés': importance de la présence du hors-groupe dans les discriminations évaluatives et comportementales, *Social Science Information*, **18**, 269–305.

Devereux, G. (1972). *Ethnopsychanalyse complémentariste.* Paris: Flammarion.

Diab, L. N. (1970). A study of intragroup and intergroup relations among experimentally produced small groups, *Genetic Psychology Monographs*, **82**, 49–82.

Doise, W. (1969a). Intergroup relations and polarization of individual and collective judgments, *Journal of Personality and Social Psychology*, **12**, 136–43.

(1969b). Autoritarisme, dogmatisme et mode d'approche des relations internationales, *Journal de Psychologie normale et pathologique*, **66**, 35–54.

(1971). An apparent exception to the extremization of collective judgments, *European Journal of Social Psychology*, **1**, 511–18.

(1972). Rencontres et représentations intergroupes, *Archives de Psychologie*, **41**, 303–20.

(1976). *L'articulation psychosociologique et les relations entre groupes.* Brussels: De Boeck.

(1978a). *Groups and individuals: explanations in social psychology.* Cambridge: Cambridge University Press.

(1978b). Images, représentations, idéologies et expérimentation psychosociologique, *Social Science Information*, **17**, 41–69.

(1979). *Expériences entre groupes.* Paris: Mouton.

(1980). Levels of explanation in the European Journal of Social Psychology, *European Journal of Social Psychology*, **10**, 213–31.

(1983). Tensions et niveaux d'analyse en psychologie sociale expérimentale, *Connexions*, **42**, 57–72.

(1985a). Psychologie sociale et constructivisme cognitif, *Cahiers de la Fondation Jean Piaget*, **5**, 127–40.

(1985b). Représentations sociales chez des élèves: effets du statut scolaire et de l'origine sociale. *Revue suisse de Psychologie*, **44**, 67–78.

Doise, W., Deschamps, J. C. & Meyer, G. (1979). Accentuation des ressemblances intracatégorielles, in W. Doise, *Expériences entre groupes.* Paris: Mouton.

Doise, W., Deschamps, J. C. & Mugny, G. (1978). *Psychologie sociale expérimentale.* Paris: A. Colin.

Doise, W., Dionnet, S. & Mugny, G. (1978). Conflit socio-cognitif, marquage social et développement cognitif, *Cahiers de Psychologie*, 21, 231–43.

Doise, W. & Frésard, M. D. (1981). Savoir, action et eclectisme, in F. Tonucci, S. Caravita & E. Detti, eds.; *La ricerca nella scuola di base.* Rome: Istituto di Psicologia (CNR).

Doise, W., Meyer, G. & Perret-Clermont, A. N. (1976). Etude psychosociologique des représentations d'élèves en fin de scolarité obligatoire, *Cahiers de la Section des Sciences de l'Education.* Université de Genéve, 2, 15–27.

Doise, W. & Moscovici, S. (1969–70). Approche et évitement du déviant dans des groupes de cohésion différente, *Bulletin de Psychologie*, 23, 522–5.

Doise, W. & Mugny, G. (1975). Recherches socio-génétiques sur la coordination d'actions interdépendantes, *Revue suisse de Psychologie pure et appliquée*, 34, 160–74.

(1979). Individual and collective conflicts of centrations in cognitive development, *European Journal of Social Psychology*, 9, 105–8.

(1981). *Le développement social de l'intelligence.* Paris: Inter-Editions.

(1984). *The social development of the intellect.* Oxford: Pergamon Press.

Doise, W., Mugny, G. & Perret-Clermont, A. N. (1975). Social interaction and the development of cognitive operations, *European Journal of Social Psychology*, 5, 367–83.

Doise, W. & Palmonari, A. (1984). *Social interaction in individual development.* Cambridge: Cambridge University Press.

Doms, M. (1978). Moscovici's innovatie-effekt: poging tot integratie met het conformisme-effekt. Doctoral thesis, Katholieke Universiteit, Louvain.

Durkheim, E. (1982). *The rules of sociological method.* (*Les règles de la Méthode sociologique*, trans. W. D. Halls). London: Macmillan.

Durkheim, E. & Mauss, M. (1963). *Primitive classification.* (*De quelques formes primitives de classification*, 1903, trans. R. Needham). London: Cohen & West.

Edlow, D. & Kiesler, C. (1966). Ease of denial and defensive projection, *Journal of Experimental Social Psychology*, 2, 56–69.

Eiser, J. R. (1971a). Enhancement of contrast in the absolute judgment of attitude statements. *Journal of Personality and Social Psychology*, 17, 1–10.

(1971b). Comment on Ward's 'Attitude and involvement in the absolute judgement of attitude statements', *Journal of Personality and Social Psychology*, 17, 81–3.

(1973). Judgement of attitude statements as a function of judges' attitudes and the judgemental dimension, *British Journal of Social and Clinical Psychology*, 12, 231–40.

Eiser, J. R. & Mower White, C. J. (1975). Categorization and congruity in attitudinal judgment, *Journal of Personality and Social Psychology*, 31, 769–75.

Farr, R. M. & Moscovici, S. (1984). *Social representations.* Cambridge: Cambridge University Press.

Faucheux, C. (1976). Cross-cultural research in experimental social psychology, *European Journal of Social Psychology*, 6, 269–322.

Faucheux, C. & Moscovici, S. (1967). Le style de comportement d'une minorité et son influence sur les réponses d'une majorité, *Bulletin du CERP*, 16, 337–60.

(1968). Self-esteem and exploitative behavior in a game against chance and nature, *Journal of Personality and Social Psychology*, **8**, 83–8.

Feffer, M. (1959). The cognitive implications of role-taking behaviour, *Journal of Personality*, **27**, 152–68.

(1970). Developmental analysis of interpersonal behavior, *Psychological Review*, **77**, 197–214.

Festinger, L. (1950). Informal social communication, *Psychological Review*, **57**, 271–82.

(1954). A theory of social comparison processes, *Human Relations*, **7**, 117–40.

(1957). *A theory of cognitive dissonance*. Evanston, Illinois: Row, Peterson.

Festinger, L., Riecken, H. W. & Schachter, S. (1956). *When prophecy fails*. Minneapolis, Minnesota: University of Minnesota Press.

Fishbein, M. & Hunter, R. (1964). Summation versus balance in attitude organization and change, *Journal of Abnormal and Social Psychology*, **69**, 505–10.

Flament, C. (1959). Ambiguité du stimulus, incertitude de la réponse et processus d'influence sociale, *L'Année psychologique*, **59**, 73–91.

(1959). Modèle stratégique des processus d'influence sociale sur les jugements perceptifs, *Psychologie française*, **4**, 91–101.

(1979). *Du biais d'équilibre structural à la représentation du groupe*. Colloque sur les représentations sociales, Laboratoire européen de Psychologie sociale, Paris, MSH.

(1984). From the bias of structural balance to the representation of the group, in R. M. Farr & S. Moscovici, *Social representations*. Cambridge: Cambridge University Press.

Flament, C. & Monnier, C. (1971). Rapports entre amitié et hiérarchie dans la représentation de groupe, *Cahiers de psychologie*, **14**, 209–18.

Flavell, J. H., Botkin, P. T., Fry, C. L., Wright, J. W. & Jarvis, P. E. (1968). *The development of role-taking and communication skills in children*. New York: John Wiley.

Fraser, C., Gouge, C. & Billig, M. (1971). Risky shifts, cautious shifts and group polarization, *European Journal of Social Psychology*, **1**, 7–30.

French, J. R. P. (1965). A formal theory of social power, *Psychological Review*, **63**, 181–94.

French, J. R. P. & Raven, B. (1959). The bases of social power, in D. Cartwright, ed., *Studies in social power*. Ann Arbor: University of Michigan Press.

Frenkel-Brunswik, E. (1949). Intolerance of ambiguity as an emotional and perceptual personality variable, *Journal of Personality*, **18**, 108–43.

Frey, D. & Irle, M. (1972). Some conditions to produce a dissonance and an incentive effect in a 'forced-compliance' situation, *European Journal of Social Psychology*, **2**, 45–54.

Furnham, A. & Argyle, M. (1981). *The psychology of social situations*. Oxford: Pergamon Press.

Gale, A. & Chapman, A. (1984). *Psychology and social problems*. Chichester: John Wiley & Sons.

Gerard, H. B. & Hoyt, M. F. (1974). Distinctiveness of social categorization and attitude toward ingroup members, *Journal of Personality and Social Psychology*, **29**, 836–42.

Gerard, H. B., Conolley, E. S. & Wilhelmy, R. A. (1974). Compliance, justification and cognitive change, in L. Berkowitz, *Advances in Experimental Social Psychology*, vol. 7. New York: Academic Press.

Gergen, K. J. (1973). Social psychology as history, *Journal of Personality and Social Psychology*, **26**, 309–20.

Giles, H. (1977). *Language, ethnicity and intergroup relations*. London: Academic Press.

Gill, R. & Keats, D. M. (1980). Elements of intellectual competence, *Journal of Cross-Cultural Psychology*, **11**, 233–43.

Gilly, M. (1980). *Maître-élève, rôles institutionnels et représentations*. Paris: Presses Universitaires de France.

Gilly, M. & Roux, J. P. (1984). Efficacité comparée du travail individuel et du travail en interaction socio-cognitive dans l'appropriation et la mise en oeuvre de règles de résolution chez les enfants de 11–12 ans, *Cahiers de Psychologie Cognitive*, **4**, 171–88.

Glachan, M. & Light, P. (1982). Peer interaction and learning: can two wrongs make a right? in G. Butterworth & P. Light, *Social cognition*. Chicago: University of Chicago Press.

Glick, J. (1974). Culture and cognition: some theoretical and methodological issues, in G. D. Spindler, ed., *Educational and cultural process*. New York: Holt, Rinehart & Winston.

Goffman, E. (1959). *The presentation of self in everyday life*. New York: Doubleday.

Greenfield, P. M. & Bruner, J. S. (1971). Culture and cognitive growth, in D. D. Goslin, *Handbook of socialization theory and research*. Chicago: Rand McNally.

Grisez, J. (1975). *Méthodes de la psychologie sociale*. Paris: Presses Universitaires de France.

Habermas, J. (1973). *Kultur und Kritik*. Frankfurt: Suhrkamp.

Harvey, O. J. & Consalvi, C. (1960). Status and conformity to pressures in informal groups, *Journal of Abnormal and Social Psychology*, **60**, 182–7.

Heider, F. (1946). Attitudes and cognitive organization, *Journal of Psychology*, **21**, 107–12.

(1958). *The psychology of interpersonal relations*. New York: John Wiley.

Herzlich, C. (1973). *Health and illness: a social psychological analysis*. (*Santé et maladie: analyse d'une représentation sociale*, 1969, trans. D. Graham). London: Academic Press.

Hewstone, M. & Jaspars, J. (1982). Intergroup relations and attribution processes, in H. Tajfel, *Social identity and intergroup relations*. Cambridge: Cambridge University Press.

Hirschman, A. O. (1970). *Exit, voice and loyalty: response to decline in firms, organizations and states*. Cambridge, Mass: Harvard University Press.

Hofstadter, R. (1945). *Social Darwinism in American thought*. Philadelphia: University of Pennsylvania Press.

Holzkamp, K. (1972). *Kritische Psychologie*. Frankfurt am Main: Fischer Taschenbuch.

Hovland, C. I., Harvey, O. J. & Sherif, M. (1957). Assimilation and contrast effects in reactions to communication and attitude change, *Journal of Abnormal and Social Psychology*, **55**, 244–52.

Hovland, C. I. & Sherif, M. (1952). Judgmental phenomena and scales of attitude measurement: item displacement in Thurstone scales, *Journal of Abnormal and Social Psychology*, **47**, 822–32.

Hovland, C. I. & Weiss, R. (1951). The influence of source credibility on communication effectiveness, *Public Opinion Quarterly*, **15**, 635–50.

Hyman, H. H. (1942). The psychology of status, *Archives of Psychology*, no. 269.

Inhelder, B., Garcia, R. & Vonéche, J. (1977). *Epistémologie génétique et équilibration*. Neuchâtel: Delachaux & Niestlé.

Inhelder, B., Sinclair, H. & Bovet, M. (1974). *Learning and the development of cognition (Apprentissage et structures de la connaissance, 1974)*. London: Routledge & Keagan Paul.

Jacob, F. (1977). Evolution et bricolage, *Le Monde*, 6th, 7th, 8th September.

Jacobs, R. C. & Campbell, D. T. (1961). The perpetuation of an arbitrary tradition through several generations of a laboratory microculture, *Journal of Abnormal and Social Psychology*, **62**, 649–58.

Jacquard, A. (1978). *Eloge de la différence*. Paris: Editions de Seuil.

Janoff-Bulman, R. & Hanson Frieze, I (1983). A theoretical perspective for understanding reactions to victimization, *Journal of Social Issues*, **39**, 1–17.

Jaspars, J. M. (1979). *Attitudes and social representations*. Paper presented at the colloquium on social representations, Laboratoire européen de Psychologie sociale, MSH.

Jaspars, J. M. & Fraser, C. (1984). Attitudes and social representations, in R. M. Farr & S. Moscovici, *Social representations*. Cambridge: Cambridge University Press.

Jaspars, J. M. & de Leeuw, J. A. (1980). Genetic-environment covariation in human behaviour genetics, in L. J. T. Van der Kamp, W. F. Langerak & D. N. M. de Gruijter, eds., *Psychometrics for educational debates*. New York: John Wiley.

Jaulin, R. (1973). *Gens du soi, gens de l'autre*. Paris: Union générale d'Edition.

Johnson, D. W. (1967). Use of role reversal in intergroup competition, *Journal of Personality and Social Psychology*, **7**, 135–41.

Jones, E. E. & Davis, K. E. (1965). From acts to dispositions: the attribution process in person perception, in L. Berkowitz, *Advances in Experimental Social Psychology*, vol. 2. New York: Academic Press.

Jones, E. E. & Nisbett, R. E. (1972). The actor and the observer: divergent perceptions of the causes of behavior, in E. E. Jones *et al.*, *Attribution: Perceiving the causes of behavior*. Morristown, N.J.: General Learning Press.

Jones, J. J. & Gerard, H. B. (1967). *Foundations of Social Psychology*. New York: John Wiley.

Kaes, R. (1968). *Images de la culture chez les ouvriers français*. Paris: Editions Cujas.

Kapferer, J. N. (1978). *Les chemins de la persuasion*. Paris: Gauthier-Villars.

Katz, I. (1973a). Negro performances in interracial situations, in P. Watson, *Psychology and race*. Harmondsworth: Penguin Books.

(1973b). Alternatives to a personality-deficit interpretation of Negro underachievement, in P. Watson, *Psychology and race*. Harmondsworth: Penguin Books.

Katz, I., Glass, D. C. & Cohen, S. (1973). Ambivalence, guilt, and the scapegoating of minority group victims, *Journal of Experimental Social Psychology*, **9**, 423–36.

Kelley, H. H. (1952). Two functions of reference groups, in G. E. Swanson, T. M. Newcomb & E. L. Hartley, eds, *Readings in social psychology*. New York: Holt.

(1967). Attribution theory in social psychology, in D. Levine, *Nebraska symposium on motivation*, vol. 15. Lincoln: University of Nebraska Press.

Kelman, H. C. (1958). Compliance, identification, and internalization: three processes of attitude change, *Journal of Conflict Resolution*, 2, 51–60.

Kogan, N. & Wallach, M. A. (1966). Modification of a judgmental style through group interaction, *Journal of Personality and Social Psychology*, 4, 165–74.

Kohlberg, L. (1963). The development of children's orientation toward a moral order. I: sequence in the development of moral thought. *Vita Humana*, 6, 11–33.

(1966). A cognitive-developmental analysis of the children's sex-role concepts and attitudes, in E. E. Maccoby, *The development of sex differences*. London: Tavistock.

Kohlberg, L. & Ullian, D. Z. (1974). Stages in the development of psychosexual concepts and attitudes, in R. C. Friedman, R. M. Richart & R. L. Van de Wiele, eds., *Sex differences in behavior*. New York: John Wiley.

Konrad, G. & Szelenyi, I. (1979). *La marche au pouvoir des intellectuels*. Paris: Editions du Seuil.

Kuhn, D. (1972). Mechanisms of change in the development of cognitive structures, *Child Development*, 43, 833–44.

Kuhn, T. S. (1962). *The structure of scientific revolutions*. Chicago: University of Chicago Press.

Labov, W. (1972). *Sociolinguistic patterns*. Philadelphia: University of Pennsylvania Press.

La Fave, L. & Sherif, M. (1968). Reference scale and placement of items with the own categories technique, *Journal of Social Psychology*, 76, 75–82.

Lage, E. (1973). *Innovation et influence minoritaire*. Paris: Ecole pratique des Hautes Etudes. Thèse de 3ᵉ cycle.

Lambert, W. E. (1967). A social psychology of bilingualism, *Journal of Social Issues*, 23, 91–109.

Lamm, H. (1973). Intragroup effects on intergroup negotiation, *European Journal of Social Psychology*, 3, 179–92.

Laughlin, P. R. & Jaccard, J. J. (1975). Social facilitation and observational learning of individuals and cooperative pairs, *Journal of Personality and Social Psychology*, 32, 873–9.

Laughlin, P. R. & Sweeney, J. D. (1977). Individual to group and group to individual transfer in problem solving, *Journal of Experimental Psychology, Human Learning and Memory*, 3, 246–54.

Leavitt, H. J. (1949). Some effects of certain communication patterns on group performance. Ph.D. thesis, Massachusetts Institute of Technology.

Le Bon, G. (1895/1916). *The crowd (La psychologie des foules)*. London: Unwin.

Lemaine, G. (1966). Inégalité, comparaison et incomparabilité: esquisse d'une théorie de l'originalité sociale, *Bulletin de Psychologie*, 20, 24–32.

(1974). Social differentiation and social originality, *European Journal of Social Psychology*, 4, 17–52.

(1975). Dissimilation and differential assimilation in social influence, *European Journal of Social Psychology*, 5, 93–120.

(1984). Social differentiation in the scientific community, in H. Tajfel, *The social dimension*, vol. 1. Cambridge: Cambridge University Press.

Lemaine, G., Desportes, J. P. & Louarn, J. P. (1969). Rôle de la cohésion et de la différenciation hiérarchique dans le processus d'influence sociale, *Bulletin du CERP*, **18**, 237–53.

Lemaine, G. & Kastersztein, J. (1971–72). Recherches sur l'originalité sociale, la différenciation et l'incomparabilité, *Bulletin de Psychologie*, **25**, 673–93.

Lemaine, G., Kastersztein, J. & Personnaz, B. (1978). Social differentiation, in H. Tajfel, *Differentiation between social groups*. London: Academic Press.

Lemaine, G., Lasch, E. & Ricateau, P. (1971–72). L'influence social et les systèmes d'action: les effets d'attraction et de répulsion dans une expérience de normalisation avec 'l'allocinétique', *Bulletin de Psychologie*, **25**, 482–93.

Lemaine, G. & Lemaine, J. M. (1969). *Psychologie et expérimentation*. Paris: Mouton, Bordas.

Lemaine, G., Matalon, B. & Provansal, B. (1969). La lutte pour la vie dans la cité scientifique, *Revue française de Sociologie*, **10**, 139–65.

Lemoine, C. (1976). L'emprise analytique des sciences humaines. Paris: Université de Paris VII. Thèse de doctorat de 3ᵉ cycle.

Leonard, F. (1975). L'équilibre cognitif. Décomposition d'une résponse. Paris: Ecole des Hautes Etudes en Sciences sociales. Thèse de 3ᵉ cycle.

Leontyev, A. N. (1981). *Problems of the development of the mind*. Moscow: Progress Publishers.

Lerner, M. J. (1971). Justice, guilt, and veridical perception, *Journal of Personality and Social Psychology*, **20**, 127–35.

LeVine, R. A. & Campbell, D. T. (1972). *Ethnocentrism: theories of conflict, ethnic attitudes, and group behaviour*. London: John Wiley.

Lewin, G. (1948). Preface, in K. Lewin, *Resolving social conflicts*. New York: Harper & Row.

Lewin, K. (1926). *Vorsatz, Wille and Bedurfnis*. Berlin: Julius Springer.

   (1933). Environmental forces, in C. Murchison, *A handbook of child psychology*. Oxford: Oxford University Press.

   (1935a). *A dynamic theory of personality*. New York: McGraw-Hill.

   (1935b). Psycho-sociological problems of minority groups, *Character and Personality*, **3**, 175–87.

   (1943). Behind food habits and methods of change, *Bulletin of the Research Council*, no. 108.

   (1948). *Resolving social conflicts*. New York: Harper & Row.

Lewin, K., Lippit, R. & White, R. (1939). Patterns of aggressive behavior in experimentally created 'social climates', *Journal of Social Psychology*, **10**, 271–99.

Lindzey, G. & Aronson, E. (1968–69). *Handbook of social psychology*. Cambridge, Mass.: Addison-Wesley.

Lloyd, B. & Gay, J (1981). *Universals of human thought*. Cambridge: Cambridge University Press.

Lorenz, K. (1966). *On aggression*. London: Methuen.

Lorwin, V. R. (1972). Linguistic pluralism and political tension in modern Belgium, in J. A. Fishman, *Advances in the sociology of language*, vol. 2. Paris: Mouton.

Lott, A. & Lott, B. E. (1965). Group cohesiveness on interpersonal attraction: a review of relationships with antecedent and consequent variables, *Psychological Bulletin*, **64**, 259–309.

Louche, C. (1974–75a). La préparation d'une négociation en groupe et ses effets sur le comportement des négociateurs et leurs représentations, *Bulletin de Psychologie*, **28**, 113–17.

(1974–75b). Les effets de la catégorisation sociale et de l'intéraction collective dans la préparation et le déroulement d'une négociation intragroupe, *Bulletin de Psychologie*, **28**, 941–7.

Luchins, A. S. & Luchins, E. H. (1961). Social influences on impressions of personality, *Journal of Social Psychology*, **54**, 111–25.

Luria, A. R. (1976). *Cognitive development: its cultural and social foundations*. Cambridge, Mass.: Harvard University Press.

McCauley, C. R. (1972). Extremity shifts, risky shifts and attitude shifts after group discussion, *European Journal of Social Psychology*, **2**, 417–36.

McDougall, W. (1920). *The group mind*. Cambridge: Cambridge University Press.

McGuire, W. J. (1967). Some impending reorientations in social psychology: some thoughts provoked by Kenneth Ring, *Journal of Experimental Social Psychology*, **3**, 124–39.

(1973). The Yin and Yang of progress in social psychology, *Journal of Personality and Social Psychology*, **26**, 446–56.

(1983). A contextualist theory of knowledge: its implications for innovation and reform in psychological research, in L. Berkowitz, *Advances in Experimental Social Psychology*, Vol. 16, pp. 1–47.

Maitland, K. A. & Goldman, J. R. (1974). Moral judgment as a function of peer group interaction, *Journal of Personality and Social Psychology*, **30**, 699–704.

Malof, M. & Lott, J. (1962). Ethnocentrism and the acceptance of Negro support in a group pressure situation, *Journal of Abnormal and Social Psychology*, **65**, 254–58.

Mead, G. H. (1934). *Mind, self and society*. Chicago: University of Chicago Press.

Meeus, W. H. J. & Raaijmakers, Q. A. W. (1984). *Gewoon Gehoorzaam*. Ph.D. thesis, University of Utrecht.

Mendel, G. (1977). *La chasse structurale*. Paris: Petite Bibliothèque Payot.

Merton, R. K. (1957). *Social theory and social structure*. New York: Free Press.

Merton, R. K. & Kitt, A. (1950). Contributions to the theory of reference group behavior, in R. K. Merton & P. F. Lazarsfeld, *Continuities in social research: Studies in the scope and method of 'the American soldier'*. New York: Free Press.

Mikula, G. (1972). Die Entwicklung des Gewinnaufteilungs-verhaltens bei Kindern und Jugendlichen. Eine Untersuchung an 5-, 7-, 9- and 11 jahrigen, *Zeitschrift für Entwicklungspsychologie und Pädagogische Psychologie*, **4**, 151–64.

Milgram, S. (1974). *Obedience to authority*. London: Tavistock.

Miller, S. A. & Brownell, C. A. (1975). Peers, persuasion and Piaget: dyadic interaction between conservers and non conservers, *Child Development*, **46**, 992–7.

Milner, D. (1975). *Children and race*. Harmondsworth: Penguin Books.

Mischel, W. & Schopler, J. (1959). Authoritarianism and reactions to 'sputnicks', *Journal of Abnormal and Social Psychology*, **59**, 142–5.

Moessinger, P. (1974). Etude génétique d'échange, *Cahiers de psychologie*, **17**, 119–23.

(1975). Developmental study of fair division and property, *European Journal of Social Psychology*, **5**, 385–94.

Montagner, H. (1978). *L'enfant et la communication*. Paris: Editions Stock.

Montgomery, R. L., Hinkle, S. W. & Enzie, R. F. (1976). Arbitrary norms and social change in high- and low-authoritarian societies, *Journal of Personality and Social Psychology*, 33, 698–708.

Montmollin, de G. (1977). *L'influence sociale: phénomènes, facteurs et théories*. Paris: Presses Universitaires de France.

Moscovici, S. (1961). *La psychanalyse, son image et son public*. Paris: Presses Universitaires de France.

    (1970). Préface, in D. Jodelet, J. Viet & P. Besnard, *La psychologie sociale*. Paris: Mouton.

    (1972). Society and theory in social psychology, in J. Israel & H. Tajfel, eds., *The context of social psychology: a critical assessment*. London: Academic Press.

    (1976a). La psychologie des représentations sociales, in G. Busino, *Les sciences sociales avec et après Jean Piaget*. Geneva: Droz.

    (1976b). *Social influence and social change*. London: Academic Press.

    (1979). *Psychologie des minorités actives*. Paris: Presses Universitaires de France.

    (1980). Toward a theory of conversion behaviour, in L. Berkowitz, *Advances in Experimental Social Psychology*, vol. 13, 209–39.

    (1982). *Psychologie des minorités actives*. Paris: Presses Universitaires de France. 2nd ed.

    (1984). *Psychologie sociale*. Paris: Presses Universitaires de France.

Moscovici, S., Doise, W. & Dulong, R. (1972). Studies in group decision II. Differences of position, differences of opinion and group polarization, *European Journal of Social Psychology*, 2, 385–99.

Moscovici, S. & Lage, E. (1978). Studies in social influence IV. Minority influence in a context of original judgments, *European Journal of Social Psychology*, 8, 349–65.

Moscovici, S., Lage, E. & Naffrechoux, M. (1969). Influence of a consistent minority on the responses of a majority in a color perception task, *Sociometry*, 32, 365–79.

Moscovici, S. & Lecuyer, R. (1972). Studies in group decision I. Social space, patterns of communication and group consensus, *European Journal of Social Psychology*, 2, 221–44.

Moscovici, S., Mugny, G. & Papastamou, S. (1981). 'Sleeper effect' et/ou effet minoritaire? Etude théorique et expérimentale de l'influence sociale à retardement, *Cahiers de Psychologie Cognitive*, 1, 199–21.

Moscovici, S. & Neve, P. (1971). Studies in social influence I. Those absent are in the right, *European Journal of Social Psychology*, 1, 201–14.

Moscovici, S. & Personnaz, B. (1980). Studies in social influence. Minority influence and conversion behavior in a perceptual task, *Journal of Experimental Social Psychology*, 16, 270–82.

Moscovici, S. & Plon, M. (1968). Choix et autonomie du sujet: la théorie de la réactance psychologique, *L'Année psychologique*, 68, 467–90.

Moscovici, S. & Ricateau, P. (1972). Conformité, minorité et influence sociale, in S. Moscovici, *Introduction à la psychologie sociale*, vol. 1. Paris: Larousse.

Moscovici, S. & Zavalloni, M. (1969). The group as polarizer of attitudes, *Journal of Personality and Social Psychology*, 12, 125–35.

Mugny, G. (1974). *Négociations et influence minoritaire*, Geneva: Ecole de Psychologie. Thèse de doctorat.

(1975). Negotiations, image of the other and the process of minority influence, *European Journal of Social Psychology*, **5**, 209–28.

(1981). *El poder de la minorias*. Barcelona: Rol.

(1982). *The power of minorities*. London: Academic Press.

Mugny, G. & Doise, W. (1978a). Socio-cognitive conflict and structuration of individual and collective performances, *European Journal of Social Psychology*, **8**, 181–92.

(1978b). Factores sociologicos y psicologicos del desarrollo cognitivo, *Anuario de psicologia*, **18**, 22–40.

(1979a). Niveaux d'analyse dans l'étude expérimentale des processus d'influence sociale, *Social Science Information*, **18**, 819–76.

(1979b). Factores sociologicos y psicologicos del desarrollo cognitivo: nueva ilustracion experimental, *Anuario de psicologia*, **21**, 4–25.

Mugny, G., Doise, W. & Perret-Clermont, A. N. (1975–76). Conflit de centrations et progrès cognitif, *Bulletin de Psychologie*, **29**, 199–204.

Mugny, G., Giroud, J. C. & Doise, W. (1978–79). Conflit de centrations et progrès cognitif II. Nouvelles illustrations expérimentales, *Bulletin de Psychologie*, **32**, 979–85.

Mugny, G., Kaiser, C. & Papastamou, S. (1983). Influence minoritaire, identification et relation entre groupes: etude expérimentale autour d'une votation, *Les Cahiers de Psychologie Sociale*, **19**, 1–30.

Mugny, G. & Papastamou, S. (1975–76). A propos du 'crédit idiosynchrasique' chez Hollander: conformisme initial ou négociation, *Bulletin de Psychologie*, **29**, 970–7.

(1980). When rigidity does not fail: individualization and psychologization as resistances to the diffusion of minority innovations, *European Journal of Social Psychology*, **10**, 43–61.

Mugny, G., Pierrehumbert, B. & Zubel, R. (1972–73). Le style d'interaction comme facteur de l'influence sociale, *Bulletin de Psychologie*, **26**, 789–93.

Mulder, M. (1972). *Het spel om macht*. Meppel: Boom.

(1977). *Omgaan met macht*. Amsterdam: Elsevier.

Murray, F. B. (1972). Acquisition of conservation through social interaction, *Development Psychology*, **6**, 1–6.

Murray, J. P. (1974). Social learning and cognitive development: modelling effects on children's understanding of conservation, *British Journal of Psychology*, **65**, 151–60.

Myers, D. G. & Bishop, G. D. (1970). Discussion effects on racial attitudes, *Science*, 788–9.

Nadler, E. B. (1959). Yielding, authoritarianism and authoritarian ideology regarding groups, *Journal of Abnormal and Social Psychology*, **58**, 408–10.

Nemeth, C., Swedlund, M. & Kanki, B. (1974). Patterning of the minority's responses and their influence on the majority, *European Journal of Social Psychology*, **4**, 53–64.

Nemeth, C. & Wachtler, J. (1973). Consistency and modification of judgment, *Journal of Experimental Social Psychology*, **9**, 65–79.

Newcomb, T. M. (1943). *Personality and social change*. New York: Dryden.

Ng, S. H. (1977). Structural and nonstructural aspects of power distance reduction tendencies, *European Journal of Social Psychology*, **7**, 317–45.

(1981). Equity theory and the allocation of rewards between groups, *European Journal of Social Psychology*, 11, 439–43.

(1984). Equity and social categorization effects on intergroup allocation of rewards, *British Journal of Social Psychology*, 23, 165–72.

Nielsen, R. F. (1951). *Le développement de la sociabilité chez l'enfant*. Neuchâtel: Delachaux & Niestlé.

Nuttin, J. (1975). *The illusion of attitude change*. London: Academic Press.

Orne, M. T. (1962). On the social psychology of the psychological experiment. With particular reference to demand characteristics and their implications, *American Psychologist*, 17, 776–83.

Osgood, C. E. & Tannenbaum, P. H. (1955). The principle of congruity in the prediction of attitude change, *Psychological Review*, 62, 42–55.

Pagès, R. (1973). L'inégalité des systèmes d'emprise à différents niveaux et leur interaction, *Epistémologie et sociologie*, 15–16, 97–117.

Pagès, R. & Lemoine, C. (1976). *L'emprise analytique: Réaction des sujets à l'analyse et à ses modalités d'appropriation ou d'aliénation*. Paris: Laboratoire de Psychologie sociale de l'Université Paris VII.

Paicheler, G. (1976). Norms and attitude change I: polarization and style of behaviour, *European Journal of Social Psychology*, 6, 405–27.

(1977). Norms and attitude change II: the phenomenon of bipolarization, *European Journal of Social Psychology*, 7, 5–14.

Palardy, J. N. (1969). What teachers believe, what children achieve, *Elementary School Journal*, 69, 370–4.

Papastamou, S. (1979). *Stratégies d'influence minoritaires et majoritaires*. Paris: Ecole des Hautes Etudes en Sciences sociales. These de doctorat de 3ᵉ cycle.

Parsons, T. (1964). *Social structure and personality*, London: Free Press.

Peabody, D. (1968). Group judgements in the Philippines: evaluative and descriptive aspects, *Journal of Personality and Social Psychology*, 10, 290–300.

Pêcheux, M. (1969–70). Sur la conjoncture théorique de la psychologie sociale, *Bulletin de Psychologie*, 23, 290–7.

(1972–73). Etude expérimentale de conditions déterminant la plausibilité d'une théorie psychologique, *Bulletin de Psychologie*, 26, 102–18.

Pennington, D. F., Harary, F. & Bass, B. M. (1958). Some effects of decision and discussion on coalescence, change and effectiveness, *Journal of Applied Psychology*, 42, 404–08.

Pepitone, A. (1976). Toward a normative and comparative biocultural social psychology, *Journal of Personality and Social Psychology*, 34, 641–53.

Perret-Clermont, A. N. (1979). *La construction de l'intelligence dans l'interaction sociale*. Bern: Peter Lang.

(1980). Recherche au Tessin: premiers résultats. Université de Genève, unpublished research.

Personnaz, B. (1981). Study in social influence using the spectrometer method: dynamics of the phenomena of conversion and covertness in perceptual responses, *European Journal of Social Psychology*, 11, 431–8.

Pettigrew, T. F., Allport, G. W. & Barnett, E. O. (1958). Binocular resolution and perception of race in South Africa, *British Journal of Psychology*, 49, 265–78.

Piaget, J. (1932). *The moral judgement of the child* (*Le jugement moral chez l'enfant*, 1932, trans. M. Gabain). London: Routledge & Kegan Paul.

(1950). *The psychology of intelligence* (*La psychologie de l'intelligence*, 1947, trans. M. Piercy & D. E. Berlyne). London: Routledge & Keagan Paul.

(1965). *Etudes sociologiques*. Paris: Droz.

(1966). Nécessité et signification des recherches comparatives en psychologie génétique, *International Journal of Psychology*, 1, 3–13. (Trans. 1972, The necessity and significance of comparative research in developmental psychology, in *Psychology and epistemology*, London: Penguin University Books).

(1971). *Biology and knowledge* (*Biologie et connaissance*, 1967, trans. B. Walsh). Edinburgh: Edinburgh University Press.

(1976a). Logique génétique et sociologie, in G. Busino, *Les sciences sociales avec et après Jean Piaget*. Geneva: Droz.

(1976b). L'individualité en histoire. L'individu et la formation de la raison, in G. Busino, *Les sciences sociales avec et après Jean Piaget*. Geneva: Droz.

(1976c). Problèmes de la psycho-sociologie de l'enfance, in G. Busino, *Les sciences sociales avec et après Jean Piaget*. Geneva: Droz.

(1976d). Postface, *Archives de Psychologie*, 44, 223–8.

(1978). *The development of thought* (*L'équilibration des structures cognitives*, 1975, trans. A. Rosin). Oxford: Basil Blackwell.

(1980). *Adaptation and intelligence: organic selection and phenocopy* (*Adaptation vitale et psychologie de l'intelligence: phénocopie et sélection organique*, 1974). Chicago: Chicago University Press.

Piaget, J. & Inhelder, B. (1956). *The child's conception of space* (*La représentation de l'espace chez l'enfant*, 1948). London: Routledge & Kegan Paul.

Piaget, J. & Szeminska, A. (1952). *The child's conception of number* (*La genèse du nombre chez l'enfant*, 1941, trans. C. Gattegno & F. M. Hodgson). London: Routledge & Kegan Paul.

Pichevin, M. R. & Poitou, J. P. (1974). Le 'biais d'équilibre': un exemple de consigne implicite, *Cahiers de Psychologie*, 17, 111–18.

Pinxten, R. (1973). Universals and anthropological research, *Communication and Cognition*, 6, 81–111.

Plon, M. (1974). On the meaning of the notion of conflict and its study in social psychology, *European Journal of Social Psychology*, 4, 389–436.

Poitou, J. P. (1974). *La dissonance cognitive*. Paris: Armand Colin.

Pollis, N. P. (1967). Relative stability of scales formed in individual, togetherness and group situations, *British Journal of Social and Clinical Psychology*, 6, 249–55.

Pollis, N. P., Montgomery, R. L. & Smith, T. G. (1975). Autokinetic paradigms: a reply to Alexander, Zucker and Brody, *Sociometry*, 38, 358–73.

Rabbie, J. M. (1974). Effecten van een competitieve en coöperatieve intergroeps orientatie op verhoudingen binnen en tussen groepen, *Nederlands tijdschrift voor de psychologie*, 29, 239–57.

(1979). Competitie en coöperatie tussen groepen, in J. M. F. Jaspars & R. Van der Vligt, *Sociale psychologie in Nederland*, vol. 2: *De klein groep*. Deventer: Van Loghum en Slaterus.

Rabbie, J. M. & Bekkers, F. (1976). Bedreigd leiderschap en intergroepscompetitie, *Nederlands tijdschrift voor de psychologie*, 31, 269–83.

Rabbie, J. M. & Horwitz, M. (1969). The arousal of ingroup–outgroup bias by a chance win or loss, *Journal of Personality and Social Psychology*, 13, 269–77.

Rabbie, J. M. & Visser, L. (1972). Bargaining strength and group polarization in intergroup negotiations, *European Journal of Social Psychology*, **2**, 401–16.

Rabbie, J. M., Visser, L. & Tils, J. (1976). De vertegenwoordiger en zijn achterban, *Nederlands tijdschrift voor de psychologie*, **31**, 253–68.

Radke, M. & Klisurich, D. (1947). Experiments in changing food habits, *Journal of the American Dietetic Association*, **24**, 403–9.

Reich, J. & Sherif, M. (1963). *Ego-involvement as a factor in attitude assessment by the own categories technique.* Norman: University of Oklahoma.

Ricateau, P. (1970–71a). Processus d'influence et niveaux d'analyse, *Bulletin de Psychologie*, **24**, 418–47.

    (1970–71b). Processus de catégorisation d'autrui et les mécanismes d'influence sociale, *Bulletin de Psychologie*, **24**, 909–19.

Riecken, H. W. (1962). A program for research on experiments in social psychology, in N. F. Washburne, *Decision, values and groups*, vol. 2. New York: Pergamon Press.

Ring, K. (1967). Experimental social psychology: some sober questions about some frivolous values, *Journal of Experimental Social Psychology*, **3**, 113–23.

Robinson, E. J. & Robinson, W. P. (1977). Development in the understanding of causes of success and failure in verbal communication, *Cognition*, **5**, 363–78.

    (1978). Development of understanding about communication: message inadequacy and its role in causing communication failure, *Genetic Psychology Monographs*, **98**, 233–79.

Rokeach, M., Smith P. W. & Evans, R. I. (1966). Race and shared beliefs as factors in social choice, *Science*, **141**, 167–72.

Rosenthal, R. (1966). *Experimenter effects in behavioural research.* New York: Appleton.

Rosenthal, R. & Jacobson. L. (1968). *Pygmalion in the classroom: teacher expectation and pupils' intellectual development.* New York: Holt, Rinehart & Winston.

Rosenthal, T. L. & Zimmerman, B. J. (1972). Modeling by exemplification and instruction in training conservation, *Developmental Psychology*, **6**, 392–401.

Ross, E. A. (1920). *Principles of sociology.* New York: Century.

Rossignol, C. & Flament, C. (1975). Décomposition de l'équilibre structural: aspects de la représentation du groupe, *L'Année psychologique*, **75**, 417–25.

Roux, J. P. & Gilly, M. (1984). Aide apportée par le marquage social dans une procédure de résolution chez les enfants de 12–13 ans: données et réflexions sur les mecanismes, *Bulletin de Psychologie*, **38**, 145–55.

Sampson, S. F. (1968). *Crisis in the cloisters: a sociological analysis.* Ph.D. thesis, Cornell University.

Schachter, S. (1951). Deviation, rejection, and communication, *Journal of Abnormal and Social Psychology*, **46**, 190–208.

Schachter, S. & Singer, J. E. (1962). Cognitive, social, and physiological determinants of emotional state, *Psychological Review*, **69**, 379–99.

Seaver, W. B. (1973). Effects of naturally induced teacher expectancies, *Journal of Personality and Social Psychology*, **28**, 333–42.

Secord, P. F., Bevan, W. & Katz, B. (1956). The Negro stereotype and perceptual accentuation, *Journal of Abnormal and Social Psychology*, **53**, 78–83.

Sherif, C. W. (1961). Established reference scales and series effects in social judgment, *Dissertation Abstracts*, **22**, 6.

(1973). Social distance as categorization of intergroup interaction, *Journal of Personality and Social Psychology*, **25**, 327–34.

Sherif, M. (1935). A study of some social factors in perception, *Archives of Psychology*, no. 187.

(1937). An experimental approach to the study of attitudes, *Sociometry*, **1**, 90–8.

(1948). *An outline of social psychology*. New York: Harper.

(1952). Group influences upon the formation of norms and attitudes, in G. E. Swanson, T. M. Newcomb & E. L. Hartley (eds.), *Readings in social psychology*. New York: Henry Holt.

(1954). Integrating field work and laboratory in small group research, *American Sociological Review*, **19**, 759–71.

(1966). *In common predicament*. Boston: Houghton Mifflin.

Sherif, M. & Cantril, H. (1945). The psychology of 'attitudes', part 1, *Psychological Review*, **52**, 195–317.

(1946). The psychology of 'attitudes', part 2, *Psychological Review*, **53**, 1–24.

Sherif, M. & Hovland, C. I. (1961). *Social judgment: Assimilation and contrast effects in communication and attitude change*. New Haven: Yale University Press.

Sherif, M. & Sherif, C. W. (1964). *Reference groups. Explorations in the conformity and deviation of adolescents*. New York: Harper & Row.

(1969). *Social Psychology*. New York: Harper & Row.

Sherif, M., Taub, D. & Hovland, C. I. (1958). Assimilation and contrast effects of anchoring stimuli on judgment, *Journal of Experimental Psychology*, **55**, 150–5.

Silverman, I. W. & Geiringer, E. (1973). Dyadic interaction and conservation induction: a test of Piaget's equilibration model, *Child Development*, **44**, 815–20.

Silverman, I. W. & Stone, J. M. (1972). Modifying cognitive functioning through participation in a problem-solving group, *Journal of Educational Psychology*, **63**, 603–8.

Smedslund, J. (1966). Les origines sociales de la décentration, in F. Bresson & H. de Montmollin, *Psychologie et epistémologie génétiques, thèmes piagétiens*. Paris: Dunod.

Smith, B. (1972). Is experimental social psychology advancing? *Journal of Experimental Social Psychology*, **8**, 86–96.

Sperling, H. G. (1946). An experimental study of some psychological factors in judgment. New York: New School for Social Research. Master's thesis.

Squibb, P. B. (1973). The concept of intelligence: a sociological perspective, *Sociological Review*, **21**, 57–75.

Stalder, J. (1975). *Lernen in kleinen Gruppen*. Bern: Inaugural dissertation, Philosophisch-historischen Fakultät.

Steiner, I. D. (1974). Whatever happened to the group in social psychology? *Journal of Experimental Social Psychology*, **10**, 94–108.

Steiner, I. D. & Johnson, H. H. (1963). Authoritarianism and 'tolerance' of trait inconsistency, *Journal of Abnormal and Social Psychology*, **67**, 388–91.

Stephenson, G. M. (1981). Intergroup bargaining and negotiation, in J. C. Turner & H. Giles (eds.), *Intergroup behaviour*. Oxford: Basil Blackwell.

Sternberg, R. J. (1982). *Handbook of human intelligence*. Cambridge: Cambridge University Press.

Sternberg, R. J., Conway, B. E., Ketron, J. L. & Bernstein, M. (1981). People's conceptions of intelligence, *Journal of Personality and Social Psychology*, **41**, 37–55.

Stroebe, W. (1979). The level of social psychological analysis, in L. H. Strickland, *Soviet and Western perspectives in social psychology*. Oxford: Pergamon Press.

Tajfel, H. (1957). Value and the perceptual judgement of magnitude, *Psychological Review*, **64**, 192–204.

(1959a). Quantitative judgment in social perception, *British Journal of Psychology*, **50**, 16–29.

(1959b). A note on Lambert's evaluational reactions to spoken languages, *Canadian Journal of Psychology*, **13**, 86–92.

(1970). Experiments in intergroup discrimination, *Scientific American*, **223**, 96–102.

(1972). Experiments in a vacuum, in J. Israel, H. Tajfel, *The context of social psychology: A critical assessment*. London, Academic Press.

(1974). Social identity and intergroup behaviour, *Social Science Information*, **13**, 65–93.

(1975). The exit of social mobility and the voice of social change: Notes on the social psychology of intergroup relations, *Social Science Information*, **14**, 101–18.

(1978). *Differentiation between social groups: Studies in the social psychology of intergroup relations*. London, Academic Press.

(1979). Individuals and groups in social psychology, *British Journal of Social and Clinical Psychology*, **18**, 183–90.

(1981). *Human groups and social categories*. Cambridge: Cambridge University Press.

Tajfel, H. & Billig, M. (1974). Familiarity and categorization in intergroup behaviour, *Journal of Experimental Social Psychology*, **10**, 159–70.

Tajfel, H., Billig, M., Bundy, R. P. & Flament, C. (1971). Social categorization and intergroup behaviour, *European Journal of Social Psychology*, **1**, 149–78.

Tajfel, H., Sheikh, A. A. & Gardner, R. C. (1964). Content of stereotypes and the inference of similarity between members of stereotyped groups, *Acta Psychologica*, **22**, 191–201.

Tajfel, H. & Wilkes, A. L. (1963). Classification and quantitative judgement, *British Journal of Psychology*, **54**, 101–14.

Tarde, G. (1904). La psychologie et la sociologie, *Annales de l'Institut international de Sociologie*, **10**, 67–81.

Taylor, D. M. & Brown, R. (1979). Towards a more social social psychology, *British Journal of Social and Clinical Psychology*, **18**, 173–80.

Taylor, D. M. & Jaggi, V. (1974). Ethnocentrism and causal attribution in a South Indian context, *Journal of Cross-Cultural Psychology*, **5**, 162–71.

Thibaut, J. & Riecken, H. W. (1955). Some determinants and consequences of the perception of social causality, *Journal of Personality*, **24**, 113–33.

Thomas, W. I. & Znaniecki, F. (1974). *The Polish peasant in Europe and America*. London: Octagon Books.

Thurstone, L. L. & Chave, E. J. (1929). *The measurement of attitudes*. Chicago: University of Chicago Press.

Touraine, A. (1978a). *La voix et le regard*. Paris: Editions du Seuil.

(1978b). *Lutte étudiante*. Paris: Editions du Seuil.

(1980). *La prophétie anti-nucléaire*. Paris: Editions du Seuil.

Touzard, H. (1977). *La médiation et la résolution des conflits* Paris: Presses Universitaires de France.

Tran Duc Thao (1973). *Recherches sur l'origine du langage et de la conscience*. Paris: Editions Sociales.

Turner, J. C. (1975). Social comparison and social identity: some prospects for intergroup behaviour, *European Journal of Social Psychology*, **5**, 5–34.

(1978a). Social categorization and social discrimination in the minimal group paradigm, in H. Tajfel, *Differentiation between social groups*. London: Academic Press.

(1978b). Social comparison, similarity and ingroup favouritism, in H. Tajfel, *Differentiation between social groups*. London: Academic Press.

(1980). Fairness or discrimination in intergroup behaviour? A reply to Branthwaite, Doyle and Lightbown, *European Journal of Social Psychology*, **10**, 131–47.

(1982). Towards a cognitive redefinition of the social group, in H. Tajfel, *Social identity and intergroup relations*. Cambridge: Cambridge University Press.

(1983). Some comments on 'the measurement of social orientations in the minimal group paradigm', *European Journal of Social Psychology*, **13**, 351–67.

Turner, J. C. & Brown, R. J. (1978). Social status, cognitive alternatives and intergroup relations, in H. Tajfel, *Differentiation between social groups*. London: Academic Press.

Turner, J. C., Brown, R. J. & Tajfel, H. (1979). Social comparison and group interest in ingroup favouritism, *European Journal of Social Psychology*, **9**, 187–204.

Van Avermaet, E. F. (1975). Equity: a theoretical and experimental analysis. Ph.D. thesis. Santa Barbara, California.

Van Avermaet, E. F., McClintock, C. & Moskowitz, J. (1978). Alternative approaches to equity: dissonance reduction, pro-social motivation and strategic accommodation, *European Journal of Social Psychology*, **8**, 419–37.

Van Avermaet, E. F. & Swerts, A. (1977). *Billijkheid en gelijkheid in het verdeelgedrag van 6-jarige kinderen*. Louvain: Katholieke Universiteit.

Vanbeselaere, N. (1984). The effects of dichotomous and crossed social categorizations upon evaluations of individual and group performances, *Abstracts, General Meeting, European Association of Experimental Social Psychology*, Tilburg. 50.

Van der Berghe, P. C. (1967). *Race and racism*. New York: Wiley Interscience.

Van Knippenberg, A. (1978). Status differences, comparative relevance and intergroup differentiation, in H. Tajfel, *Differentiation between social groups*. London: Academic Press.

Vaughan, G. M. (1978). Social categorization and intergroup behaviour in children, in H. Tajfel, *Differentiation between social groups*. London: Academic Press.

Villette, M. (1975). L'accès aux positions dominantes dans l'entreprise, *Actes de la Recherche en sciences sociales*, no. 4, 98–101.

Vygotsky, L. S. (1962). *Thought and language*. Cambridge, Mass: M.I.T. Press.

Waller, M. (1973). Die Stereotypität vs. Personnorientierheit des Verhaltenserwartungen von Kindern in Abhängigkeit von deren Alter und der untersuchten Verhaltensdimension, *Zeitschrift für Entwicklungspsychologie und Pädagogische Psychologie*, **5**, 1–15.

(1978). *Soziales Lernen und Interaktionskompetenz*. Stuttgart: Klett-Cotta.

Walster, E., Berscheid, E. & Walster, G. W. (1976). New directions in equity research, in L. Berkowitz & E. Walster, eds., *Advances in Experimental Social Psychology*, vol. 9. New York: Academic Press.

Wolf, H. E. (1979). *Kritik der Vorurteilsforschung*. Stuttgart: Ferdinand Enke Verlag.

Wolf, S. (1977). The effectiveness of dependence and consistency as sources of minority influence, Duke University. Doctoral dissertation.

Wundt, W. (1902). *Outlines of psychology*. Leipzig: Wilhelm Engelmann.

Zavalloni, M. (1964). Types directs contre types indirects de jugement et échelles socio-psychologiques, *Bulletin du Centre d'Etudes et de Recherches Psychotechniques*, 13, 199–210.

Zavalloni, M. & Cook, S. W. (1965). Influence of judges' attitudes on ratings of favourableness of statements about a social group, *Journal of Personality and Social Psychology*, 1, 43–54.

Zigler, E. & Butterfield, E. C. (1968). Motivational aspects of changes in IQ test performance of culturally deprived nursery school children, *Child Development*, 39, 1–14.

Zillmann, D. & Bryant, J. (1974). Effect of residual excitation on the emotional response to provocation and delayed aggressive behaviour, *Journal of Personality and Social Psychology*, 30, 782–91.

Zillmann, D., Johnson, R. C. & Day, K. D. (1974). Attribution of apparent arousal and proficiency of recovery from sympathetic activation affecting excitation transfer to aggressive behavior, *Journal of Experimental Social Psychology*, 10, 503–15.

Zimbardo, P. G. (1970). The human choice: individuation, reason and order versus deindividuation, impulse, and chaos, in W. J. Arnold & D. Levine, eds., *Nebraska Symposium on Motivation*, vol. 17. Lincoln: University of Nebraska Press.

Zimmerman, B. J. & Lanaro, P. (1974). Acquiring and retaining conservation of length through modeling and reversibility cues, *Merrill-Palmer Quarterly of Behavior and Development*, 20, 145–61.

Index

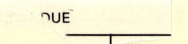